the
Vigorous
Mind

the Vigorous Mind

Cross-Train Your Brain to Break Through Mental, Emotional, and Professional Boundaries

Ingrid E. Cummings

Health Communications, Inc.
Deerfield Beach, Florida

www.hcibooks.com

**Library of Congress Cataloging-in-Publication Data
is available through the Library of Congress.**

© 2009 Ingrid E. Cummings

ISBN-10: 0-7573-0698-5
ISBN-13: 978-0-7573-0698-3

Publisher: Health Communications, Inc.
          3201 S.W. 15th Street
          Deerfield Beach, FL 33442–8190

Cover design by Andrea Perrine Brower
Interior design and formatting by Lawna Patterson Oldfield

for my parents

"Let's emulate those
among us who resist
being cognitively sedentary.
There's absolutely
no reason to be mentally
malnourished."

—Ingrid Cummings

CONTENTS

PART ONE

Part One includes Chapters 1 through 3. Chapter 1 sets up the book's backdrop, raison d'être, and tools needed for your cross-training endeavor. In Chapter 2, we'll explore a little-discussed feature of modern society: the disappearance of generalists in favor of specialists. Chapter 3 takes a look at kaizen, a deceptively simple technique for making headway on goals—and in our case, the goal is to structure a more vigorous, more generalist mind.

1

HOW TO USE THIS BOOK, AND HOW I CAME TO WRITE IT

Life itself is the proper binge.

—*Julia Child (1912–2004), chef*

The Proper Binge

Doesn't it make sense that we should all feel pretty good about ourselves? After all, we've acquired so much of what we've always desired: spouses, kids, careers, friends, homes, cars, education, electronics, shoes galore, and microwave ovens with innards that twirl around and around. It's scary almost, how well we're doing, even when you factor in economic frazzles and the volatility in so many sectors of our lives. So of course, things aren't exactly *perfect*, but we never counted on perfect. We did somehow expect, though, that we'd feel a little better about things. Instead, around midlife (your mileage may vary), almost without fail, burnout sets in. Maybe severely, maybe mildly. The blahs. Stagnation. Just at the point in life when we should feel proud and accomplished and something approaching happy, we begin to feel . . . flat. There's no mystery why the haunting song "Is That All There Is?" was a hit. It oozed ennui, that corrosive disillusionment so many adults experience. We feel it, most of us, but we try to deny it. And our culture offers up lots of ways to tamp it down, things that are quite contrary to Julia Child's proper binge noted above. "Improper binges" could include drink, drug, demon chocolate, antidepressants, shopping for more shoes, or buying microwaves that are even fancier in their ability to spin the food around yet still leave cold spots in it. No, the problem isn't that things aren't perfect. *The problem is that we've lost our ability to be seduced by the world.* Children are enthralled by everything, because it's all new. As adults, though, we believe we've been there, been everywhere; done that, done everything; bought the T-shirt, bought the iPod. We've become blasé. We've started to flatline. And we don't know how to fix it.

Is it any wonder so many of us experience burnout and low-grade depression in midlife? Sit up, because this is the big reveal: *we are starved for mental stimulation.* A core belief of mine is that we all simply want to feel better about ourselves. Becoming just a little smarter, a little more well-rounded, a little more engaged with the underappreciated treasures of this wide, wide world—that will do the trick very nicely, thank you. Yet, for the most part, we deride ourselves, noting our failings, our shortcomings, our underachieving smallness. But it's absolutely possible to feel better about ourselves without resorting to antidepressants or antianxiety medications. Just as the world offers up plenty to be disheartened about, so does it offer up all the raw materials to cross-train our brains.

What does it mean to "cross-train" your brain? At the most basic level, it means to make a point of exercising all of your brain, not just the comparatively small part you take out for a spin every day in your job as a chemist, organic farmer, or automotive designer. When you visit a personal trainer for purposes of physical fitness, you generally exercise every major muscle group in your body before you consider yourself to have "worked out." Yet, on the mental side of the equation, we let scads of our precious brain bandwidth lie dormant with nary a thought as to the damage that chronic inactivity is doing to us. Just as we should be cross-training our bodies (swimming, if we're primarily a runner; lifting weights, if we're primarily a gymnast), so should we be cross-training our brains (working crosswords if we're primarily a social worker; gardening if we're primarily an aesthetician).

"Brain exercise" is a vital function that has unfortunately been relegated to a secondary role—playing second fiddle to the universally hailed imperative for physical exercise. We all know that an agile, well-stimulated brain is better conditioned to fend off the ravages of mental dementia and Alzheimer's disease than a sluggish, understimulated brain. We know it, but we don't do enough about it.

Cross-training our brains leads to becoming a generalist. A generalist is a gloriously restless person whose penchant for a variety of diverse interests allows him or her to acquire all kinds of skills, curiosities, and enthusiasms. And, generally speaking, generalists are the people who are best positioned to fight back the blahs that come a-callin' on almost everybody eventually. Cross-training your brain—adopting the habits and worldview of a generalist even as you continue to pursue your career as a specialist—is the antidote to mental malnutrition. Plus, complementing your professional specialty with a series of unrelated pursuits will trigger a higher skill level at your profession—I know that sounds paradoxical. Cross-training will also put the brakes on the midlife melancholies and career burnout. Better health and improved joie de vivre will result.

This book is for people who suspect they've become cognitively malnourished and want to reverse course. It's written for those who feel strangely flat and don't have an inkling why. It's for anyone who wants to broaden his or her horizons by building a more vigorous mind. I have in mind the reader who can hear Peggy Lee crooning "Is That All There Is?" and wants to lash out in resistance—but doesn't quite know where to start.

But Can It Be Done?

It's the big question, and I've been tormenting myself with it for years now: is it meaningful—or even possible—to be a successful generalist in this day and age? That is to say, can we develop vigorous minds, a "true fabric of self," in our leisure hours? In our modern era, with its abundance of knowledge, is it reasonable, let alone relevant, to eschew specialty in favor of diversity and embrace a broad range of interests? Is it feasible to feed one's mind based on a da Vinci–like curiosity about all aspects of the world, or is that a hopeless anachronism? Particularly with so many of our lives already spun nearly out of control with activities and obligations, is becoming a cross-training generalist a realistic pursuit?

This book is not going to argue in favor of a return to general-practice physicians or do-it-all lawyers or the like. Specialists are the individuals who, in the most concrete ways, have moved civilization forward in quantum leaps. They are some of society's highest-contributing citizens. Albert Einstein was an überspecialist in physics. Michael Jordan is a superspecialist in basketball. Thomas Keller is a chef of such singular magnitude that he's said to have attained monk status. Bill Gates is a computer software megawonk who has enabled me and countless others to pursue our life's work while sitting in airport terminals. (Yes, this is a good thing.)

My point is that the pendulum has swung too far in the direction of super-specialists. This has led to a pervasive, as-yet-unacknowledged dulling of our brains, as we're exercising only that comparatively small portion required to perform cosmetic dentistry or tax law or plumbing. Imagine if you exercised only your bicep muscle. This is not the profile of a fit person! The same goes for your brain. Chances are you're exercising just one or two "muscles" within your large and mostly fallow brain: your oral surgery muscle, your furniture refinishing muscle, your horse training muscle—however you spend the bulk of your workday. Almost no one in this day and age can be said to have a brain that's fully "fit"—*almost* no one. My task, in this book, is to make you one of the "almosts" by providing you with the tools to build a fully fit brain that will go along with your fully fit body—to cross-train your brain by using and stimulating all of its potential. (And if your body's not fully fit—well, join the crowd. We'll find a way to work that in as well.)

The idea is to build a more complex, interconnected brain that can be deployed in service to your work, your leisure—anything. "You've tapped into a big hot issue in neuroscience," says Indiana University School of Medicine Professor Charles Goodlett. I spoke with Goodlett, a neurobiologist, while researching this book. The big hot issue concerns "experience-dependent neuroplasticity," which refers to changes in brain structure that occur at the molecular level when you learn something new.

And here's the wildly counterintuitive good news: by strategically engaging in activities that have no apparent connection to your professional specialty, you can actually become more proficient in your field. Want to become a better engineer? Go rock climbing. Want to be a better administrator? Learn to cook. Practicing judo can make you a more inspired teacher. Taking chess lessons might make you a better landscaper. Getting into carpentry could lead to innovations as a radiologist.

"The idea that the brain is changed by new experiences isn't particularly novel," Professor Goodlett told me. "But your notion—learning skills that are quite different from one's everyday occupation, and how that can improve one's emotional status, adaptability, and cognition—is new. The ideas you're suggesting are very current with major research themes."

A Three-Ring Circus

I write this book as a retort to the edict that we must all be specialists in one field or another in order to forge a successful life in the contemporary world. In our professional pursuits, I concede specialism, up to a point—more on that later. But many of us would go stir-crazy if we were somehow limited to just watercolor, or auto repair, or antique collecting in our after-work hours. By all rights, we should all be so stimulated by the sheer multitude of things to do, learn, and be in this life that we're concerned we'll never get around to doing everything. Life is a three-ring circus, and too many of us are content to operate in just one tried-and-true ring. A close-up shot is a fine thing, but those of us who get frustrated by its narrow confines need to experience the sweeping panorama. I'm going to demonstrate the value of "going big." What we're after is a full-tilt assault on the bounds of what you think is possible in your life—because too much specialization is, frankly, detrimental to your well-being and emotional, cognitive, intellectual, and psychological development. You'll soon see the remarkable benefits that accrue by engaging in a diverse range of pursuits, rather than limiting your focus to just one thing.

If you didn't much like the three-ring circus metaphor, try this one on: a bunch of pots simmering on the stove, instead of a single pot boiling—an image that suggests the exquisite tension we'll be exploring between being a specialist and being a generalist in our modern culture. Our Western world is overrun with specialists: people with expertise a mile deep and an inch wide. This is not entirely bad, of course. You certainly want to benefit from the skills of a single-minded specialist if you fall ill with some rare disease or if you encounter an abstruse legal problem or if a complex tax issue is weighing on your mind. It's not even really possible—in a certified, sanctioned sense—to be a standard-issue generalist anymore. Consider the profession of medicine: If you introduce yourself as a "doctor," you will surely be asked, "What kind?" Under pressure to specialize, medical students commit themselves to one area of expertise—for example, pediatrics. Then they discover an interesting niche as a pediatric oncologist. Soon they realize that the real action—the money, the prestige, the most challenging cases—is in, perhaps, pediatric oncology coupled with a subspecialty in orthopedics. On and on it goes, an endlessly attenuating focus. Would you believe a particular orthopedic surgeon is busy with a practice that specializes in only *left* shoulders? It's true.

A blog entitled Creative Generalist offers this input:

> Specialists are inevitably and relentlessly becoming even more specialized. Science has moved from being a handful of scientific disciplines—physics, biology, chemistry—to being broken down into hundreds of specialist components. Postgraduates don't study biology anymore; they study distinct branches of biology. In media, television has gone from consisting of a few large networks to a selection of cable stations to a thousand channel universe comprised of highly specialized niche channels.

In *The Vigorous Mind,* I will argue for a return to a Renaissance perspective, when the ideal was to be well-rounded—a notion that sounds delightfully quaint today. The Greeks were among the first to embrace the ideal of what Roman poet Juvenal termed *mens sana in corpore sano*, which translates to "a healthy mind in a healthy body." Today's Renaissance person takes the Greek ideal to the next level, with a wide range of accomplishments and intellectual interests. For example, he or she may be a successful executive who can put together a gourmet meal, advise the president of a Fortune 500 company, play the piano, and quote Shakespeare—someone such as math genius Alan Clark, who was named dean of the School of Science at Purdue University at the age of thirty-two, went on to become president of Clarkson University, and studies Renaissance painting and Greek literature; or Fulbright Scholar Ingrid Bengis, a Maine fishmonger, professor of English at the State University of St. Petersburg in Russia, author of *Combat in the Erogenous Zone*, and a singer in an amateur opera company.

It's my hope that, inspired by the stories of these and other contemporary Renaissance men and women, you will learn to become your own "brain trainer" by cross-training your own personal factory-issued brain. I can hear you resisting me already: "I don't have enough time as it is!" I am thoroughly sympathetic to this objection. But kinetic engagement (frenetic busyness) is very different from cognitive engagement. Whether you're a soccer mom, a time-crunched executive, a questing baby boomer, or an ambitious empty nester looking for more wattage in your life, this book will demonstrate how you can make time in your harried schedule to engage in a veritable smorgasbord of pursuits. What are the net results of cross-trained cranial nourishment? The consequences are improved physical and mental health and a more exalted experience of life. That's your payoff. And that's worth fighting for.

L'Arc de Triomphe

The key to achieving a vigorous mind is a technique I call "Triumph in Twenty," which is a strategic immersion in activities of your choice for twenty or fewer minutes a day.

The secret is consistent, incremental baby steps, in the spirit of the newly rediscovered Japanese belief system called *kaizen*. Kaizen is an ancient Japanese Zen philosophy that advocates taking small steps to accomplish large goals. For our purposes, in this Vigorous Mind program, the intention is for you to make accelerative progress toward your cross-training goals by committing just twenty minutes of concentrated attention per day to a topic of your choice. What can you get done in twenty minutes? You can learn a few of the fundamentals of chess. You can pick up five new words of French. But, as with the power of compound interest in your bank account, the cumulative progress created by those twenty intense minutes of attention every day can be astonishing.

The Curse and Blessing of Leisure

How shall I spend my time? If we think of life as a brimming buffet table, most of us sample only a limited number of dishes. The unprecedented volume of information, sometimes called "content" (Internet, cable television, video-on-demand, DVDs, magazines, music, classes, theater, books— need I mention books?), has created an avalanche of alternatives available to anyone who's ever asked that fundamental question: "How shall I spend my time?"

How to optimize what we so blithely call our "free time" has been an issue for thousands of years. We may have been led to believe that our earliest ancestors were constantly stalking wildebeests or gathering roots and berries, but evidently not. Cave paintings attest to time spent in that least barbaric of activities: drawing. That noted gentleman of leisure, Aristotle, declared that one of the central challenges facing man was how to fill his leisure hours. Kings at court played games, threw parties, and indulged in hunting as sport. These days, free time is distributed more democratically—at least in theory. Most individuals who are prosperous complain as readily as anyone else about how busy they are and how little free time they have. *The truth is that most of us have much more free time than we acknowledge.* The old maxim that "you make time for what's important" is true. If we designate a task or activity as critical, lo and behold, it will get done.

As leisure activities (spectator sports, shopping, vacations, working out, surfing the Internet) have become ever more central to our lives, it's useful to ask ourselves what is the purpose of that leisure. Is leisure simply the opposite of work? Or could it represent an opportunity for something more substantial, such as personal growth and development? Some might object to that notion, saying it suggests that leisure would then become like work. Yet, it's fascinating to note that people studied by renowned author and psychologist Mihaly Csikszentmihalyi, in his landmark book *Flow: The Psychology of Optimal Experience*, reported greater levels of satisfaction while at work than while at play. And, Csikszentmihalyi writes, "when supposedly enjoying their hard-earned leisure, people generally report surprisingly low moods." This perplexing contradiction suggests to me that our leisure hours could use a little strategic oomph. Specifically, we need to use our leisure time to cross-train our brains—give them the workout they're not getting at work—so we can move further toward "generalist" on the generalist/specialist continuum. The writer W. L. Phelps said, "Those who decide to use leisure as a means of mental development, who love good music, good books, good pictures, good plays, good company, good conversation—what are they? They are the happiest people in the world." The big picture of this book, *The Vigorous Mind: Cross-Train Your Brain to Break Through Mental, Emotional, and Professional Boundaries,* is about joining that group of people.

My prescription to beat back the unsung malady of our time—mental malnutrition—is to embrace a much wider vista of life than you are likely doing currently. Whether that manifests in your personal life or your professional life is up to you (odds are, it will be your personal life, but you'll see how to make the straight-line connection later). It's

> *"It is in his pleasure that a man really lives. It is from his leisure that he constructs the true fabric of self."*
>
> —Agnes Repplier (1855–1950), essayist

certainly reasonable to select a specialty for your profession, which you will then supplement by complementary pursuits (and all pursuits are complementary, as we'll see). Not only will you become more skilled in that profession, but you will also forestall midlife burnout and be happier and healthier. So if you've ever had a yen for Zen, a penchant for pottery, or a feel for fashion, you need to pursue that interest—study it a little; take a class; talk to an expert; roll up your sleeves; try your hand.

How I Came to Write This Book

How did I come to claim this bold endeavor, this zeal for cross-training brains? To understand that question for myself, I had to confront my past in search of the source of this desire to strategically structure a fully faceted life.

I have never considered myself particularly well educated, and have always been self-conscious about it. Despite the fact that I have a master's degree in communications, I have felt a gnawing, chronic lack—some vague unease that my schooling, if not my brain, was somehow inadequate. Perhaps ungraciously, I will partly blame the educational climate in the '70s, when I was in high school. Hard as it is to believe now, students were actually encouraged to leave school after lunch and go work at the mall, at a junk-jewelry kiosk or a hamburger joint. Although I never joined the throngs of my classmates who departed the school grounds at 1:00 PM for the reputed "real-world education," those extra few hours of daily schooling I stuck around for still seemed to make no scholar out of me.

I recall that Latin was offered as an elective. Being jejune and presuming Latin was, too, I heedlessly elected not to take it , and no counselor pressured me otherwise. Likewise, it would have been wonderful to have been exposed to French in grade school, when the language window in the brain is open wide. When I finally took French in ninth grade, I was a quick study, but by then the biology of the brain had foreclosed on perfect fluency. My wish is that Latin and grade-school French had been mandatory, as well as humanities classes . . . and art appreciation . . . and advanced science and math . . . and music. A few of those classes were offered here and there as electives, but in my school, kids—like kids everywhere—tended to avoid anything that was challenging if they could get away with it. The larger disincentive was the potential threat a tough class would pose to the sanctity of the almighty grade point average. For me, in those days, it was about grades, not education.

It must be said, if I wasn't as well educated as I could have been, it was in large measure my own fault. I was typical of most teenage girls of that era, I suppose, in my shortsighted distractions that included boys, clothes, the daily drama of the high school social scene, boys . . . and, of course, boys.

And the distractions continued. College made me crazy. I was forced to choose a major, naturally, which was torturous to me, as an incipient, sublimated Renaissance person who wanted to learn everything. Turns out they wouldn't grant a degree for something so whimsical and nebulous and impractical as "sublimated Renaissance person." I buckled and took a lifeless major in business administration, narrow in scope and dull to boot—not to mention all wrong for me. My burgeoning love for academics withered completely under pressure to get a job after graduation. A powerful emphasis was placed, economically and parentally, on securing gainful employment.

Is my pursuit of a vigorous mind the result of my own personal vendetta against my ho-hum education? Or might I be onto something bigger than simply compensating for my wasted youth? I'm not sure I know, but regardless, the practical questions drown out all else. Is embarking on this quest to become the ultimate "well-rounded person" relevant to the harried, hassled lives most of us live in this postmodern era? Is it folly to try to "cross-train" my brain? Is it unreasonable and unachievable? Or is it a return to a more organic, sane, humanistic approach to life?

Even after my formal education ended—come to think of it, *especially* after my formal education ended—I remained in this uneasy state of yearning. I'd fizzled out as a scholar, and now it was time to see if I'd fizzle out as a working professional. Several unsatisfying jobs in the business world later, the realization began to take shape: *This isn't my thing,* I thought. *I should've been a liberal arts major. I missed the boat.*

In my thirties, feeling out of sorts and stymied in dreary jobs, I found myself sitting across the desk from an official at the local state university. I announced that I wanted to enroll in a master's degree program in liberal arts . . . or humanities . . . or whatever they may call it. He looked at me, genuinely perplexed. "There is no such degree offered here," he said. Undaunted, I replied, "Okay, let's create it." My enthusiasm was met with a big sigh and a forlorn shake of the head. It would be a battle with the statehouse, given that this was a state-funded institution. I didn't have the stomach for a fight. I just wanted to study Monet. And so another couple of years passed. I nabbed a master's degree in communications along the way, funded fully by my generous employer since it pertained to my job at the time.

By now a desultory "professional," I found that my liberal arts itch resurfaced as a desire to teach. I wound up as an English, media, and communications instructor at the university level, where I saw students being counseled to choose a major early and "specialize or die," as the current wisdom dictated. I was witnessing the early stages of budding cross-trainers being quashed. I made the same sad observation in noncredit adult education classes I taught—an increasing and relentless drive toward professional specialization is damaging to the best interests of sharp people.

Eventually, things evolved and improved for me. I founded my own communications firm, which has surprised some observers by not fitting into any narrowly defined market segment. (As you might have guessed, I greatly prefer a broad sweep of diverse clients.) It's more fun, it's more interesting, and it reflects the way my brain is organized. Meanwhile, I was still teaching. As part of the academy, I became increasingly frustrated with the lack of interest in or respect paid to interdisciplinary studies. I decided that if I couldn't teach the kind of classes I'd always wanted to take myself, I'd find a venue other than the collegiately sanctioned one. So I devised a series of workshops, seminars, and lunch-and-learns, offering them to continuing education groups, local leadership academies, churches, Junior Leagues, bookstores, and similar locales. No grades, no credits—just education.

Those workshops eventually developed into my Da Vinci Devotee salon, where directed conversation and the exchange of ideas were the order of the evening. From there evolved the idea for this book, as I realized I was cross-training the brains of men and women who found that scratching some of those unacknowledged itches did just what they wanted: it made them feel better about themselves. And by extension, it made them feel better about the world at large and better at what they specialized in for a living.

As an outgrowth of this activity, my public speaking career began to take off, assisted by the resurgence of interest in history's premier Renaissance man, Leonardo da Vinci. From there, I've gone on to create and host a popular weekly radio show called *Rubicon Salon* (WICR-FM, Indianapolis) that highlights intriguing local and national personalities known for diverse accomplishments.

During the last few years, I've observed a disturbing, if not surprising, trend. In my work as a radio host, journalist, public speaker, and corporate trainer, I've noticed how agitated and restless the most specialized of my students, friends, and acquaintances were becoming. These are people who by all rights are at the top of their game professionally, doing good work in impressive-sounding, highly specialized jobs, yet they were entering a dead zone emotionally. Their work, the one thing they figured they could count on as a source of satisfaction in this uncertain world, that bedrock touchstone—their *livelihood*—was simply not doing the trick for them anymore. It occurred to me that the reason was because they were not getting enough mental exercise, either on the job or in their free time. Their careers, although often high paying, prestigious, and meaningful (at least to an outsider looking in), had become boring, quotidian, dull, unstimulating, and repetitive. The irony is, the people who are in the position to have these high-powered, highly specialized careers are usually the brightest and most questing among us, who long to ramble all over creation and to let their minds take flight—yet they are stuck in a narrow silo. Think back to your high school classmates. The best and brightest often opted for medical school or law school, remember? You may have been one of them. Once those people get ensconced in thriving practices as physicians or attorneys, these formerly supersmart whiz kids are at risk for midlife dysthymia, or low-grade depression, since they've squeezed most of their brainpower down to a thin sliver, in service to their chosen specialty.

I was motivated to write this book because I have felt the tug: the agitated yearning to experience more of the scope of life, a greed for the full sweep of what's possible to know, to do, to see, to be. After reading about David Denby's Great Books reading campaign in his bestseller *Great Books: My Adventures with Homer, Rousseau, Woolf, and Other Indestructible Writers of the Western World*, I was incapable of saying simply, "How nice for him to be able to indulge himself that way." I wanted to emulate him, pull threads from his experience and weave them into my own tapestry. But I didn't want to embark only on a Great Books reading campaign. I wanted to see if a "Great Learning" campaign was remotely achievable in the context of my hectic professional and personal life.

It must be said that declaring a liberal arts major in college doesn't inoculate anyone against the midlife glums, the "is this all there is?" existential crisis. Even liberal arts majors get the blues. They get sucked into the maw of daily tedium just like the rest of us. In fact, it could be that the humanities, history, and English majors among us have it even worse, since they experienced an enticing exposure to the buffet table before having to retreat to a lifeless diet of uninspiring gruel.

One fortunate aspect of endeavoring to become a well-rounded and cross-trained renegade is that you have by now likely acquired the experience to put what you're learning in context. Sure, I missed out on *Pride and Prejudice* in high school, but I wouldn't have understood it anyway. And that holds for so much more than just literature. I was immature when I was seventeen, without enough life under my belt to truly appreciate most things. The more salient point is that we absorb the juice from our culture only when we're good and ready. A friend mentioned that he had indeed taken Latin in high school. "What a waste," he recalls. The teacher appears when the student is ready, it is said, and it's so true. My friend wasn't receptive to Latin at seventeen; now, he'd eat it up. I wasn't receptive to *Pride and Prejudice* in high school; now, I cling to Jane Austen as if she's carting around the Rosetta stone itself.

Over time, my thoughts about "vigoring up" my mind continued to coalesce. Intuitively, I knew I was on the trail of something significant. My brain was getting stronger and nimbler. And so were the brains (and lives) of my coaching clients. But I needed to speak with scientists doing research on the human brain to validate my hunch that there was a connection between cross-training the brain and staving off mental malnutrition. And indeed, the brightest lights in neuroscience have embraced these notions about cross-training the brain. *The Vigorous Mind* owes much of its strength to its basis in very current scientific research in the field of neuroscience: it's thrillingly possible to build a better brain, and by extension, create a richer quality of life.

Yearn, Baby, Yearn

After years of trial and error, it finally became clear to me: I don't fit in well where the scope of endeavor is limited. Unfortunately for me, in the real world of ordinary employment, the scope of endeavor is limited almost by definition. These days, a job is by definition a narrow slice of a business that is itself a narrow slice of its industry. Yet, after all these years of rending my garments and gnashing my teeth, I've finally hit upon my niche: my niche is eschewing niches. I've also discovered the pitfalls and frustrations and limitations that are inherent in pursuing a path that has not been beaten down. I am beating my own path—a Renaissance path, one with countless tangents and dead ends and offshoots and eddies, yet a path that is ultimately interconnected. I remain in a state of yearning, but at least I can now identify what I'm yearning for: a bigger bite of life; arms long enough and strong enough to embrace art, music, literature, technology, and science; a deeper understanding of the life of the mind, the body, and spirit.

The good news is that it's never too late. We can all hop in a dinghy and paddle out to join that boat we thought we'd missed. We can always go back to school or engage in self-study to remedy the failings of a craven and mis-spent youth. I will devote the rest of my life to filling in the perceived gaps in my education and experience. I intermittently soldier through the Great Books that were never assigned in school. They've been waiting for me for twenty-five years. That's the great thing about Great Books—they're patient. I study a little Latin. I've learned chess. I travel and read history and biog-raphy. I write bad poetry and study dream interpretation. I plant vegetables and go camping. I dabble in art, too. I dabble, period, in the spirit of an unapologetic dilettante. I feel like a water bug, happily skittering across the surface of everything, content to not be a wood borer. And you know what? I've held the blahs at bay. Some days you get the bear; some days the bear gets you—true, but I've got the upper hand on the bear most days. Churchill (a dedicated cross-trainer, by the way) called the enemy the Black Dog. I pre-fer the Dark Lady. If the Dark Lady comes calling, by now I know what to do to show her the door: sit down at the piano, pick up a word puzzle, plan next year's vegetable plot, write a short story. I feel certain that, in addition to winning the war on dysthymia, I am more mentally agile now than I've ever been in my life, even at an age when cognitive deterioration is (sigh) expected. Plus, I have significantly more intellectual scope to offer my clients, and I'm more successful, professionally, every year.

The Road Map for This Book

The Vigorous Mind is divided into three parts. Part 1 consists of the first three chapters. Chapter 1, which you're reading now, sets up the book's premise, promise, and backstory. In Chapter 2, we'll explore what it means to be a generalist and figure out if you're cut out of generalist cloth or spe-cialist cloth. If you're innately a generalist, you'll be able to locate the cross-training slipstream a little more readily. If it turns out you're a natural-born specialist, I'll help you tap into your as-yet-undiscovered "inner generalist." (The generalist/specialist polarity is a fascinating binary that's becoming more germane to our world every day.) The point is that this book can be meaningful to everyone, whether they identify as a generalist, a specialist, or someone who's never really given the matter any thought. Chapter 3 unpacks the major how-to tool that will power your Vigorous Mind program: using kaizen to "Triumph in Twenty." Part 2, the next seven chapters, consists of the seven imperatives you will need to consider as you embark on your Vigorous Mind venture. Part 3 returns to a macro perspective with some honest and perhaps surprising observations about choice as it concerns your vocation (how to make a living as a generalist); your learning style (a manifesto about becoming an autodidact); and the real story about your leisure time (how to wring the most advantage from it).

Several exercises appear at the conclusion of each of the Imperative chapters. My suggestion is to scan through the exercises and choose one or two to complete before you continue. You'll find they'll help you lock in the learning from that chapter and will allow you to move forward with more assurance.

This book is for all those contrarian souls who just don't or won't conform to the specialist mold. That is to say: amateurs, Renaissance men and women, liberal arts lovers, iconoclasts, renegades, nonconformists, dissenters, dabblers, defiant individualists, freethinkers, the idiosyncratic, the nonlemmings, the vigorously minded, and anybody who chooses to join the contrarian crusade.

So to answer the question posed earlier in this chapter: do I believe it is reasonable, desirable, even possible to cross-train your brain in a postmodern world that glorifies specialists? Based on my own experience and that of many of my clients, the answer is a heartfelt—even fervent—yes. I

———

"Iron rusts from disuse; water loses its purity from stagnation and in cold weather becomes frozen; even so does inaction sap the vigor of the mind."

—Leonardo da Vinci (1452–1519)

———

am therefore proposing a return to a liberal arts gestalt; to the preeminence of humanist thinking, before the M.B.A. ruled and super-specialization became the byword for success; a "great synthesis," if you will. I have found it to be the most gratifying, life-affirming, fulfilling course I could have charted for myself, my clients, and my readers.

2

BRIDGING THE FULFILLMENT GAP

A generalist is somebody who knows less and less
about more and more until he knows nothing about everything.
A specialist is somebody who knows more and more about less
and less until he knows everything about nothing.

—*Anonymous*

The human brain has not evolved to create specialists. It has evolved to create people like Mitch Albom and Leonard Lopate and Kristin Chenoweth, each of whom we'll meet in this chapter. In order to survive as a species, *Homo sapiens* had to be good at lots of things. Our long-ago ancestors did everything well: find food, establish shelter, even draw on their cave walls as an outlet for expression. Our hardwiring evolved to consist of both a rational, scientific side and an artistic, expressive side. To this day, we all persist in having the *ability* to do everything well, even though we may identify more with either our rational or our artistic side—each, perhaps, to the exclusion of the other. In an era characterized by an overabundance of readily accessible information, it would be a shame to not explore both sides of our brains.

Even if you're fortunate enough to have a talent for music, for instance, I firmly believe that you can become an even better musician if you study a little architecture. What happens is that you begin to see an amazing interconnectedness between things—the artificial walls between fields of study drop away. The fixed laws of geometry and math that govern the construction of a building also govern the time signature on a piece of music. A building's floor plan can be represented as an equation of unyielding angles and numbers; likewise, there are only so many beats in any given measure in a piece of music—mathematically, you're bound by that delimiter. In both music and architecture, once you've honored the "givens," you're free to add flourishes in the form of grace notes, trills, and sharps . . . or architraves, crown molding, and fluting. Ultimately, you'll experience the big epiphany, the dizzying metaphor: music "is" architecture.

For example, Bill is an accountant who races motorcycles on the weekends. Despite the rather startling juxtaposition, the reality is that the devil-may-care, *Easy Rider* facet of Bill's personality loosens up his perspective on debits and credits and helps him become a more competent (even more creative) C.P.A. Or consider a priest who studies improv. Improvisation helps Father see beyond the surface of things to perceive motivation and subtext and to draw people forth, not to mention enabling him to be a better speaker from the pulpit. So cross-training one's brain—taking up activities quite unlike what you ordinarily do for a living—is actually an eminently practical endeavor.

We tend to turn a blind eye to the panoply of choices available to us, probably because we're in a constant, overstimulated state of overwhelm. There exist more books, magazines, and blogs than anyone could ever hope to read; five hundred channels on television, and not

> *"Listen to your life.*
> *See it for the fathomless mystery*
> *that it is. In the boredom and pain of*
> *it no less than the excitement and*
> *gladness: touch, taste, smell your way*
> *to the holy and hidden heart of it*
> *because in the last analysis,*
> *all moments are key moments*
> *and life itself is grace."*
>
> —Frederick Buechner, theologian

all of it lousy, contrary to prevailing opinion; plays, movies, classes; restaurants, parties, festivals. Rather than revel in our choices, too many of us turn inward in defeat, frozen in a state of indecision/nondecision, choosing the comfort of the couch over a strategic selection of the world's treasures, all available for the asking. Choice can indeed be "de-motivating." Shoppers offered free samples of six different kinds of jams were more likely to make a purchase than shoppers offered free samples of twenty-four, according to author Barry Schwartz in *The Paradox of Choice*.

The Cognitive Revolution

It is an article of faith these days among academics, athletes, lawyers, physicians, and professionals of all stripes that the way to get ahead is to ignore the smorgasbord of interesting diversions the world offers and to instead focus on a single pursuit. For those who think generalists have faded away, gone off to the Land of a Little of This, a Little of That, behold Leonard Lopate, radio talk-show host and so-called five-star general of generalists. "I think that almost every topic in the world has an interesting angle," says Lopate, who has been called a conversational acrobat. Lopate has hosted *The Leonard Lopate Show* on WNYC for more than twenty years. It's a daily broadcast conversation of uncanny breadth that serves as an on-air salon of New York's intellectual life. Through the years, Lopate has interviewed poets, actors, physicists, novelists, comedians, painters, chefs, and former presidents—sometimes all in the same week—as well as dancers, scientists, historians, grammarians, curators, filmmakers, do-it-yourself experts, and more. He has spoken with John Updike, Doris Lessing, Bill Bradley, Mark Morris, and Francis Ford Coppola. While every good talk-show host has to be able to chat about a range of subjects, Lopate seems to go for "maximum thematic dissonance" between segments. For example, during one recent broadcast, he started with a discussion on Senegalese hip-hop; moved on to chat about Hindu-Muslim relations in Gujarat, India; and then spent a few minutes on the composer Harold Arlen before wrapping up with a conversation about a

"Try to know everything of something and something of everything."

—Lord Brougham (1778–1868),
British statesman

documentary on Hollywood's role in shaping public opinion about the Holocaust. "He can leap from literature to baseball to quarks," says a friend. "He's a polymath because it's in his bones."

Talk-radio host Mitch Albom calls himself the "Renaissance man of Talk Radio." He's the bestselling author of *Tuesdays with Morrie*, a nationally syndicated sports columnist, and an accomplished songwriter and lyricist. As if that weren't enough, his background includes stints as an amateur boxer, nightclub singer, and pianist. Albom's profoundly moving experience with an old professor helped Albom get back in touch with his Renaissance-style capacity for wonder. "With Morrie, I was transported to being the way I was back in college—wide-eyed. That was Morrie's magic."

Susan Sontag (1933–2004) was an American "new intellectual," writer, and leading commentator on modern culture. She wrote innovative essays on diverse subjects such as camp, photography, AIDS, and revolution, as well as having published novels and short stories and written and directed four feature-length films. She had a great impact on experimental art in the 1960s and 1970s. Said Sontag in the *New York Times*, "I'm interested in various kinds of passionate engagement. All my work says to be serious, be passionate, wake up."

The Detrimental Drift

Anthony Kronman, writing in *Education's End: Why Our Colleges and Universities Have Given Up on the Meaning of Life*, notes that graduate students are taught to accept the limits of specialization and to see them as the price that must be paid for the opportunities they afford. It's a steep toll. The loss of wholeness is dehumanizing.

Without question, the further you persevere through the university system, the more narrow your scope of scholarship must necessarily become. We all start out in grade school studying the full spectrum of subjects: reading, science, music, writing, physical education, art, math, history, social studies. If you continue to plod through the scholastic system all the way to the promised land of the Ph.D., though, you will be required to abandon any notion of broad-based study. You will be obliged to declare a specialty, in the form of a doctoral thesis—an area of study of such constricted scope that it may seem almost comical. Here are a few examples of doctoral theses. Their titles betray the inch-wide, mile-deep nature of advanced academic study:

- Women, Property, Power, and the State in Medieval England, 1154–1227
- A Protestant Theological Inquiry into a Classical Confucian Idea of Offering Sacrifices to Ancestors
- Agent-Based Simulation of a Recreational Coral Reef Fishery: Linking Ecological and Social Dynamics
- An Exploratory Look at Career Criminality, Psychopathy, and Offending Persistence: Convergence of Criminological and Psychological Constructs?
- A Study of the Cross-Cultural/Racial Ministry of a Korean Immigrant Pastor in the United Methodist Church
- Between East and West: The Bulgarian Francophone Intellectuals— Julia Kristeva, Maria Koleva, and Tzvetan Todorov
- Defining the Mobilization of Social Capital for Low-SES Minority Youth Participants in the Summer Bridge Program by Program Leaders

This isn't ludicrous, of course. The necessity is quite self-evident. With the sheer amount of knowledge that's available to us expanding exponentially every year, no one can reasonably expect to attain the status of expert other than in a limited field. Thomas Jefferson was said to know everything there was to know in his era. Probably the same is true of the leviathan Leonardo da Vinci. But in our era, let's be realistic: mastery of *all* isn't in the cards. So to truly do a subject justice, to thoroughly give it its due, you must chip off just a tiny fragment and then pulverize it into a state of atomic dissection. We've likely seen the last of bona fide Renaissance men such as Jefferson and da Vinci. Nevertheless, broadening the scope of one's interests is not only meaningful, possible, reasonable, and relevant, it represents a vital component to living a more balanced and satisfying life.

According to the aptly named website Shift Happens, studies show that half of what engineering students learn their freshman year will be obsolete by the time they're juniors. The half-life of a specialist is now measured in weeks or months, so it's obviously incumbent upon specialists to keep up with advancements in their fields. But specialists are in danger of making themselves obsolete by burrowing into a field that is so constrictive that everything they've learned quickly becomes outdated and useless. Bobby Fong, president of Butler University, predicts that 40 percent of students will eventually work at jobs that do not now exist, because "the contours of life are changing so quickly."

> *"Failure is only the opportunity to more intelligently begin again."*
>
> —Henry Ford (1863–1947)

The Frenchman Boris Vian (1920–1959)—novelist, poet, playwright, songwriter, jazz trumpeter, screenwriter, actor, and general scourge of anyone failing to have enough fun in Paris in the postwar era—said, "One should be a specialist in everything." He did his best to live up to this dictum.

Young children are often asked what they want to be when they grow up. (Comedienne Paula Poundstone quipped that adults are always asking kids what they want to be when they grow up because they're looking for ideas.) However well-meaning, this question suggests that children must begin to eliminate possibilities at the time when they should instead be learning of the very existence of those possibilities. In any case, how can we expect children to know what they want to do in their adult careers, especially those among them who are budding generalists? Childhood should be the bastion of sweeping possibilities.

College students are encouraged to declare their majors earlier and earlier. And if you dare to declare an undergraduate major in liberal arts, you're likely to be hooted off the quad. You may as well proclaim you're majoring in "You want fries with that?" These days, the prevailing belief seems to be that a formerly

"The nearest way to glory— a shortcut, as it were—is to strive to be what you wish to be thought to be."

—Socrates (c. 470–399 BC)

respected, well-rounded college degree in liberal arts is tantamount to unemployment, and it's this sad fear and loathing of liberal arts that's turning undergraduate education in our country into vocational education. College is not about getting a well-rounded education anymore; it's about getting your ticket punched so you can grab the fattest job and paycheck you can possibly manage.

While the total number of bachelor's degrees rose by almost 40 percent between 1970 and 1994, the number of degrees in English *declined* by 40 percent, according to *Harvard Magazine* in a 1998 article titled "Humanities in the Age of Money." And it may get worse: only 9 percent of high school students today indicate an interest in majoring in the humanities. One university was so desperate to restore enrollment in its College of Arts and Sciences that it hired an advertising firm to come up with a "Think for a Living" campaign. Some of the slogans they came up with include:

- Do what you want when you graduate or wait two years for your midlife crisis.
- Insurance for when the robots take over all the boring jobs.
- Okay then. Follow your dreams in your next life.
- Yeah, like your parents are so happy.

Writing about the Renaissance revival in the *New York Times* in 2002, William Norwich says, "Since World War II, when technology and science helped America win the war and maintain its freedom, both academia and business have rewarded compartmentalization, aiding and abetting the widening division between things literary and things scientific." Steven B. Sample, the president of the University of Southern California, witnessed the same thing in 1993. Bemoaning the demise of the Renaissance man, Sample observed, "This increasing shift toward specialization led inevitably to the abandonment of the classical curriculum. Knowledge was no longer associated with virtue, nor with religion or gentlemanly ways. Instead, knowledge became associated with power, wealth, prosperity, and political dominance."

My contention is that the abandonment of liberal arts learning is damaging to the intellectual and psychological health of the individual, and I am promoting a return to the broad-based exploration we were all offered in our tender years. It's almost inevitable: *adults drift once they emerge from formal education.* Once you're saddled with the detritus of adult life—bills to pay, spouses to please, kids to raise, bosses to placate, lawns to mow, houses to clean, meals to cook, jobs to tolerate, deadlines to meet—the most we think we can do is wistfully recall what a wonderful thing it was to be continually exposed to a flow of new topics, new people, and new points of view. Even if school wasn't exactly Mecca, we never appreciated it for what it was, did we?

This book, on one level, is a love song to the poor, downtrodden, beleaguered liberal arts. I'm nostalgic for childhood, when we were not only free to study anything we wanted, but we were obligated to, as part of an educational system (even if a mediocre one) that recognizes it's appropriate, healthy, desirable, and vital for children to learn about all kinds of diverse subjects, even though we may never end up working in those fields. Who knows what value this "forced" exposure to all things may have engendered? Maybe Bill Gates's nimble brain was molded and nurtured based on an early exposure to topics that seemingly had nothing to do with the future field of computer science: music, poetry, literature, biology. I would like to think so.

Our society exposes its youth to a broad range of subject matter because broad learning is the very foundation of education. I contend that adults would be more well-rounded if they heeded less the siren call of "riches in niches" and returned to the intentional diversity of education found in the lower grades.

Divergent Thinking

Gurus in the world of business advise us to diversify our financial portfolios in order to maximize our profits. Yet, those same business gurus preach the mantra of "specialization" and "finding your niche." That business paradigm (specialization equals success) is not the optimal model for squeezing the most fulfillment out of our personal lives. Just as diversifying one's portfolio can maximize one's monetary gains in the business world, diversifying leisure-time activities can lead to long-term gains in one's personal life. Being a generalist holds great promise, especially because the world is such a boundlessly engrossing playground for those with agile, curious minds. Having that kind of mind is a fortuitous gift. So few of us are tending to the big picture; most of us are caretakers of such a narrow slice of the pie that you can actually astonish your colleagues by presenting an astute macroanalysis of a given topic. With all the information (and misinformation) floating around, somebody needs to play the role of gatherer and analyzer. For example, if your business is computer software, someone on your team should possess the ability and desire to look up from his or her keyboard at the wider world beyond, antennae quivering, sniffing the breeze for opportunities and threats, poised to generate linkages and perceive trends that could impact the software business—to notice the advantageous circumstances in Africa, the spiraling increase in video gaming among baby boomers, the myriad applications for voice recognition software. This person is blessed with a restless and omnivorous imagination. Consider this colleague to be your extrapolator, the member of the team who perceives the intersection of trends in software development with trends in population growth, demographics, fashion. I hope it's obvious that this kind of "intersectional thinker" should be regarded as a priceless member of your team.

It's for exactly this reason that you have to appreciate the generalists. But it takes all kinds, and a world full of generalists is certainly not what we're after. There's a Japanese proverb that says if you try to chase two rabbits at once, you'll lose both. So we generalists must pay proper homage to our mirror-image brethren.

Generalists view the world as if from an airplane flying at thirty-six thousand feet, and thus excel at identifying opportunities and threats. Specialists are implementers, thriving at the grassroots level. Specialists are subject to the bias that comes from soaking in their own vat of expertise. For example, surgeons tend to recommend surgery. Exercise physiologists counsel exercise. Massage therapists advocate for massage. Specialists generally default to a reductionist view of the world. It may fairly be said that this kind of excessively narrow, reductionist view of our planet's environment has contributed to our global-warming crisis. When you're thinking only about your individual needs, it's easy to slurp up more than your share of oil, for instance. If you're focused just on today and your desires, it's easy to dismiss recycling, wind power, electric cars—these are big-picture ideas, the kinds of ideas that are all about conserving resources for everyone and developing new energy sources for the future. Gaia theory, which proposes that living and nonliving parts of the earth are viewed as a complex interacting system that can be thought of as a single organism, is a generalist theory—a theory about the connections between things.

> "Vision without action is merely a dream. Action without vision just passes the time. Vision with action can change the world."
>
> —Joel A. Barker,
> independent scholar and futurist

Science writer Gary Taubes, writing in *Good Calories, Bad Calories*, his monumental work of scholarship about the myths of the weight-control industry, had this to say about the damaging effects of specialization: "Evolution of medical science has suffered enormously, although unavoidably, by the degree of specialization needed to make progress. 'Each science confines itself to a fragment of the evidence and weaves its theories in terms of notions suggested by that fragment,' observed the British mathematician and philosopher Alfred North White-head. 'Such a procedure is necessary by reason of the limitations of human ability. But its dangers should always be kept in mind.'"

Generalists, on the other hand, frequently fall victim to their own blind spots. Generalists are subject to missing nuance due to their lack of in-depth expertise. Generalists typically are not grade-A implementers or detail hounds. So specialists are about depth; generalists are about breadth. At the risk of oversimplifying: generalists define problems and specialists solve them. Clearly, generalists and specialists complement each other. You want some of both at work. You want some of both in your own makeup, ideally.

"I force specialists to speak in terms that I, a generalist, can understand," says Susan August, a technical analyst at InnoPath Software in Silicon Valley. "It's my job to collapse the 'Tower of Babble' that specialists construct around themselves."

"At last count there were more than twenty thousand different disciplines, each of them staffed by researchers straining to replace what they produced yesterday," says John Burke, host of the long-running British television show *Connections*. "You are more than likely to achieve recognition if you make your particular research niche so specialist that there's only room in it for you. So the aim of most scientists is to know more and more about less and less, and to describe what it is they know in terms of such precision as to be virtually incomprehensible to their colleagues, let alone the general public." Hence, the role of the generalist—to translate and transcend.

Yet, I think it's instructive to consider leaving behind the binary notion that you must be one or the other, generalist or specialist. A blend of the two ways of being is possible. I call this third way the "Vitruvian Capability," named after the *Vitruvian Man*, Leonardo da Vinci's famous 1492 journal sketch of a nude male figure superimposed in two positions, arms outstretched, legs akimbo. The positioning strongly suggests an incorporation of both depth and breadth. The sketch further calls to mind a unification of art and science, given that the *Vitruvian Man* is simultaneously inscribed in a circle and a square— strongly evocative symbolism from history's preeminent Renaissance man.

Intellectual Promiscuity

Journalist Bryant Gumbel was once described in *Sports Illustrated* as "a friend you can take to any party, for there is no subject on which he is not conversant. You have the world's best Trivial Pursuit partner, a Jeopardy fiend, one of last of the Renaissance men. You also have the Beau Brummell of this age, an impeccable dresser, a man with more than 100 suits, some with the tags still uncut, a man who wouldn't think of leaving the house without color-coordinated tie, cufflinks, underwear, and socks. You have a whiz in the kitchen, a connoisseur of champagne, a global citizen, a 12-handicap golfer, a father of two, and a multimillionaire."

Tyler Cowen, a professor of economics at George Mason University, runs a popular blog called Marginal Revolution, which covers an astonishing range. He's been described as a world-class polymath who whips through graphic novels and 816-page bricks such as *Africa: A Biography of a Continent*, listens to everything from Bach to Brazilian techno, searches out exotic cuisines all over the world, and still finds time to travel to remotest Mexico to update his collection of amate paintings. For him, deep immersion in culture defines the good life, and his readers get the vicarious benefits of his cultural opinion. He's been called a "cultural billionaire."

Kristin Chenoweth is a singer and Tony Award–winning musical theatre, film, and television actress. Some of her best-known roles have included Glinda in Broadway's *Wicked* and Annabeth Schott in television's *The West Wing*. Chenoweth admitted to the *New York Times*, "I maybe have a bit of career ADD. But I always did 5 million jillion gazillion things a day." That may be what it takes to satisfy a personality that combines, in one tiny frame: "faith in Jesus, sexpot allure, strict professionalism, insane girly-girliness, triple-threat talents, and a steely, restless need to exploit them all to the fullest. Her persona is like a bag of puppies, each ambition tumbling over the others in a desire to get out."

Another avatar of "generalism" is Snoopy, of the *Peanuts* comic strip. He's an astronaut who ventures to the moon, a yet-to-be-published novelist, and a hunter. He is everything his imagination can create—an anteater and a partridge in a pear tree, a piranha, Hucklebeagle Finn, Mickey Mouse, a fierce snow snake, a riverboat gambler, Dr. Beagle and Mr. Hyde, an authority on dragonflies. He gives kisses sweeter than wine and travels to the Sahara and France. He is a devotee of the absurd, yet he remains unjaded. He is Snoopy, jack-of-all-beagles.

A Vigorous Mind Sampler Platter

A vigorous mind is a thing much to be desired. Yet, oddly, there is plenty of resistance to the idea of it. Why? The four obstacles listed below represent forces we all need to overcome in order to attain a vigorously cross-trained, generalist state of mind. These are our Four Horsemen of the Apocalypse:

1. **Mental Malnutrition.** Without attention to continued learning, mental malnutrition can easily set in. Call it "brain entropy." Think back to your last year in high school or college . . . wherever you were when you stepped off the merry-go-round of formal education. Ask yourself: Am I mentally sharper today than I was then? Chances are, you'll ruefully conclude that when you were under the gun to perform mentally—producing assignments, making presentations, and studying for tests—you were more cognitively agile, more incisive, and more perceptive then than you are today, when you're slammed with routine, not-very-stimulating tasks, and a not-always-mentally challenging job. Indeed, the day we graduate from formal schooling, there is a propensity to become "brain stale" unless we take active measures to reverse that entropy. Beware the "ides of entropy."

2. **Anti-Intellectualism.** A robust strain of anti-intellectualism runs through our popular culture—and I hate it. I was reading a magazine article—a popular magazine, not a scholarly journal—and the author used the word "exogenous." She went on to define it ("oriented

outside yourself"), but what got me was that she then apologized for using it at all, as if using a seldom-heard word was worthy of shame, embarrassment, reproach, censure, and disgrace. We live in a peculiar era, when dumbing down is considered polite and politically proper. To be openly interested in a life of the mind is considered elitist or effete. No looking uppity! The untapped brainpower of our citizenry is absolutely appalling. And it's a source of pride for too many. Philistinism exists. It is our opponent.

3. **Groupthink.** The third factor to be overcome is groupthink. Groupthink is the absence of independent, critical thinking. It is "thinking" that defers to the group, thinking that cedes creativity, imagination, and personal responsibility to the great gray group. Groupthink puts consensus and conformity first, above individual spunk, outspokenness, boldness, or initiative. It's going along to get along. And it's everywhere.

4. **Lack of Time.** The fourth factor that militates against us developing a vigorous mind is a perceived lack of time. This objection is so dominant, reasonable, pervasive, understandable, logical, and amenable to improvement that I've dedicated an entire chapter to it. (See Chapter 6.)

Addressing these obstacles opens up a vista of possibilities for a richer, more textured experience of life, allowing room for the budding of latter-day Renaissance men and women.

The Secret Life of Generalists

Philosopher and bestselling author Tom Morris told me that in his own life as a philosopher, "If I'm reading just philosophy I'll become a real boring person. I need to be reading science fiction and science and poetry in order to be a lively creative person in my own specialty." Life, he says, is supposed to be a series of adventures, yet "people allow inertia to hold them in place." Morris has bemoaned the fact that as adult life creeps up on us, all we ever seem to talk about with friends is what the kids are up to, what's on sale at the mall, and how our local sports team is doing. What an arid departure from younger days of yore, when we'd talk late into the night about all sorts of weighty things—life, death, love, meaning, happiness, good, and evil. The irony is that once we're older, we actually have meaningful contributions to make to these kinds of discussions, but we tend not to make time to talk about real topics. Virtually all my clients have decried the very same lack of substance in their lives. People are "restless to re-engage with their more exalted selves," says Morris. People want to experience life on a higher plane. Most pop-culture formulas for success have turned out to be empty promises. Still, we all crave a way of living that will result in sustainable and energizing satisfaction with life. As Morris says, "Our time on this earth is not to be wasted."

Aristotle concluded that happiness is action. Dressed out a little further: happiness is participation in something that produces fulfillment. "The soul ever yearns to be doing something," said Cicero. It is not having but doing that is most intimately related to the fullest experience of being. We are at our best and feel our best when we are engaged in a worthy task. Challenge is pleasure. Those of us who are intrigued by the notion of building a more vigorous mind for ourselves are challenge-mongers. And, I submit, we inhabit an enhanced position to extract the maximum dosage of fulfillment from life. That's the metagoal of this book.

When you broaden your cognitive horizons, that dormant little imp called "the joy of discovery" kicks in. You find that learning about kinetic energy in a physics class is exhilarating; seasoning your conversation with a few showy German words such as *schadenfreude* or *gemütlichkeit* can make for fun at parties; learning about perspective in a drawing class is stimulating and makes you feel more alive; indeed, learning anything, purely for its own sake, is truly worthwhile and makes you more human. For example, if you're an accountant and have been specializing in accounting your entire adult life, I'd recommend you expose yourself to the life sciences or to the Civil War or to

French cooking or to beekeeping. In other words, steer away from a laserlike focus on one endeavor and steer toward the direction of a wider palette.

The world is an infinitely faceted place. Take advantage of the riches. Don't deprive yourself of the bounty that is the legacy of generations of scholars who have come before. If your life is busy but bland, you can reverse that mental malnutrition and replace it with a banquet of Renaissance-style learning— and find your way back to joy.

An Eclectic Itinerary

I understand that some people seem to be born with a strong, seemingly genetic tropism to become therapists or symphony orchestra conductors or handymen or pharmacists or soccer players. But those "destinies" may actually be economically based choices they've consciously or unconsciously made, rather than a manifestation of inborn hardwiring to spend their lives in that occupation. My fear for these people is that their work might become their undoing if the day comes that they're bored, restive, depressed, blasé.

Talented, supremely accomplished individuals such as Albert Einstein, Michael Jordan, Thomas Keller, and Bill Gates have moved the ball forward in their chosen fields by quantum leaps, making the world a better place for all of us. I certainly do not forecast or advocate a trend away from specialists such as these paragons—in our professional lives, that is. For the sake of civilization, we would not want to see that happen. We would not want to relinquish the contributions that experts/specialists are in a position to make. But there's a potentially devastating downside to devoting your life on a wholesale basis to being a one-note specialist. Although you're in a primo position to make stellar advancements in your field—advances that could potentially enhance the lives of millions—those accomplishments might come at the expense of your own personal betterment and fulfillment. For example, a medical doctor in Hawaii named Jane Fyrberg says she loves medicine and her patients but commented, "It narrows your life to focus on one area for so long. There are wonderful things you can't experience when you're immersed in medicine or law. [Things such as] playing violin in a symphony, or studying hula—not the tourist hula, but the traditional hula that's serious and sacred."

Whether you're a specialist-type or a generalist-type and whether you became that way by nature or by nurture, all are welcome under the Big Top. In any case, I'm advocating that all of us compensate for our specialized careers by taking a page from the generalist handbook. Generalists are too fidgety, too intellectually promiscuous, too tempted by the all-you-can-eat buffet of life's offerings to be satisfied with specializing in one topic. Individuals seeking to develop a truly vigorous mind won't settle for limitations.

A Wider Wingspan

We're all familiar with *Roget's Thesaurus*. Peter Mark Roget (1779–1869) had the sort of edgy intellect that solved London's water-filtration problem, invented the log-scale for slide rules, and organized an immense collection of words into categories, according to the ideas they represent.

In our era, Steve Isenberg was an academic standout as a student at the University of California, Berkeley. He became New York mayor John Lindsay's chief of staff in the '60s, then, with no experience, dove into newspaper publishing, eventually becoming an executive at the *Los Angeles Times* and *Newsday*. Now teaching literature at the University of Texas, Isenberg says, most humbly, "There are certainly times when I feel I didn't drive on every piston, didn't take the best route, didn't have the wingspan I wanted. Still, on the other hand, does life have only one winner's circle?" I'm struck by his lovely notion: wingspan. We all want to enlarge our wingspans—emotionally, psychologically, intellectually.

As a dyed-in-the-wool generalist, I actually sort of envy my specialist friends. Life must be so much easier for them. They recognize at some point, probably early in life, that they're meant to be cellists, economists, divorce lawyers, interior designers, or businesspeople. Then they proceed to spend the rest of their professional lives doing what they feel they were called to do.

Minimal regrets, few second thoughts, misgivings held at bay, only a touch of the midlife gloomies, no discernible burnout. Not that life is necessarily a bed of roses for these specialists, but at least they feel a deep-rooted assurance that they're doing work that is well-suited to them—that when it comes to their career, they're dwelling in the very center of their strike zone.

Legions of the rest of us, though, are the proverbial square pegs trying to fit into round holes. It's said that the average twenty-something today will have ten different jobs before age forty, and upward of seven distinct careers in the course of his or her working life. If you're born to professionally sprawl across lots and lots of vineyards sequentially, it can be tough to squish yourself down into the confining little space required to be a bond trader or a TV producer or an upholsterer. It could begin to feel like occupational suffocation. You may start out as a copier machine salesperson, then get antsy. You stumble into producing documentaries. That peters out. You get wind of an opportunity to invest in a start-up company that makes environmentally friendly lightbulbs. A falling-out with your partners results in a return to sales, this time involving advertising on blogs. Then day-trading beckons, and you do that part-time in the evenings and on weekends. The economy falters, and you respond by taking classes in calligraphy. Meanwhile, you get a gig as a lobbyist for the engineering industry. Onward through the darkness. . . . Does this sound like an admirable career path? Does this sound like a person with a plan? Does this sound like the kind of professional life you'd want for your children, or yourself? Probably not. It does bring to mind the quip that "generalist" is a charitable word for people who can't make a career decision. Yet, you must admit, there is a sort of frenetic, life-is-short, go-for-the-gusto vivacity about it. The behavior of some generalists can indeed appear fractured. The trick is to learn how to position this kind of ricocheting so it doesn't appear random . . . herd it into a cohesive unit and untangle its outward appearance so a cohesive theme emerges. We'll discuss generalists in the workplace in Chapter 12.

Meanwhile, imagine if Einstein, Jordan, Keller, and Gates had each dabbled in a whole slew of other disciplines. Imagine Jordan working at

Microsoft, Gates toiling as a chef, Einstein playing power forward. Jordan actually did take a swing at baseball, and he was aggressively average at it, even playing only at the minor league level. But chef Keller, computer guru Gates, and relativity majordomo Einstein all seem to have devoted their lives purely to the disciplines of their choice. What if they had not? What if Keller had dabbled in cooking, grown stagnant, and gotten into ceramics? We likely wouldn't have the opportunity to share in his Zen-like mastery of culinary art and science. What if Einstein had not pursued physics with his single-minded intensity? We wouldn't have mind-bending physics classes and nuclear energy. What if Bill Gates had thrown only half his energies into personal computers, and had investigated architecture with the rest of his time? Think what the world would have missed. Some superspecialists are so inspiringly, ethereally talented that it's hard to imagine cross-training (or anything else) could make them appreciably better at what they do. Yet I can't help wonder . . . might these paragons of specialization have made even more sensational contributions to civilization if they'd allowed themselves to sample ample fare from other spheres?

For the rest of us mortals, we need all the help we can get. So, throughout this book, I will serve as your personal learning consultant, helping you plan your returning-to-learning program. I'm an educational broker—aiding readers in tailoring the right learning program for them. But this isn't high school anymore. This time around, it's going to be fun. You'll be in charge, and a universe of choices will dazzle you. This time around, no lockers, no hall passes, no social-strata angst, no lunch ladies terrorizing you in the cafeteria. We'll be dealing in an enhanced Sturm und Drang. We'll never get around stress, but it's time to start dealing with a higher *quality* of stress in our lives: the generative kind, not the debilitating kind.

From What Cloth Are You Cut?

At some point, you'll want to ask yourself a fundamental question: which was I born to be—a specialist or a generalist? Of course, this begs a fascinating question: is one born a Renaissance person or can this trait be acquired? This debate can be framed by the existentialist versus essentialist debate. According to a conversation I had with Jungian analyst Gary Sparks, an existentialist says, "We come into the world and create ourselves." An essentialist, such as Carl Jung, says, "We come into the world already created; the essential you (your 'self') is inborn. You're there a priori." The goal in psychotherapy is to bring people to that self. According to Sparks, Jung's theories say that all of our problems stem from us being untrue to who we are. So if you're a generalist forced to live and behave like a specialist, or vice versa, you're heading toward disintegration.

There's nothing inherently better about being a natural-born generalist, rather than a specialist, or vice versa. The trick is to determine your type, then build your life around it. Don't fight your innate self—you'll lose. Be who you are. Do what you are. The pop-psychology rudiment about "changing" oneself is valid only up to a point. We can learn new behaviors, yes, but we won't be changing our core selves.

Further, even if you determine that you are, in fact, a dyed-in-the-wool specialist/expert by nature, you can nonetheless experience a bad case of the professional blahs in your career, because so much of your powerful and vigorous brain is lying fallow as you overexercise the tiny corner of your brain that's responsible for landscape architecture, appliance repair, or software design. *Everyone's* prone to midlife career flatlining.

You don't want the person who cuts your hair to also be the person who fixes your car. For your locks, you want someone who has studied hair inside and out, who has a passion for the work, who has been doing it for years— someone who loves it so much he or she would do it even without being paid. We don't want to work with those who are disgruntled. We want to deal with those who are fully gruntled!

But what does this kind of slender, lifelong focus do to the hairstylist? Isn't it a rather thin gruel to sustain a life of the mind on? What toll does it exact? After twenty years of cutting and styling hair, our hairstylist may be getting burned out and bummed out, perhaps even suffering from some low-level, nonspecific depressive malaise. What she really needs are foil highlights of the cognitive variety, but she's not quite able to put her finger on the problem. After all, she's gaining accolades for her skill, drawing legions of devoted clients, earning more money than she ever expected, and enjoying professional status among her peers. The irony is that this hairstylist had a true passion for her craft when she started out. Sadly, there is nothing out of the ordinary about her predicament. It represents a career trajectory that's so common it's pervasive, so typical it's axiomatic. So expected it's hardly noticed. What results is a terrible dilemma. The world needs specialists—those with the temperament for a professional life consisting of one primary lifelong concentration. But these poor souls may be on paths that are leading them toward profound dissatisfaction.

Behold the antidote: self-development. Self-development through continued learning is the fundamental strategy for successful living. Although it may be elemental, it's nevertheless a vastly underused tactic. Our hairdresser should not necessarily ditch the salon for a job selling condos in the suburbs, but should instead bring fresh energy to her hair art by taking up some other energy-producing interests that are not remotely similar to blow-dry's, perms, and gypsy shags.

Let me be clear here: despite what you may assume, I am not trying to dissuade anyone from becoming a specialist in their career. Even if you consider yourself to be an inborn generalist, working as a specialist is virtually a given. These days, there are precious few want ads that read "jack-of-all-trades wanted; someone who does a lot of things at a mediocre level." On the other hand, if you query employers, they will indeed say that they desire well-rounded, well-educated employees they can train in the particulars of the specific job at hand. They want employees who can communicate to colleagues and customers, who can make connections between departments, who can get along with coworkers and clients, who are bright and curious, and who have a good work ethic. What I can wholeheartedly advise is that everybody, whether an innate specialist or an innate generalist, strive to become a Renaissance activist in their free time as a way to enhance professional experience and personal fulfillment. That is this book's prescription, and there's valid brain science at play that makes this more than just a feel-good, pop-psychology patch du jour.

You're a Generalist If . . .

- Your mind wanders horizontally during meetings, veering off to generate nonrelated thoughts.
- Your personal library resists cataloging because it's so eclectic.
- You frequently use metaphors to express yourself.
- You become bored easily.
- People refer to you as having attention-deficit disorder.
- Your home or office is filled with projects started, abandoned, half-completed—but not forgotten.
- Interconnections are the point.

You're a Specialist If . . .

- Your mind wanders vertically during meetings, excavating ever deeper into the intricacies of the topic at hand.
- Your personal library is approaching the definitive collection of books on a given topic (for example, Will Shortz, crossword puzzle editor at the *New York Times*, owns an astonishing array of books, all on puzzles).
- Metaphors annoy you.
- You have a high threshold for boredom.
- People refer to you as intense.
- You're good about closure: you tend to finish whatever you start.
- Interconnections seem beside the point.

Insectile Inspiration

When was the last time you heard someone described as well-rounded in a conversation that was not, god help us, about the obesity epidemic? The term *well-rounded* needs resurrecting. I want to make it hip, cool, chic, smart, savvy, and sexy to be a "water bug," a person who sees life as one big, mouthwatering combo platter—the ultimate mixed grill. A water bug skitters across the surface of life's bountiful diversity in a reasonably skilled, more or less talented, and above all curious way. The water bug doesn't even break the surface of the water, content to remain on top of it. That bug's got Renaissance instincts. Being a water bug is about finding enrichment in sampling the diversity of that big, enticing pond, especially if you're temperamentally inclined to be a generalist. If by nature you're a specialist or expert type—in keeping with the insect imagery, a "wood borer"—you're inclined to drill down deep into one subject, and you would be aghast at the surface-skimming, superficial tendencies of us water-bugging generalists. The wood borer burrows far below the surface of a topic, learning all it can about that one silo of its world, not particularly interested in sampling the variety platter of life.

The world needs both water bugs and wood borers. The awe-inspiring feats of the specialists and experts of this world have been granted ample treatment in the proliferation of books about "genius" on the market today. Yet, the surface-skimming Renaissance person has not been nearly as celebrated as his wood-boring specialist cousin. Generalists are derided as being jacks-of-all-trades, masters of none—but what is the matter with that, I ask? I would be honored to be referred to as a jack-of-all-trades. Mastery is overrated. A friend mentioned to me that when attempting to speak with new acquaintances, he finds that he can't really get up enough steam for a good conversation, since "the only thing people can talk about is their own thing."

The Diligent Dilettante

I like the term *brain cross-trainer*, even though it's devoid of the insectile imagery conjured by our friends the water bugs and the wood borers. Our hapless fellow mentioned above—the guy who's vaulted from sales to lobbying to day trading to calligraphy—might be said to be cross-training his brain. He's taken the Greek ideal of the well-rounded, cross-trained man to the next level, buoyed by a range of interests the ancient Greeks could not even have fathomed. Additionally, today's cross-trainer (or "artful dabbler," you might say) is not particularly inclined to pursue any given activity to the point of becoming expert at it.

Another word I aim to rescue from unjust derision is *dilettante*. I submit that this fine French word is overdue for some connotation cleansing. To be called a dilettante is a putdown; it suggests you're taking up an art, activity, or subject merely as a trifling amusement, the way the idle rich might. Well, I think any of us should be flattered to be referred to as a dilettante—redolent as it is of French sophistication and superciliousness. Think fine wine and stinky cheese. And while we're mucking about in the dictionary, I'll coin a couple of neologisms to denote carefree generalists: *desultorians* and *superficialists*.

What do all these terms really mean? *Renaissance man* is the term we're used to hearing. Conventionally speaking, a Renaissance man is an immensely curious person with interests, talents, and achievements spanning a broad spectrum of human endeavor, from art to science to music to philosophy to fitness—someone who craves self-improvement and is willing to delve into new areas of interest with gusto. Other terms over the years have included *Uomo Universale*, or "Universal Man"; Nietzsche's *Superman*; and the Greeks' *Ideal Man*. The ancient Greeks portrayed the Ideal Man as being proud; strong, both physically and in terms of character; forthright; independent; war loving; skilled in combat; cunning; inventive; and ruthless with his enemies, if necessary. The Renaissance archetype built on that of the Ideal Man, broadening the definition to describe a man who also possessed all the knowledge and skills of the various arts from grammar, rhetoric, and philosophy, to art, music, poetry, and architecture. That's where we get the modern notion of the Renaissance man.

Renaissance man is a term that could use a refresher, for glaring reasons. Women are in on the act, too, obviously and fully. We will therefore refer to Renaissance women where applicable. When referring to both men and women who nurture a Renaissance sensibility, we will use the term *Renaissance person*. The Renaissance signifier is customarily used to describe the scope of someone's cognitive interests and abilities, but for our purposes it includes any and all abilities, including physical fitness and less tangible attributes such as spiritual fitness.

Before we continue, we need to make an important distinction between a Renaissance person and a mere hobbyist. "Some people say that the modern-day Renaissance man is an investment banker who likes to go horseback riding on the weekend, or something like that," says Orit Gadiesh, as quoted in Frans Johansson's *The Medici Effect*. "That's not a Renaissance man, that's a man with a hobby. A Renaissance man is someone that can see trends and patterns and integrate what he knows." Gadiesh also makes a salient point about the fine art of wasting time: "You have to be willing to 'waste time' on things that are not directly relevant to your work, because you are curious," she says. "But then you are able to, sometimes unconsciously, integrate them back into your work." (The philosopher Bertrand Russell would understand. He said, "The time you enjoy wasting is not wasted time.") Gadiesh, named one of the one hundred most powerful women in the world by *Forbes* magazine in 2006, calls herself an expert at being a generalist, or an "expert-generalist," a term she coined to describe someone who's adept at generating innovative strategies and insights.

The world desperately needs thirty-six-thousand-feet big-picture assimilators, as well as those who process their worlds from just an inch away. Although I've emphasized the revolutionary ideas, concepts, and breakthroughs that specialists/experts have supplied to society, generalists contribute in a big way, too. Perhaps their contributions aren't always as readily apparent or obvious as those of experts, but what generalists do better than anyone is *make connections* between disciplines—they see the broader pic-ture. They are "systems thinkers," and their perspective is vitally impor-tant. (Chapter 12 will provide a look at systems thinking in the context of cross-training.) This ability—almost a drive—to forge connections between disciplines is what separates bona fide generalists from gadfly hobbyists.

Experientially Empathic

Specialization is the organizing principle in nearly every productive human activity today. Fine. But we need some balance. Thus, it's encouraging to note that a number of colleges and universities are beginning to recognize the value of exposing their students to cross-disciplinary studies (and by this I'm referring specifically to the humanities, which constitute cross-training for most students, since so few of them study the humanities as their major). In a much-discussed opinion piece titled "Will the Humanities Save Us?" pub-lished in the *New York Times* in 2008, educator Stanley Fish cites a number of bloggers who lament that too often in the past, universities have "defaulted on the obligation to produce well-rounded citizens." Another blogger, though, weighs in with the other side of the issue: "When a poet creates a vaccine or a tangible good that can be produced by a Fortune 500 company, I'll rescind my comment." Perhaps the fault lies with "humanities depart-ments who are responsible for the leftist politics that still turn people off." Someone else blamed "the absence of a culture that privileges learning to improve oneself as a human being."

Fish says the issue the bloggers implicitly raise is that of justification. "How does one justify funding the arts and humanities? You can't argue that the arts and humanities are able to support themselves through grants and pri-vate donations. You can't argue that a state's economy will benefit by a new reading of *Hamlet*. You can't argue—well you can, but it won't fly—that a graduate who is well-versed in the history of Byzantine art will be attractive to employers (unless the employer is a museum)." In terms of Fish's per-spective about the value of being well-rounded, he (misguidedly, in my opinion) states, "[The well-rounded] ideal belongs to an earlier period, when the ability to refer knowledgeably to Shakespeare or Gibbon or the Thirty Years War had some cash value (the sociologists call it cultural capital). Nowadays, larding your conversations with small bits of erudition is more likely to irritate than to win friends and influence people."

At one time, justification of the arts and humanities was unnecessary because, as Anthony Kronman is quoted in the Fish piece, "It was assumed that a college was above all a place for the training of character, for the nurturing of those intellectual and moral habits that together form the basis for living the best life one can." It followed that the realization of this goal required an immersion in the great texts of literature, philosophy, and history, even to the extent of memorizing them. "It is to a version of this old ideal that Kronman would have us return," Fish continues, "not because of a professional investment in the humanities (he is a professor of law and a former dean of the Yale Law School), but because he believes that only the humanities can address 'the crisis of spirit we now confront' and restore the wonder which those who have glimpsed the human condition have always felt, and which our scientific civilization, with its gadgets and discoveries, obscures."

Apropos to all this is the cultural intelligence movement. Proponents of the cultural quotient, or CQ, posit that it's your cultural background that impacts on your ability to be successful socially and in the business world. Compare CQ to IQ (intelligence quotient), or EQ (emotional intelligence quotient). People with higher CQs are regarded as better able to blend into diverse environments than those with lower CQs. Cultural intelligence looks at which of your behaviors are specific to you as an individual as opposed to your culture. Understanding this critical difference can form the basis of better business practices.

Speaking of workplace acumen, Jim Collins has written a much-praised business book called *Good to Great*, in which he asserts that the best companies follow a simple, focused formula: no spinning off of unrelated businesses. That means no unrelated acquisitions, no unrelated joint ventures. In other words, if a proposed undertaking doesn't directly correlate with the company's mission, you don't pursue it. Perhaps this is good for business, but I can't agree when it comes to one's personal life. With all due respect to Collins and his formula for success in the professional realm, I propose that a Renaissance person can go from good to great by deliberately launching unrelated interests, strategically pursuing unrelated personal-growth acquisitions, audaciously engaging in gloriously unrelated joint ventures, and boldly doing what "doesn't fit."

Sidney Harman, one of the founders of audio giant Harman Kardon, has had great success with my formula. Harman believes that in the business world, exploration and curiosity can lead to greatness. He claims that business schools, which focus on specialization, are shortchanging not only the students but also the parents who are funding those educations. The assumption is that the arts are the "stuff" one turns to when the work has been done; Harman, though, believes that if business leaders integrated music and the arts more into their work, they would be better prepared in times of change. He says, "My company succeeds on such a platform and I recommend it heartily."

Challenge Is Pleasure

Harman has it right. Whether it's a business setting or a personal one, however, a transition from intense focus to cross-training won't be a snap. You'll likely encounter some degree of frustration as you get your Vigorous Mind program under way. Don't be surprised or resistant. It's part of the process; indeed, it's a good sign. *Optimal frustration* is a term from developmental psychology that refers to the way children learn, but I'm going to borrow it because it's wonderfully relevant to our thesis. The basic premise is that the task a child is facing should always be a little difficult, thereby forcing a degree of concentrated attention. In other words, the task should be a bit of a struggle. Few people appreciate the gift that is optimal frustration. Whether children or adults, it's actually satisfying to struggle. We're born to struggle. We *need* to be struggling. It's how to keep our brains alive—growing and thriving. *Challenge is pleasure.*

Note, too, that if you're drawn to topics or ideas outside your usual realm, you need not be annoyed at your scatteredness and assail yourself with protestations of "there I go woolgathering again." All those "distractions" are, in truth, your oxygen, your mother's milk. They've snagged your attention precisely because—somehow, in some way—they're connected to each other. A common thread unites them. Thus, all those distractions are hounding you to draw the lines between them, to connect the dots, to create the big picture. Rejoice in your so-called distractions, because they are your friends and your fuel and your raw material. You are a linkage creator, and they are your links.

> *"Do not wait; the time will never be 'just right.' Start where you stand, and work with whatever tools you may have at your command, and better tools will be found as you go along."*
>
> —Napoleon Hill (1883–1970), author of *Think and Grow Rich*

Symptom Checklist: Would Cross-Training Benefit You?

To determine if you would benefit from cross-training, answer the following questions:

Do you feel you're not as creative as you could be?

Do you hit a mental wall when confronted with a problem?

Do you seize upon your first impulse, rather than wrestling over competing alternatives?

Do you experience a pang of envy when you meet people who have traveled or read more than you?

Do you look back at your younger self and wonder where your zest for living has gone?

If you answered yes to one or more of these questions, then you're an excellent candidate for a Vigorous Mind program of reengagement.

Eat Up

There *is* such a thing as a free lunch. You can find it in Beethoven's "Ode to Joy," in the joie de vivre of Susan Sontag's essays, in the exuberance of "irrational physicist and curious character" Richard Feynman's merry and intuitive commentary on what constitutes authentic knowledge. In *The Vigorous Mind* I will demonstrate that it is ultimately a courageous act to claim the entire world as your oyster.

> *"The most important choice you make is what you choose to make important."*
>
> —Michael Neill, author and creator of GeniusCatalyst.com

> *"The only joy in the world is to begin."*
>
> —Cesare Pavese (1908–1950), poet, novelist, and literary critic

Michelangelo believed that his statues were waiting for him inside the blocks of marble he carved with hammer and chisel. Likewise, a better life—a rebirth to Renaissance, if you will—lies inside each of us, if only we can learn to wield our hammer and chisel with care and diligence . . . and with a wee bit of derring-do.

EXERCISES

The following four exercises will allow you to assess your capacity for Renaissance-style growth and help you develop a cross-training program that's right for you. Granted, these things resist a pure empirical analysis, but the exercises can help you establish a baseline from which to start your program.

1. Renaissance Quotient "Gap Analysis"

Ask yourself how accomplished, comfortable, or satisfied you are in each of the following eight sectors, known as the "wheel of life." Then determine what headway you would like to see yourself make in the categories that speak to you most urgently. Take a fearless moral inventory of yourself by checking the boxes that represent needed improvement and noting beside each box, on a scale of 1 to 5, how urgent the need is (1 = least urgent; 5 = most urgent).

- ❏ Career
- ❏ Money
- ❏ Health
- ❏ Friends and Family
- ❏ Significant Other
- ❏ Fun and Recreation
- ❏ Physical Environment
- ❏ Personal Growth

Now, ask yourself the same questions in terms of the following general knowledge sectors. Assess your basic level of knowledge, comfort, and satisfaction. Go with your impulsive, top-of-mind thought. The purpose is to begin to formulate a framework for the topics you'll want to start exploring. Check the boxes that represent needed improvement, noting beside each box, on a scale of 1 to 5, how urgent the need is (1 = least urgent; 5 = most urgent).

❑ Science
❑ Art
❑ Music
❑ Literature
❑ History
❑ Athletics
❑ Spirituality

2. The Big Bailiwick

Spending no more than twenty minutes, create a "Bliss List" of twenty to fifty activities you'd love to try (or return to) if only you had the time, energy, strength, courage, and so on. Don't self-edit—let the ideas spill out at will. Jumpstart your thinking by taking note of what kinds of magazines you linger over at the newsstand, which newspaper articles or blogs really get you thinking, and whose life you're envious of and why. Immersed in all these choices and impulses are clues about the kind of activities that could help develop the cross-training program that's right for you.

3. "Yeah, But"

Next, draw a line down the middle of a piece of paper and list on the left side all the activities from your Bliss List. The right side is for your "Yeah, Buts" (yab-buts)—the excuses, fears, and "irrational rationale" that instantly bubble up to keep you from your "Big Bailiwick." Share your list with a friend to get some objective feedback. In two days, return to your list and notice if you feel differently about some of those "Yeah, Buts."

4. To Thine Own Self Be True

If the exercises above leave you cold, maybe you're a natural-born specialist. Ask friends and family how you strike them: as a specialist in something or as a generalist in everything. Chances are they'll have insights about you that are difficult for you to perceive about yourself. That said, I maintain that you know, at some level, which camp you fall into. Allow yourself to journal on the question and see if you surprise yourself with what you write.

3

USING KAIZEN
TO TRIUMPH IN TWENTY

"The secret of getting ahead is getting started.
The secret of getting started is breaking your complex
overwhelming tasks into small manageable tasks,
and then starting on the first one."

—*Mark Twain (1835–1910)*

It's time to get down to strategy. Realistically, how does an already bursting-at-the-seams wannabe self-learner heed the call to cross-train his or her brain? The key is a technique I call "Triumph in Twenty." Audiences unfailingly come alive when I present this elegantly simple strategy to them. Triumph in Twenty calls for strategic immersion in one or more activities of your choice—tennis, knitting, writing, photography, or wherever your interests lie—for twenty minutes a day (although, truth be told, ten will do the trick). The cumulative results, much like compound interest in your bank account, can be absolutely astounding. Compound interest is the unsung eighth wonder of the world. We tend to forget its magic—its transformational capability.

The secret is consistent, incremental baby steps, in the spirit of the Japanese belief system called *kaizen*. Kaizen is an ancient Japanese Zen philosophy that advocates taking small steps to accomplish large goals. It's not a new idea, nor is it complicated, but it's certainly underappreciated. Similar to courage, according to novelist George Konrad, it's "only an accumulation of small steps." The kaizen intention is for you to *stay in action* around your cross-training goals by committing a mere twenty minutes a day, two or three days a week, to whatever it is you choose to do. Think of it as snacking or grazing. A little bit here and there. But instead of junk food, we'll be snacking on activity.

> *"If you think you are too small to be effective, you have never been in bed with a mosquito."*
>
> —Bette Reese, pilot

Don't be put off by what may, at first, seem like a recipe for an interminable slog. Spending just twenty minutes a day may strike you as requiring "forever" to reach any substantial goal. Not at all. What will cause you to take "forever" to reach your goal is waiting until you have an entire weekend to devote to it. That seldom happens, as you well know.

Toyota has successfully embraced kaizen in a business context. They've perceived that progress, or innovation, is an incremental process. Headway is seldom made by blinding epiphanies or quantum leaps. Better cars (or better selves) are more typically built by continuous daily attention to improving the small things. That's kaizen.

> *"We are what we repeatedly do. Excellence, then, is not an act, but a habit."*
>
> —Aristotle (384–322 BC)

The business world has been rigidly bifurcated, like a corporate Janus Effect: the scientific people run the algorithms and attend to all the techie stuff, while the humanists take charge of human resources and marketing and other soft-side disciplines. Kaizen has historically resided on the scientific/technical side of the house, but there's no reason why it can't saunter over and get cozy with the PR types. Kaizen has monster applicability to social science, yet oddly enough, it has never been fully employed in this setting.

Kaizen is representative of the mystical, pared-down East—think Japan, with its unknowable, Zen-like wisdom and strange bean-curd ice cream. Japan's bountiful legacy is one of reserve, in the spirit of Zen Buddhism. In historical

> *"True life is lived when tiny changes occur."*
>
> —Leo Tolstoy (1828–1910)

Japan, meditation was revered, along with a life of humility, labor, service, prayer, and gratitude. The mythos was mystic, inward-focused, minimalist, calm, accepting. Kaizen was born in a culture that honored attunement with the life force and, above all, mindfulness.

Kaizen is the fine art of cutting grand goals down to size—the amazing power of taking one step at a time, putting one foot in front of the other. This notion is sophisticated and elegant in its simplicity, yet it's been neglected. We live in a fast-paced culture, and we want to rush to get to the finish—quickly. There's something in us that resists the slow and steady. But slow-and-steady progress is how you develop a vigorous mind. It's how you accomplish any goal, for that matter.

Get Your Motor Runnin'

Grace Duffy really, really wanted to rally. She wanted to join the half-million-plus devotees flocking to the annual pilgrimage of the faithful in Sturgis, South Dakota. Sturgis is famous as the location of one of the largest annual motorcycle events in the world. Motorcycle enthusiasts from around the world congregate in this usually sleepy town during the Sturgis Motorcycle Rally every summer and exercise their motorcycle muscles in good cheer. Problem was, Duffy was a two-wheeled rookie, never having piloted a motorcycle in her life. But she had a plan.

First, Duffy embarked on a three-weekend training intensive on motor-cycle safety, buying a small Suzuki motorcycle she called her "training wheels." During the week, she practiced on her own, every day, referring to a training video the guys at the bike shop had given her. She strictly limited each practice session to just twenty minutes. "I practiced curves, U-turns, starting, stopping, and avoiding objects on the road," she recalls during conversation with me. Of course, she didn't work on every single one of those skills during each session, since she was scrupulous about limiting her training to just twenty brief minutes at a time. This duration was short enough, reasonable enough, that she never questioned her ability to fit it into her frenzied schedule as an overworked business consultant. (It's fine if you choose to go beyond twenty minutes, by the way, but don't sabotage yourself by thinking you need to.)

> *"Life gives you a chance at the brass ring. And, if you miss it—gives you another and another and another, ad infinitum."*
>
> —Rusty Berkus, poet, from "Life is a Gift"

By sticking to that completely accessible training regimen—the sort of routine that seems doable to most of us—Duffy achieved mastery over that little Suzuki, and went on to buy the Harley of her dreams. And, yes, she joined her husband and achieved her big goal: successfully riding that Harley from Florida all the way to South Dakota. She credits careful preparation for her triumph. "Those short practice sessions were sufficient for me to gain confidence to ride by myself on the Harley all the way to Sturgis," she says. "It's kaizen."

Chop and Carry

The Japanese say "chop wood, carry water," referring to the realization that everything we need—whether it's a spiritual journey or a Renaissance quest—is present and available to us in our everyday lives, here and now. It also suggests the need to do what needs to be done—to simply do the work

without overthinking it. Thus, the phrase
implies the almost sacred resoluteness of
kaizen.

The journey of a thousand miles begins with a single step.

—Wisdom of the Tao Te Ching

A Tibetan lama who crossed the
Himalayas on foot during the Chinese
occupation of his country was once asked
how he had managed such a difficult journey. He replied, with disarming
simplicity, "One step at a time."

Of course, one significant difference between crossing the Himalayas and
embarking on a Vigorous Mind program is that it's clearly apparent when
you've completed your Himalayan adventure. Our Vigorous Mind venture
has no endpoint—it's ongoing; it's a way of life; it's a worldview. Nonetheless, that one-step-at-a-time ethos is still fully applicable.

Lather, rinse, repeat. That's the essence of Triumph in Twenty. (Notice there's
no off-ramp in that formula. I visualize people in the shower, shampooing to
infinity.) Triumph in Twenty is kaizen made manifest. Once you've decided
what you want to study, and how you want to go about it, you dig in. Per
kaizen, you start small—very small. How small is up to you. Perhaps you want
to know more about chess. It's absolutely okay to jot down a note to yourself
to "look into chess." That counts as an action. Or look up a phone number of
the local chess association; call a friend who's mentioned playing chess; surf the
Internet for online opportunities to play; get a book on chess from the library.
You may regard these as laughably small actions, perhaps even negligible, but
they're fully in the spirit of kaizen and can vault you past the inertia that's keeping you from accessing the treasure chest of life's possibilities.

Our lives are measured out in coffee spoons, wrote T. S. Eliot. Small actions,
well taken, make up a life. The quotidian is where the juice is. Thunderous
breakthroughs are almost always the result of a cumulative aggregation of small
steps and seemingly trifling achievements. Looked at this way, kaizen is simply
a higher-octane variant on divide-and-conquer.

Kaizen is what powers the miracle of compound interest. Let's say we're
saving for retirement. Making small but regular deposits into your savings

account represents the continuous, incremental baby steps you'll need to make—in other words, the kaizen. For example, let's say I deposit $1,000 into a savings account. If I earn 5 percent on that $1,000 investment the first year, and I reinvest that interest back into the account instead of buying a new pair of Manolos, then in the second year, I would earn 5 percent interest on the $1,000 I started with as well as on the interest that I reinvested. This cycle continues in the third year, and so on. After ten years, that original $1,000 is now worth a handsome $1647.01.

This miracle of money management happens because your interest is itself drawing interest—the essence of what's known as "the accelerator." This is truly and literally exponential growth. No less a mathematical guru than Albert Einstein is said to have called compounding the most powerful force in the universe—and this is a guy who knew his powerful universal forces.

It's been said there are two types of people in the world: those who understand compound interest and those who are doomed to pay it. For our purposes, the two types of people represent those who understand and harness the power of kaizen and those who pooh-pooh it.

Another factor relevant to our banking analogy is that you naturally want to secure a savings account with the highest rate of interest available. In terms of building a vigorous mind, the interest rate is analogous to the degree of passion you exhibit in your study of photography, weaving, candle-making, whatever. The more into it you are, the faster the entire process will progress. Your passion serves as the catalyst in the equation.

So let's apply this banking analogy back to our topic—cross-training your brain via kaizen. For one thing, in our example, our investor consistently resisted the impulse to pull money out of the bank to buy a fetching pair of Jimmy Choos or a new video-game system. If you're practicing the violin for just

"Don't give up. Keep going. There is always a chance that you will stumble onto something terrific. I have never heard of anyone stumbling over anything while he was sitting down."

—Charles F. Kettering
(1876–1958), inventor

twenty minutes a day for three days a week, even though you might initially be tempted to dismissively snort that you'll never learn the violin at that rate, persist. Don't quit.

Rest assured you are learning the violin more quickly than you perceive. What's going on is that you're building on what you learned yesterday. You're not starting from scratch each day. The first day you learn about the components of the violin—a baby step, fully in the spirit of kaizen. The next day, you remember what the parts are called and go on to learn how to hold the instrument—kaizen again, of course, since these are small, easily accomplished tasks. The third day, you've got the parts down pat and are getting a little more comfortable with holding that Stradivarius, even as you learn what the role of the bow is. Each day you're building on yesterday's foundation, which in turn was built upon the previous day's foundation. A recent issue of the *Harvard Business Review* proclaimed that "expertise is actually the fruit borne of consistent practice." Quite soon, you'll be bowing away like Perlman playing "Turkey in the Straw."

Take note, however, that if you put that fiddle aside for a lengthy period, you will indeed lose headway. You'll find that you'll have to backtrack and refresh yourself on fingering, bowing techniques, vibrato. Inertia works both ways: a body in motion tends to stay in motion; a body at rest tends to stay at rest. You'll likely not have to go back to the very beginning since, as they say, "you never forget how to ride a bike," but you will have abdicated the power of the accelerator if you toss that violin behind the dirty clothes hamper for too long. That's why I recommend you book several violin sessions a week for yourself. One or two sessions would work, at minimum, and ten minutes each session could even do the trick. The operative principle is *small doses of exposure at regular intervals*. That's channeling kaizen and the power of compound interest (not to mention Itzhak Perlman). Assuming you're not already a professional violinist, you are cross-training your brain with every scratchy, amateur squawk you coax out of that instrument.

NEURO NUGGET

Change hurts. People change when ready. Ask don't tell. Pay attention. Expect good things. Practice. That's the essence of an article called "The Neuroscience of Leadership" from *Strategy + Business* magazine, summer 2006. "I suppose if you didn't learn these lessons between your kindergarten teacher and your high school football coach (or equivalent) then the neuroscience explanation might help you," says author Jon Miller. "One of the true geniuses of the Toyota Production System is their insistence on asking people to think about their work and to come up with improvement ideas. Called the Creative Idea Suggestion System, this approach generates about one implemented improvement idea per person per month, year after year. This has the effect of giving people the jolt of satisfaction at solving a problem while expecting change to happen around them (expectation shapes reality), as well as getting people to pay attention to their work. Not bad for a product of 1950s motivational theory. It's safe to say that complacency is the enemy of kaizen. Dr. W. Edwards Deming, esteemed expert on production practices, said it another way: 'It is not necessary to change. Survival is not mandatory.'"

Building on whatever it is we've learned previously is so obvious as to be self-evident. It's the same way we learned to walk, talk, read, write, and send a spaceship to the moon. But for some reason, we give the back of our hand to the power of kaizen-style baby steps and their role in accelerative learning—quite possibly because the method is so infuriatingly self-evident and fundamental. But it works. How do you eat an elephant? By ingesting one little incremental, kaizenlike *amuse-bouche* after another. Yet, I have had clients say to me, "I'll never learn to play the violin because I can't devote every single weekend for the rest of my life to it." Triumph in Twenty is the solution for those of us juggling big dreams alongside big jobs and big families. It's the way to dabble in lots of different things when we don't bask in the luxury of unlimited time. A little dab'll do ya. It's also the right answer for those of us who, frankly, aren't motivated to achieve Julliard-caliber expertise. The glory of Triumph in Twenty is its kaizen-fueled accelerator. But it depends on your making Triumph in Twenty a habit.

If the violin isn't something you'd choose as part of your cross-training regimen, you could consider it a hobby and be as desultory about it as you like. The difference between a hobby and Triumph is Twenty is the difference between a haphazard, unstructured approach and a sincere, structured intent. For our purposes, once you've committed to the violin, you've signed on to Triumph in Twenty. At some point of your choosing, when you've extracted everything from the violin you want to get, you can move on to something else. I would hope you wouldn't let the violin drop off your radar altogether, however. Typically, you can keep the skill alive with an occasional session, even as you move on to another round of Triumph in Twenty with another interest that's beckoning.

"People do not decide their future. They decide their habits, and their habits decide their future."

—Anonymous

Make Triumph in Twenty a habit. Stay in the game. Persist. Consider: You can learn a few of the fundamentals of lace making in twenty minutes. The Chinese language will yield five new words to you in the space of twenty minutes. You can speed-walk around the block—twice—in twenty minutes. In the same way that compound interest can allow for eye-popping financial returns, so can the cumulative progress represented by Triumph in Twenty blow your mind with what you'll be able to

"Think only about the present and focus on micro-goals. Just make it to that stop sign up ahead; OK, now make it to the tree up the street; and so on."

—Dean Karnazes,
ultramarathon runner

accomplish. You *build* on your progress—this simple fact is so often not acknowledged. This is how you step ever so gently into the slipstream, where resistance is reduced and, better still, you are tugged along by that powerful forward force called momentum.

Strategic Vectoring

Building a more vigorous mind often proceeds by way of what I call strategic vectoring. We're all familiar with the way Web surfing happens—how one topic leads to another, browsing from one link to another. That's frequently the way a Renaissance person acquires new interests. Assembling birdhouses leads to furniture design leads to boat building, and so on. You can choose to be less random and more strategic about your vectoring if you choose. Whether you generate your interests erratically or deliberately, you'll have four decisions to make: approach, topics, frequency, and pattern.

Approach

Your approach will depend on whether you wish to "train" or "cross-train." *Training* refers to activity that makes you more proficient at your primary occupation. So if you're a retail store clerk, training might call for customer service skills or inventory management. If you're a lawyer, training could involve continuing legal education classes in mediation skills or immigration options. It is a natural and commendable desire to become more adept at your occupation. If you're a physician, you spend as much time as you're able with medical journals, educating yourself on the latest studies, drugs, trends, and controversies in your specialty area. If you're a shoe designer, you probably spend a substantial portion of your free time attending trade shows, exchanging industry news with colleagues and competitors, and traveling to manufacturing facilities. If you're a parent, you scour books, magazines, and blogs dedicated to all aspects of parenting. Now, odds are, you and/or your employer are already taking care of your on-the-job training, in which case you're ready to move on to cross-training. But if that's not the case, or if you're anxious about the notion of cross-training in areas that are new to you, then straight training can ease you into the habit of strengthening your brain.

This book is predicated on the idea of cross-training, not training. Ultimately, I strongly recommend that everyone move up to cross-training, since that's what activates the highly desired neural activity in the brain. Sign up for a cooking class, even if you rely on take-out at home. Study music composition, even though you may never have played an instrument.

Topics

It's up to you to select which activities you choose to engage in—I set forth no prescriptions. These can be interests that seem similar to your primary occupation, if you wish. (For instance, if you're a high school Spanish teacher, you may wish to learn more about the geography of Central America.) If you're engaged in cross-training, however, your choices are much more vast—limitless, in fact. As a high school Spanish teacher, you'll reap the greatest benefits of the Vigorous Mind program if you stir your brain up with stamp collecting or woodworking or website construction—endeavors that have no apparent connection to teaching Spanish. That's how to access all your brainpower and bring it to bear on your primary occupation.

Frequency

You'll need to make a decision about how often you'll partake in your personal Triumph in Twenty. Once a week or twice during the week? Weekends only? Every day? I recommend a minimum of two times a week, and a maximum of five. If you leave this decision to chance, we all know what will happen. Other "stuff" will rush in to fill the time, even if that stuff is junk TV or Web surfing. As we've seen with the power of compound interest, maintaining traction is key. So start small to ensure that you can reliably honor the commitment. Lots of self-help programs are shot down by too much, too soon. Make a commitment here—even if it's a small one—and call on your weekly planner to be the enforcer. Suffice it to say that human beings need structure. In that manner, we're all a little like adolescents—we think we hate structure, when we actually crave it. (You'll learn more about making time for kaizen in Chapter 6.)

Pattern

Finally, you'll need to make a choice about which pattern of activities you'll want to pursue: one activity for a few months, or several topics at once. If you decide to follow the first, single-dimensional pattern, you might want to delve into a study of World War II, devoting twenty minutes a day, four days a week, for as long as you wish. If you choose, instead, the second, multi-dimensional pattern, you might engage in Pilates, poetry, and pottery, each activity once a week, for maybe six or twelve months. It's completely up to you. This program has lots of variables, and you're in charge of all of them. Your attention span is what governs the pattern of your involvement, as well as how many topics you're interested in, your work and family obligations, and financial constraints.

> *"Yard by yard, life is hard.*
> *Inch by inch, life's a cinch."*
>
> —Anonymous

Tortoise, Not Hare

Kaizen is a way of life, not a short-term process or program. It assumes that continual improvement is the goal of living, that every aspect of our lives deserves to be constantly improved. That sounds awfully tiring, doesn't it? Think about it too much, like I've been doing, and you're inclined to want to lie down and take a nap. Being under the gun to produce constant improvement in every single sector of my life sounds way too ambitious for a sorry slug like me. But kaizen is effective because it's sneaky. Since its changes are designed to be so small as to be almost undetectable, it can safely slip in under your defenses. The way we defend ourselves against self-improvement is fear. And kaizen will end-run your fear, bit by tiny little bit.

Surely you've heard the expression, "If it ain't broke, don't fix it." The kaizen philosophy is that everything, even if it "ain't broke," can be improved. *Quelle différence!* Think of it this way: minute course corrections in an airplane's trajec-

> *"Wisdom is knowing what to do next, skill is knowing how to do it, and virtue is doing it."*
>
> —David Starr Jordan
> (1851–1931), educator

tory can make all the difference; that's the way the pilot gets you to San Francisco, in fact: tiny adjustments along the way to accommodate wind speed and direction, turbulence, storms, and so on. Kaizen has nothing in common with splashy quantum leaps or megablockbuster improvements. You would not get from transistor radios to iPods all at once via kaizen. Yet, "thinking big" is ingrained in the American cultural mystique. This is likely the explanation for why kaizen has historically been a tough sell in America— we're impatient; we want things *now*. I get crazy waiting for the microwave to count itself backward from sixty. What am I supposed to do during those sixty seconds? (Kitchen-floor yoga, I've decided.)

There's nothing *wrong* with thinking big, of course. It's implementing the big-thinking schemes that seems to invariably fall short. We read almost daily about high-flying companies announcing grandiose expansion plans. They're going to open forty-nine new outlets and hire 717 employees in thirty states. Has anyone ever tracked the follow-through ratio on these proclamations? Although it may seem contradictory, I'm actually an advocate of big-thinking goals (BHAGs: Big Hairy Audacious Goals), but may I suggest a measured program of kaizen-flavored implementation? Yes, breakthroughs can happen in one swell foop, as they say, one epiphanic burst of inspiration, the way Mozart and John Lennon and Bernie Taupin composed certain of their iconic songs, for example. But quite possibly the best things in life take time to develop: cheese, wine, love, people . . . and skill at playing the violin.

Zen It Out

Kaizen is sort of like haiku: a Japanese concept that's been adopted and adapted for Western purposes—although I'll grant you, some of its mystical muscle has been lost in the process of assimilation. Like many things Japanese, there is something ineffably numinous about kaizen. It's almost as if an element of meditation whistles softly beneath its surface, an essence of listening to your inner self and respecting your own intuition. To that point, I have to admit that I've frowned at that familiar quote used earlier in this chapter ("The journey of a thousand miles . . .") and thought, "Yeah, sure—but what *is* that step?"

"Bird by bird."

—Anne Lamott, author
and political activist

Kaizen implies a "knowingness" about the next action step—that's the meditative aspect of it. If you quiet yourself and thaw the fear-freeze that's seized you, then simply ask yourself what is the first (or next) minuscule step to take, you'll find you have a pretty good idea what to do. And it's important to realize that within the universe of baby steps, there are conceivably many legitimate "next steps." The point is to just take a step—don't obsess about whether or not it's the "correct" one. There could be dozens of valid next steps as you move through your exploration of astronomy or fashion design or deck building.

Making a conscious effort to achieve your goals requires you to have *thought* about them. Maybe you have some gonzo "Mt. Fuji" goals, or endgame goals. Maybe you haven't yet formulated any big goals, but still want to do a little cross-training of your brain. In either case, you need only decide what tiny, incremental step you're going to *take today* in pursuit of that goal. Whether your goals are large or small, you have to be *thinking* to use kaizen—in fact, to will yourself to generate a new thought counts as a mini-step toward the achievement of a goal. Thinking is not only necessary for kaizen; it *is* kaizen. "The ancestor of every action," said Ralph Waldo Emerson, "is a thought."

"You've got to *think* that new small baby-step action before you can do it," says Grace Duffy, our motorcycle mama from earlier in this chapter. "If you believe in it first, then you'll see it—which is just the opposite of Missouri's state motto, 'Show me.' If we can first visualize something, we can eventually do it." That's encouraging to those of us seeking to develop our minds: we've got to first believe we can do it, against all odds, because there aren't too many people modeling it for us. This book includes numerous short profiles of both contemporary and historical individuals who have been bound and determined to live a wide-angle life, and I hope they spark you up. But you must first *believe* you can emulate them before you'll take the necessary actions.

To be sure, kaizen doesn't stop at thinking. It's all about action, and although thinking is necessarily the first action step, it's only the first. You'll need to move from thinking to doing, obviously. What's less obvious is that you'll then have to go from doing to habitual doing. Some kaizen experts call that "holding the gains."

Let's say you succeed in losing weight. (Congratulations—your prize is the toughest job you'll ever have—maintaining the loss. It's ironic that the kaizen way of expressing "maintaining the loss" is "holding the gains.") You may have accomplished your goal by literally eating just one fewer calorie per day than you did the day before, then two fewer calories the next day, and so on. Or perhaps, as an exercise-phobic, you first worked up the nerve to drive by a gym, recognizing that jumping right into an exercise program— or even walking in to inquire about membership—was too big a leap to make. Sometimes simply buying workout clothes is the first step—or even just making a note to buy the clothes. Whatever the case, you know what your first (or next) step needs to be. You probably don't need a guru to tell you; you already know in that small quiet place inside. Maybe that knowing is blocked from your consciousness, but kaizen says that if you "Zen it out" just a little, you will know.

So, by using kaizen, you've lost the weight—but you can't just revert back to status quo. Whatever changes you made in food, exercise, or thinking patterns need to stay made, even as you continue to look for additional baby steps to make. Kaizen doesn't sleep, any more than entropy sleeps.

Kaizen is the enemy of—and antidote to—entropy. We all want to avoid kaizen's opposite, *kaiaku*, which literally means "change for the worse." Kaiaku, or entropy, is chaos, disorder, dissipation of energy. It's what happens to anything you're not mindful of—it inexorably goes to pot. (The good thing about entropy, as the quip goes, is that it requires no maintenance.) Some everyday examples of entropy: setting aside your violin for three years, letting the ice melt in your drink, allowing clutter to overtake your home or office, permitting relationships to flag if you're not attentive to them, failing to keep up an exercise regimen. We can also experience entropy within our psyches. This is equivalent to mental malnutrition, the "brain starvation" I referred to earlier—the sad consequence of getting so woven into the adult world of relentless responsibility and narrowly defined jobs that we lose touch with our better selves, our formerly well-rounded selves.

Kaizen, in its dogged, persistent way, is the world's best antidote to entropy. Nothing can ever defeat entropy, but keeping it at bay via small incremental steps consistently taken—that's cookin' with gas; that's the strike zone.

Kaizen and the Law of Attraction

We've seen that kaizen starts with a thought, or that it can even consist of a thought. This notion of "thinking as action," bizarre as it sounds, is quite *au courant*. In March 2006, a film called *The Secret* was produced that explores the "Law of Attraction," and was later developed into a book by the same name. It's having quite a cultural moment itself. The movie and book continue to sell at a furious pace, and both have gained widespread attention in the media, from *Saturday Night Live* to *Oprah*. Like kaizen, an ancient philosophy rooted in Zen, the Law of Attraction is an ancient Eastern belief system that's being recycled for contemporary consumption.

The Law of Attraction is this: As you sow, so shall you reap—meaning that whatever you put out into the universe will be reflected back to you.

What this means from a practical standpoint is that we always attract into our lives whatever we think about most often, believe in most strongly, expect on the deepest levels, and imagine most vividly. When we are negative or fearful, insecure or anxious, we often attract the very experiences, situations, or people we're seeking to avoid. If we're positive in attitude, expecting and envisioning pleasure, satisfaction, and happiness, we tend to attract people and create situations and events that conform to our positive expectations. So consciously thinking about what we want to have or achieve can help us to manifest it in our lives. As you think, so shall you be.

How important is mental attitude to Triumph in Twenty? It's big. Mental attitude controls, on a grand scale, the space we occupy in life, the success we achieve, the friends we retain, and the contributions we make to posterity. And perhaps the most convincing evidence of the importance of mental attitude is the fact that it's the one and only thing over which anyone has been given the complete, unchallengeable privilege of personal control.

Thinking is a skill that the vigorous-minded owe it to themselves to . . . well, think about. It's germane to our topic—in moderation, as we'll see. The Law of Attraction simply states that you are what you think about, and then you *get* what you think about. Therefore, you can manifest what you want by thinking the right thoughts. Thinking negative thoughts will derail you, block your progress toward your goals. The Law of Attraction implies that you can actually control your reality by thinking the right kinds of thoughts. I have wondered if the Law of Attraction would allow us to think our way to being higher-functioning cross-trainers. Or is it yet another instance of over-promising and underdelivering?

The Law of Attraction asserts that the experience of life is manifested through our predominant thoughts, feelings, words, and actions. It suggests that we consequently have direct control over our experience of reality—the contents of our consciousness—through our thoughts alone, given that our thoughts lead to our actions. If I radiate joy, love, positivity, abundance, and hope, that's what I'll attract back in return. If I emanate a miasma of despair, negativity, nihilism, scarcity, and fear, I'll attract those kinds of energies into my life.

Because the Law of Attraction purports that what you get is what you think about, it's easy to see how legions of followers have been tempted into subscribing to it. After all, what could be more enticing? Its sheen has led some enthusiastic proponents to think—compulsively—about wealth, love, happiness, prosperity, money, wealth, cash, and money. Wealth, too.

What most bothers me is that within this discussion of how to bring peace, love, joy, and abundance into your life, there seems to be no recognition of an old-fashioned and, admittedly, rather unpopular idea: hard work. I'm all for thinking good thoughts—especially when they concern the development of a vigorously cross-trained brain. I completely agree that positive thoughts are essential. It just seems somehow correct to me that if you sow upbeat thoughts, you'll reap upbeat results. And the inverse seems correct, too. But that's not the end of the story.

No one can just sit around on the back porch thinking a whole slew of happy thoughts and then expect the universe to open its purse strings and let fly with the good stuff. That's called wishful thinking. It's a fine thing to do; in fact, thinking that you want a new car or a new job or a new boyfriend or a new outlook is the necessary first step, as we've seen in kaizen. But you can't stop with that first baby step, as we've also seen in kaizen. You've got to go forth and make it happen. It's like they say: Pray hard to catch the bus—then run like hell.

So I take the Law of Attraction with a grain of salt. It's fine as far as it goes, but embedded within the law is an unappealing naïveté ("presto: the universe will support me and my wishes") and a lack of personal responsibility that *you* determine if your goals are going to be met, based on your hard work, not the whims of the universe. You'll never get the job done without the Law of Attraction on your side, but you'll also never get the job done with *just* the Law of Attraction on your side.

> *"Creating an adult life is a continuous act of will."*
>
> —Anonymous

Your Brain as a Grab Bag

There is a juicy tension beginning to make itself known, roiling around just beneath the surface of our topic. I have quite intentionally juxtaposed two whopper-sized concepts: the first is large-scale Renaissance cross-training of your brain; the second is small-scale "baby steps."

This ambitious juxtaposition can be symbolized by a global comparison of East versus West. The word *Renaissance* is associated with that period in history—think Italy in the fifteenth century—when the world emerged from the ghastly drear of the Middle Ages and, with flamboyance, fecundity, and built-up brio, embraced art, music, science, and Ben & Jerry's (whoops, that came later). Artists, philosophers, and explorers in Florence began to recover the ancient genius from before the fall of Byzantium and found there the ideas and images of the Greeks, Romans, and Hebrews. The lost legacy of the world's past thoughts and dreams was born again into their time, and from this stimulus, to this very day, we are still staggered and stirred. The Renaissance era is an example not of incremental, kaizenlike advances, but of blasting breakthroughs, explosions of realized potential. Another order of reality appeared to the world as painters, sculptors, musicians, architects, engineers, and scientists were consumed by visions of what could be, their pent-up inspiration pouring forth like geysers of human capability.

The key to making headway on a goal is a balance between kaizen and epiphany. Kaizen represents regular, predictable, incremental gains; in contrast, an epiphany is a breakthrough—a seemingly spontaneous eruption of insight you can't directly elicit. You definitely can and should set out to implement kaizen on any given day; however, you cannot set out to have a breakthrough or epiphany on Thursday at 10:00 AM. Put your faith in the former; hope for the latter.

"That all things are possible to him who believes; that they are less difficult to him who hopes; that they are more easy to him who loves; and still more easy to him who perseveres in the practice of these three virtues."

—Brother Lawrence (c. 1614–1691), Carmelite monk

In the years before Henry Ford conceived of his famous assembly line, the process of manufacturing followed the so-called English System. This system centered around a craftsman producing each part of a product individually and then assembling those parts into the finished product. Then a world-changing event took place. A Ford engineer named William C. Klann visited a slaughterhouse in Chicago, where he observed what was referred to as a *disassembly line*. On this line, animals were moved along a conveyor as one worker removed the same piece from each animal, over and over. Klann drew a comparison between cows and cars—his famous "slaughterhouse revelation." Although one was being taken apart, and the other put together, he perceived the parallels. The slaughtering process was efficient, compared to the inefficiency of one worker disassembling a cow entirely on his own. He reported his observations to Ford; skepticism prevailed, but Klann was given the green light to try his conveyor idea. This turned out to be a breakthrough of earth-shattering proportions, resulting in the modern moving assembly line in which interchangeable parts are added in a sequential manner to create a finished product. The assembly line is now widely considered to be the catalyst that initiated the modern consumer culture and all its attendant marvels and misfortunes. For our purposes, it's instructive to realize that before and after the breakthrough idea of an assembly line, a million kaizenesque adjustments were being made to the process, as you can well imagine. Epiphany and kaizen. Evolution and revolution. They work best when they work together.

"Continuous improvement, or kaizen, is like brushing your teeth daily, or working out every day," says Tom Pearson, a business consultant who helps corporations implement kaizenlike continuous process improvement. "Brushing your teeth and exercising are routine things you habitually do while you wait for that big breakthrough." Implicit in Pearson's thought is that a breakthrough may never quite arrive—there's no guarantee—but that's okay, because you'll do just fine plodding along making small but steady progress using kaizen. Yes, proud poky plodders we shall be. "Kaizen operates like the tortoise, not the hare," notes Grace Duffy. "Both are good; both are desirable. But kaizen is evolutionary, not revolutionary."

I'm quite smitten with the marriage of the lofty Renaissance movement with the rubber-meets-the-road notion of kaizen. The Renaissance was a sudden, epiphanic blossoming. Kaizen was under it, behind it, before it, and after it. The two form a sweeping, ambitious synthesis.

> *"Life is a succession of moments. To live each one is to succeed."*
>
> —Corita Kent (1918–1986), artist and author

Mentors and Coaches and Gurus, Oh My!

Now, I'll grant you, the violin example from earlier in this chapter is somewhat specious. Most of us would need a teacher to get us off on the right foot with the violin, and violin instructors don't typically sell their lessons in ten- or twenty-minute chunks of time. But in terms of your practice time, the Triumph in Twenty methodology is perfectly valid. At some point, even the most devoted autodidact may want to seek out a mentor. Most of us can go only so far on our own, before our skills level off. As Grace Duffy puts it, "I can do only what I believe I can do. I may need outside influence to change my paradigm to a new and more advanced vision of performance." But you'll find that plenty of other endeavors, although less technical, can be successfully undertaken with little or no outside instruction. Cooking, physical fitness, and reading immediately come to mind. The beauty of our civilization is that there's always an expert or coach waiting in the wings to guide you along, no matter what the endeavor. Call upon them when you need an injection of expert inspiration.

Sometimes, though, the best learning takes place when we make discoveries on our own, rather than being spoon-fed by a guru. Whether you're interested in learning about the works of Charles Dickens, playing golf or the violin, scrapbooking, or preparing and eating raw foods, here's a list of readily available resources that you might want to consider:

Books. Published books are usually written by experts and are, therefore, usually reliable. As such, they're an excellent resource of high-level information that can help you get started on just about any topic.

Book discussion clubs. You may be able to get more out of what you read if you meet with a group of like-minded individuals who are reading the same, or similar, books. Not only will you have the opportunity to discuss what you've gleaned from your text, but you'll most likely learn a great deal from the insights offered by others. When organized properly, a book club can be a good resource for learning more about a given interest.

E-books. Electronic books are relatively new and are therefore not as plentiful as printed books, although that's beginning to change as the technology develops. The advantages of e-books is that they can be searched automatically and cross-referenced, and they are highly mobile, as long as you have a portable online reading device. E-books offer a good—though limited—resource for quality information.

Magazines. It's seems there's a magazine for just about every interest, from somewhat specialized periodicals (*Popular Mechanics, Discover, Time*) to highly specialized publications (*T'ai Chi, Dairy Goat Journal, Bead & Button*) to scholarly journals (*The Kenyon Review, The Chronicle of Higher Education*). Because the possibilities are practically limitless, magazines are an excellent resource for breadth and depth of information.

Newspapers. Don't overlook newspapers as a fertile source of ideas and information; keep in mind, however, that daily publications are best at putting current events in perspective, so you might not always find what you're looking for, depending on what's considered newsworthy at the time. Newspapers are a good resource for learning more about an enormous range of topics.

The Internet. The alpha and the omega for vigorously minded crosstrainers. Surfing the Internet takes you places you never imagined (all without leaving your chair), and there's almost nothing you can't find with a few clicks of the mouse. Just remember that what you find might not always be true or complete or even palatable. Though the reputable sources represent good resources, much else of what's available is dross.

Online databases. Databases offer much of the information you can find on the Web, but they're much more reliable and, therefore, they're an excellent resource of information on a broad range of topics and interests. Examples include: InfoTrac, DemographicsNow, Grolier Online, NoveList, ReferenceUSA, and LexisNexis.

Blogs. Web logs, or blogs, are websites that often include commentary, descriptions of events, or other material. They can be excellent conglomerations of information, depending on the knowledge and reliability of the bloggers. You can start one of your own to chronicle your Vigorous Mind venture, and become a resource for friends and family to emulate.

Electronic mailing lists, or e-lists. These include newsletters, discussion lists, and online bulletin boards intended for a large group of people who are united by a common interest. Subscribers to these services can post questions, answers, and comments, composing a sort of online dialog. Some e-lists are regulated by moderators, who help ensure a high average quality of posts, thereby increasing reliability and validity.

Chat groups. Online chats allow for conversation in real time. There's no lack of chat groups available for just about every taste or interest. Chats are a fair resource for information; the quality of information depends on the knowledge and reliability of those in the group.

Coaches. As you embark on your cross-training, you may find that you need a hired gun to hold you accountable. A coach doesn't have to be an expert in your given area of interest, but he or she can guide you in staying focused on your goals. Coaches are an excellent resource for information and inspiration.

Classes. Classes taught by knowledgeable professionals are also an excellent resource. Taking a class for credit will surely motivate you to keep your nose to the grindstone of your choice; noncredit classes—such as most continuing education classes—can offer the same quality of information, with perhaps a little less rigor. Both types are great for meeting people with similar interests.

Online/televised classes. Some cable television networks will bring classes right into your living room, and many universities now offer computer-based online courses that can be completed for credit. These are good resources—and convenient, too.

The buddy system. Try setting up a partnership with a friend. The beauty of the buddy system is that the other person's presence creates an expectation you'll show up, too. This is especially beneficial when you're undertaking a physical fitness program.

MasterMind groups. To nurture the "life" in your life of the mind, create a MasterMind group—a small confederation of people gathered for mutual betterment. Albert Schweitzer said, "In everyone's life, at some time, our inner fire goes out. It is then burst into flame by an encounter with another human being. We should all be thankful for those people who rekindle the inner sprit." When you're trying to generate an idea or an approach that's bold and memorable, it may help to model or emulate someone you admire. I've heard this called "being a consultant to yourself." In his 1937 classic *Think and Grow Rich*, Napoleon Hill invited "imaginary friends" to join his MasterMind group. Each night before falling asleep, Hill would close his eyes and imagine himself to be in the company of nine "invisible counselors" modeled after his nine greatest heroes: Ralph Waldo Emerson, Thomas Paine, Thomas Edison, Charles Darwin, Abraham Lincoln, Luther Burbank, Napoleon Bonaparte, Henry Ford, and Andrew Carnegie. "My purpose," wrote Hill, "was to rebuild my own character so it would represent a composite of the characters of my imaginary counselors." Hill would then ask each member of his "cabinet" to bestow upon him some quality of theirs that he especially admired. For instance, he asked Emerson for understanding of nature; Napoleon, the ability to inspire men; Lincoln, a keen sense of justice, and so on.

Videos/DVDs. Videos and DVDs are valuable resources not only for their informational content, but also because they're visual how-tos that are particularly helpful for hands-on tasks that may be difficult to master when you have only written material to follow. When you're having trouble visualizing how to cast off in knitting (or fishing), check out a how-to video from your local library.

Books on tape. These are good resources for auditory learners who can absorb information while they're sitting in traffic, taking a walk, folding laundry, or are otherwise engaged. The classics by osmosis—why not?

Conferences and conventions. Birds of a feather flock together. Conferences and conventions are an excellent resource of information related to a particular topic, and they provide opportunities for people with common interests to participate in discussions or listen to lectures about specific areas of study.

Lectures, symposia, and public events. The eclectic offerings at New York City's 92nd Street Y are unparalleled in depth, breadth, quality, and value. Prominent leaders in science, art, entertainment, business, culture, and health speak on issues of the day. Regularly perusing their catalog is itself a treat. Robert Pirsig popularized the term *Chautauqua*, an educational gathering that includes lectures, concerts, and dramatic performances. I once attended a Chautauqua featuring a performance of actors channeling Churchill, Marilyn Monroe, Gandhi, and Einstein, all commenting on contemporary world affairs. Perhaps a troupe in your city could be persuaded to follow suit—the establishment of which would make a great Renaissance activity.

What the heck, just plunge in on your own and see what happens. Sometimes this is the most fun and most efficient, leaving you open to the power of serendipitous discoveries.

"Every action we take, everything we do, is either a victory or defeat in the struggle to become what we want to be."

—Anne Byrhhe, educator

EXERCISES

The following exercises are designed to build your kaizen muscle and establish a pattern for integrating Triumph in Twenty into your weekly routine.

1. Triumph in Twenty

Refer to your master Bliss List from Chapter 2. Choose three activities, and try approaching them using the Triumph in Twenty technique. If you want to sneak up on it, take a baby-size action step while you're waiting for a phone call, a lunch date, a doctor's appointment, or the microwave. These are small windows of time just begging to be kaizen'd.

2. Triumph in Twenty, Part Two

Jot down the next kaizen-inspired action step you will commit to taking for three projects in your life. Or better yet, take those action steps.

PART TWO

Now that we've learned a little bit about the latent power of our leisure time, established the complementary benefits and liabilities of generalists and specialists in our society, and introduced the concept of kaizen and its cousin Triumph in Twenty, it's time to turn to Part 2.

In Part 2, we'll unpack the seven imperatives that constitute the experience of a fully faceted cross-trainer. To develop the kind of nimble mind we all want, you'll want to develop a relationship with all seven imperatives. Some will, naturally, be more or less second nature to you; other will represent a stretch for you (indeed, stretching is itself one of the imperatives).

The seven imperatives are designed to head off the most pervasive, insidious, and undiagnosed malaise of our society: brain entropy. You'll see that the imperatives are decidedly not specific activities I'm prescribing for you to engage in as a way of achieving brain health—things such as partaking of daily exercise or solving brain teasers or devising new routes to work. These are all fine things, but they are details, and in this program, details are left up to you to select. Rather, the imperatives that follow represent something much more sweeping: global attributes that you'll want to incorporate into your character. The imperatives are not "things to do"; they are more like "ways to be." The seven imperatives represent, in toto, the kind of worldview or state of mind any true Renaissance person makes a point of cultivating.

The following chapters will introduce you to the seven imperatives. They are:

- The Curiosity Imperative: Don't Take "Yes" for an Answer. This is nonnegotiable! The most conspicuous trait of any cross-trainer, curiosity underpins all else.

- The Individuality Imperative: To Thine Own Self Be True— Or Not. Make the program work for you. This is custom work, not one-size-fits-all.

- The Selectivity Imperative: Be Selective but Open-Minded— There *Is* Enough Time. We attack the crucial lack-of-time objection.

- The Empathy Imperative: Share the Riches. Go forth, spread the word, and share the wealth.

- The Stretch Imperative: Put Something on the Line. Expect sore mental hamstrings once in a while.

- The Spirituality Imperative: Peak Experiences and Constructing a Worldview. This is where we put the pursuit of a vigorous mind in a big-picture context.

- The Courage Imperative: The Audacity to Be an Amateur. No one ever said this would be easy. Remember, challenge is pleasure.

These imperatives are consistent with the kind of vigorous and cross-trained mind that characterizes a *Uomo Universale*. Without further preamble, let's get curious and get started.

4

IMPERATIVE #1:
THE CURIOSITY IMPERATIVE

Don't Take "Yes" for an Answer

> I could not, at any age, be content to take my place
> by the fireside and simply look on. Life was meant to be lived.
> Curiosity must be kept alive. One must never,
> for whatever reason, turn his back on life.
>
> —*Eleanor Roosevelt (1884–1962)*

We start with the sine qua non trait of any serious cross-trainer: curiosity. It's the single nonnegotiable characteristic of all Renaissance thinkers.

While not necessarily a full-fledged Renaissance woman herself, Terry Gross of National Public Radio has exuded the benchmark quality of curiosity through her enviable exposure to interesting writers, books, ideas, and thoughts on her radio interview show *Fresh Air*. Writer Paul Schneider says, "In an age of micro-specialists—salad-course editors and foremost authorities on Serbo-Croatian transgender epic poetry—Terry Gross is a great beacon of voracious Renaissance curiosity. She reminds us, her listeners, that this great big world is overflowing with the most extraordinary range of talent, art, achievement, and perspective, all of which is accessible and worthy

"One can remain alive long past the usual date of disintegration if one is unafraid of change, insatiable in intellectual curiosity, interested in big things, and happy in small ways."

—Edith Wharton
(1862–1937), author

if we're only curious enough to ask with an open heart and listen with an open mind."

Certainly the most celebrated example of a curiosity-driven Renaissance man was Leonardo da Vinci. One of the greatest artists of all time, he filled his notebooks with minute observations of nature; with schemes for mechanical inventions and engineering projects, ranging from military projectiles to airplanes; and with anatomical studies and sketches. Da Vinci was a painter, sculptor, engineer, astronomer, anatomist, biologist, geologist, physicist, architect, philosopher, and humanist. Truly a cognitive acrobat, he moved easily from art to science and back again. Only in a culture with no rigid boundaries between the two spheres could this take place. (Like many of his contemporaries, he believed that painting was a scientific activity that called on the principles of arithmetic and geometry.) There were practical considerations for investigating so many areas of interest. During the Renaissance, it was advisable to be competent in a variety of fields because the artists in greatest demand with noble employers were those with drafting, engineering, and architectural talents, as well as creative and aesthetic flair. Da Vinci did not reject specialization; it's just that the concept had not yet been invented.

"All men, by nature, desire to know."

—Aristotle (384–322 BC)

Edward Tufte is variously described as the "Galileo of graphic design," the "da Vinci of data"—and a rock star, to boot. Although his doctorate is in political science, this man is eclectically curious. Technically, he's a professor (at Princeton) and statistician, but that's a mighty meager description for someone who extracts input from art, economics, and history to do his work. That work is often labeled "information architecture" or "analytic design"—otherwise stated, his expertise is in the presentation of informational graphics such as charts and diagrams. He achieved fame through his criticism of the way Microsoft's PowerPoint software is typically used—or, shall we say, misused. Tufte's criticism of PowerPoint has extended to its use by NASA engineers in the events leading to the Columbia space shuttle disaster.

And consider Buckaroo Banzai, who is a fictional character in the movie *The Adventures of Buckaroo Banzai Across the 8th Dimension*. He's a Renaissance man driven to know the whats and whys of all kinds of things: neurosurgery, particle physics, race car driving, rock 'n' roll, comic books. Buckaroo is considered the last best hope of the human race. I admire his curiosity.

> *"What a large volume of adventures may be grasped within this little span of life by him who interests his heart in everything."*
>
> —Laurence Sterne (1713–1768), from his novel *A Sentimental Journey*

The Exemplar of Curiosity

As befits a discussion of the most important trait a brain cross-trainer can cultivate, I present to you the crown prince of consummate curiosity, Richard Feynman. Feynman, who died in 1988, was a great scientist and a winner of the Nobel Prize, remembered as much for his unquenchable vitality and sense of humor as for his laboratory work on liquid helium. A playful spin of a plate in a cafeteria led him to his breakthrough work on the spin of electrons and his 1965 Nobel Prize in Physics. His lighthearted approach to life made his lectures at the California Institute of Technology a delight and his scientific accomplishments all the more intriguing. Feynman was curious about everything. Once called a "puckish genius," he painted; he traded ideas with Einstein and Bohr; he calculated odds with professional gambler Nick the Greek; he used his talent as a lock picker to demonstrate how lax security was; he accompanied ballet performances on his bongo drums. His life story has been described as a combustible mixture of high intelligence, eternal skepticism, raging chutzpah, and unlimited curiosity.

"This is so interesting!" was Richard Feynman's cri de coeur and mantra for life. Feynman was born in1918, in Queens, New York. A late talker (in common with other famous physicists Edward Teller, Carl Sagan, and Albert Einstein), he must have given his parents cause for concern: a three-year-old with a vocabulary of zero. As a child, he enjoyed repairing radios and demonstrated a knack for engineering.

Author Kay Redfield Jamison analyzed Feynman with respect to his exuberance, noting that his zesty curiosity about science and life in general made for a rapier intuitive intellect. Feynman understood that all the world's a stage, and his was the lecture hall. As a lecturer/performer, he shared with his audience dramatic fireworks as well as data, yet he seems not to have made the mistake of substituting impact for information. He urged students to assemble their own worldview, to fabricate a unique universe of ideas. Feynman's father, Melville, passed along the genes for curiosity and challenging orthodoxy. Still, Richard wasn't so much a whiz as he was a galumpher, and it was all such fun to him. Physicist Freeman Dyson observed, "I never heard him give a lecture that did not make the audience laugh." When asked how long he worked each week, Feynman couldn't really say, because he never knew when he was working and when he was playing. "Science is done for the excitement of what is found out," he said, an assertion that made its way into his book *The Meaning of It All: Thoughts of a Citizen Scientist*. "It is almost impossible for me to convey in a lecture this important aspect, this exciting part, the real reason for science." Furthermore, you cannot understand science unless you "understand and appreciate the great adventure of our world . . . This tremendous adventure is a wild and exciting thing."

Life, for Feynman, was the fabulous pursuit of truth and beauty and joy. His life was a testament to the notion that exploration leads to pleasure and that such pleasure, in turn, leads to more discovery; that wonderful mysteries lure one "to penetrate deeper still . . . turn over each new stone to find unimagined strangeness leading on to more wonderful questions and mysteries—certainly a grand adventure!" He dazzled his audiences with intellectual capework and riveted them with his wit and energy, infusing his audiences with his own joy in discovering the "beautiful things" of nature.

As a free spirit and true eccentric, Feynman chased down all kinds of interests: biology, art, hieroglyphs, painting, juggling, playing the bongos, and pulling practical jokes. He discovered the combination to a locked filing cabinet by using the numbers a physicist would use (27-18-28, after the base of natural logarithms). Once, he repaired to an isolated section of a mesa to drum in the style of American natives and "maybe dance and chant a little." (These antics did not go unnoticed, and rumors spread about a mysterious Indian drummer called "Injun Joe.") Dyson wrote that Feynman was "half-genius, half-buffoon," but later revised that to "all-genius, all-buffoon." During his lifetime and after his death, Feynman became one of the most publicly known scientists in the world.

Sometimes called the "Great Explainer," Feynman gained a reputation for taking great care when explaining scientific explanations to his students, and for assigning himself a moral duty to make the topic accessible. His principle was that if a topic could not be explained in a freshman lecture, it was not yet fully understood.

Feynman frequently expressed a long-standing desire to visit the Russian land of Tuva. His efforts to circumvent the complex Soviet bureaucratic system that kept Tuva sealed, and also his attempts to write and send a letter using an English-Russian and Russian-Tuvan dictionary, as well as his earlier efforts to translate Mayan hieroglyphics, all demonstrate his lifelong passion for puzzles.

Although Feynman's professional life focused on physics, he loved the arts and keeping company with artists. Using the pseudonym "Ofey," he became interested in drawing at one point, which resulted in an exhibition of his work. He turned his enthusiasm to drumming at another point in his life. With persistence and practice, he learned to drum in the samba style, even attending a samba school. Standard orchestral music did nothing for him, but he had such an innately strong sense of rhythm that his brain seemed to function as a chronometer, allowing him to "tell time" instinctively and without a watch. When it came to arithmetical equations, he was said to have some degree of mixed sense perception, or *synesthesia*, where the black-and-white letters and numbers in certain mathematical formulations appeared in color to him.

A dynamic Renaissance man, Feynman's charisma stemmed from his fascination with every aspect of life. Of his curiosity gene, he said, "I'm an explorer. I like to find out." Feynman was one of the most singular characters to roam the earth in the twentieth century—my exemplar for the Curiosity Imperative.

The Pleasure of Finding Things Out

Curiosity is the cornerstone of a vigorous mind. It cannot be overstated how powerful is the simple act of asking a seemingly naïve question. It triggers a consideration of something altogether new, depositing a speck of impurity into the mix, like the impurity that begets a pearl in an oyster. Curiosity opens up avenues that lead to new intersections. But only a receptive mind can conjure something as radical as a naïve question. You have to be open to the unexpected so that, should you wander into a discovery, you'll recognize it and act upon it.

Curiosity is about cultivating an open mind, then expanding it further still. Be curious. Be avid. Be keen. Be *relentless*. Ask more questions. Curiosity is about asking why, when, who, how, what, and where; introducing skepticism and risking the fallout that skepticism usually generates; getting in touch with every child's birthright—seeing everything in this old world for the very first time and wondering, wondering, wondering. Ask yourself, "What is the big picture here?" Generalists are good at observing the "everythingness" of life and seeking out the particular something that a specialist can pursue. A generalist, as we've seen, is a divergent thinker in touch with a large realm of possibilities. Those possibilities exist at the intersection of multidisciplinary, multi-industry, multicultural thinking—exactly the kind of thinking that our narrowly focused lives tend not to have enough of. Record producer David Foster recently told the graduates at Berklee College of Music in

Boston to expand their horizons while pursuing their artistic passions. "Be open to things other than music," said Foster, who's won fourteen Grammy Awards. "Remember the first words you learned in grade school: look and listen. Learn as much as you can about everything."

Searchlight Curiosity

Historically, curiosity has been a revered trait. In addition to Feynman, other avatars of curiosity include Sir Francis Bacon (1561–1626), a Renaissance man in England, who rather grandly wrote, "I have taken all knowledge to be my province." Sir Walter Raleigh (1554–1618) was a soldier, statesman, explorer, poet, and a courtier to Queen Elizabeth I. Another great example of the Renaissance ideal is Leon Battista Alberti (1404–1472), who was an architect, painter, poet, scientist, mathematician, and also a skilled horseman. And most people will agree that Winston Churchill (1874–1965), the wartime prime minister of Great Britain, was a Renaissance man: soldier, statesman, scholar, historian, writer, painter, wit, and maker of memorable phrases. In the history of the United States, surely the preeminent Renaissance man was Thomas Jefferson (1743–1826), author of the Declaration of Independence, third president of the United States, architect of the University of Virginia and of Monticello, inventor of many ingenious and useful household improvements, and guardian of the liberties of the people.

At the time of the Renaissance, a man of the aristocracy received an all-around education that prepared him for curiosity about all aspects of his life. He was trained in the "manly arts" of fencing, riding, and combat; as a courtier, he had to be adept in conversation, ready to turn out a sonnet or a song, and be able to play a musical instrument; as a statesman, he had to have a classical education, a proficiency in languages, and skill in diplomacy. There was no division at that time between a man of action and a man of learning and the arts. A Renaissance man was expected to be both. Fueled by boundless curiosity, it was assumed that one could develop one's potential, covering both the arts and the sciences. It is interesting to note that *Renaissance man* is unfailingly used as a term of admiration, even awe, in literature, including passing references. No villain, no matter how many-sided or famous, has ever been called a Renaissance man.

Curiouser and Curiouser

There's curiosity and then there's curiosity *squared*. Most animals are curious to a degree (cats being famous for their curiosity, of course). Curiosity is innate in the human animal, consistent with our drives for self-preservation and reproduction. For example, our ancient ancestors called upon their curiosity in order to seek out new food sources: Is this plant poisonous? Are rocks edible? What will happen if I put this pig over a fire? Curiosity can thus confer a survival advantage to certain species, and can be found in their genomes. But modern humans seem to be losing touch with the power and importance of curiosity in our lives when, in fact, we have the capacity to get caught up in an endless loop that our friends the lower animals don't fuss about— getting curious about curiosity itself, which is the essence of abstract self-awareness and self-consciousness.

Human beings who are most alive, though, go beyond a superficial level of curiosity to seek out the next level of wondering. We are curious about the underlying structure of the world, the level that lies below the obvious. We not only want to know the answers to "yes or no" questions, but also answers to the "why" questions, the causes or reasons behind what we know. This knowledge of the world is intrinsically rewarding; it is delightful even when it can't be put to immediate practical use. Science is the name we've assigned to the systematic study of curiosity about our world.

The Curious Business

"What is the single most important quality that suits you for a career in science?" asks V. S. Ramachandran, director of the Center for Brain and Cognition at the University of California, San Diego. "People often say 'curiosity,' but surely that can't be the whole story. After all, everyone is curious to some degree, but not everyone is destined to be a scientist." Ramachandran is immensely curious about ancient Indian archaeology, art, linguistics, the cultivation of orchids, anthropology, ethnology, paleontology, gastropod taxonomy, inorganic chemistry, botany, and entomology. But generic curiosity isn't sufficient. "I would argue that you need to be obsessively, passionately, almost pathologically curious. Or, as Peter Medawar once said, you need to 'experience physical discomfort when there is incomprehension.' Curiosity needs to dominate your life."

Whatever happened to our childlike state of curiosity—the kind of awe that Ramachandran has and that Feynman maintained throughout his life? What is it about growing up that tamps down and displaces curiosity with boredom, disinterest, and indifference? Some people might place the blame for its loss on our system of schooling, which tends to reward the right answers more than the right questions, so that teachers feel under pressure to "teach to the test." A student who brings the class to a halt with his or her relentless questioning (a difficult scenario to imagine, given the apathy of so many students today) is impeding the teacher from slogging through the state-mandated curriculum. School, as many of us experienced it, placed no premium on a questing intelligence; it was not about education, but about process, not about curiosity, but about its antithesis: the teacher-sanctioned correct response. The forced march of public schooling too often quashes inquisitiveness in favor of the tyranny of the "right answer."

Only as adults do we finally realize that there is no "right answer," and to remain focused on that mirage keeps us from looking at more creative ways to solve the problems we face. The higher the quality of question we ask, the higher the quality of answer we will receive. In fact, the questions that engage our thought on a daily basis influence the quality of our lives, especially as brain cross-trainers seeking mental vigor. Don't take "no" for an answer. Don't even take "yes" for an answer. The answer is always "why?" or "tell me more."

As adults, the favorite whipping boy for our lack of mental vigor is probably lack of time. I believe that lack of time is actually a stand-in for lack of the proper perspective about time. More on that in Chapter 6.

The Width of the World

Respected *New York Times* columnist Thomas L. Friedman, author of *The World Is Flat*, has set forth a formula that brilliantly captures the importance of curiosity: Your Curiosity Quotient plus your Passion Quotient is greater than your Intelligence Quotient (CQ + PQ > IQ). Friedman states, "Give me the kid with a passion to learn and a curiosity to discover and I will take him or her over the less passionate kid with a huge IQ every day of the week." IQ still matters, says Friedman, but curiosity and passion matter even more.

It's perplexing, then, that curiosity has gotten such a black eye over the years. No doubt because it can lead to peril, curiosity is the object of many cautionary stories and adages. Pandora's curiosity loosed a host of woes upon the world when she opened a box. Faust's curiosity led him to sell his soul for secret knowledge. I much prefer to revere curiosity as the motor of motivation—the force that propels learning and advancement and civilization.

> *"One thing life taught me— if you are interested, you never have to look for new interests. They come to you."*
>
> —Eleanor Roosevelt (1884–1962)

The biblical "fall" of mankind is popularly associated with illicit curiosity for forbidden knowledge. The Mormons have a fascinating approach to this—they seem to accept it with more equanimity than other Christian denominations. According to John Tanner of Brigham Young University, "Latter Day Saints do not understand the Fall as a precautionary tale against curiosity, nor condemn Eve for desiring godlike knowledge. Rather, we proclaim that humans can and should strive to become like God, whose glory is intelligence. We affirm that we ought to learn all we can in this life and expect to continue learning in the next. For us, lifelong learning is not simply a practical expedient for a flat world. It is a theological imperative for this world and the world to come."

Go Ahead and Kill the Cat

Keep in mind our thesis: Deliberately seeking out new experiences and knowledge across a broad range of subjects cross-trains the brain. That full-brain stimulation provides us with a rich mosaic of perspectives to call upon when we pursue our own little sliver of the world, that niche where we spend our working days. Being a generalist, in other words, helps you become a better specialist. Here are a few reasons why curiosity will make you better at what you do and who you are, whether you're an organic farmer, short-order cook, sommelier, bond trader, work-at-home mom, postmaster, or you-name-it.

Curiosity broadens horizons. By swallowing a curious vitamin every day, that "vitamin C" will stretch the bounds of your mental vision, enabling you to perceive more possibilities—on the surface, underneath the surface, beyond the surface.

Curiosity is a catalyst for proactivity. If you're always reacting to things, you need to kick it up a notch. Become cognitively proactive. Do this by asking questions. Ask curious questions. Never accept "yes" as an answer. Want a better answer? Ask a better question.

Curiosity props open the doorway of your brain. When you flex your "curious muscle," you energize your brain. And the next time you generate a new idea, your fired-up brain will embrace it more quickly. Otherwise, your flaccid brain may not even recognize its own brainstorms. I believe most of us have had astonishing ideas that we didn't even acknowledge, due to the fact that we're the victims of mental malnutrition.

Curiosity fends off "groupthink." Groupthink is, in essence, conformity. It's the dark underbelly of consensus. Groupthink suggests an abdication of personal responsibility, surrendering the opportunity to think for oneself. At about the age of nine I decided never to believe anything because it was convenient. I began reversing every statement to see if the opposite was also true. Yes, I was one annoying kid. This is now so much a habit with me that I hardly notice I'm doing it anymore. As soon as you put a "not" into an assertion, a whole range of other possibilities opens out. The best and most subversive place to drop a "not" in is while you're reading women's magazines, when they give fashion and beauty advice. Try it. For example, what follows is some random "wisdom" from the world of glamour mags, along with its negation:

- Try putting hair conditioner on unruly brows! (It's pointless to put hair conditioner on unruly brows.)

- Short women should avoid wearing capris. (Short women have no reason to avoid capris.)

- Purple eye shadow is just the thing for fall! (Purple eye shadow is *never* the thing for fall.)

- The peasant look is flattering to every body type. (The peasant look is flattering to no body type.)

- Women over forty should not wear shorts. (Woman over forty should wear shorts if they choose to.)

- Brows should always be plucked in a tidy clean arch—no stragglers. (Brows should *not* be plucked in a tidy clean arch unless you're a slavish conformist.)

I learned later that this technique is actually Hegel's dialectic. For example, when Henry Ford made a commitment to develop an "unbreakable" glass for car windshields, his highly educated engineers reported that it was "impossible." Undaunted, Ford directed them to find someone who didn't know it was impossible. The plant recruited some curious engineers who had not yet accumulated a mass of limitations based on what they knew. This group devised the formula to manufacture shatterproof glass. A commitment to curiosity and a "not bomb" dropped into the proposal solved a seemingly unsolvable problem and has saved who knows how many lives in the decades since the invention of shatterproof glass.

Curiosity generates thrills. Here, I'm referring to an antidote to the pervasive dulling of our outlooks that historically strikes around midlife but is occurring sooner and sooner in the life cycle (often called the "quarter-life crisis"). My prescription is a daily dose of kaizen in the name of curiosity. You can't cowboy up your life unless you're curious.

360-Degree Living

Penicillin was born out of mold. Chemotherapy drugs were derived from mustard gas used as chemical warfare in World War I. X-rays were discovered by a researcher who was exploring cathode rays. Antidepressants were developed during research on antituberculosis agents. The invention of Teflon has been described as "serendipity, a flash of genius, a lucky accident" that occurred as scientists were working with refrigerant gases. Viagra was initially studied for use in high blood pressure and chest pain. Silly Putty is a silicone plastic, marketed today as a toy for children, but originally created by accident during research into potential rubber substitutes for use during World War II. Minoxidil was first used exclusively as an oral drug to treat high blood pressure, but it had the remarkable side effect of restoring hair loss. Botox was originally developed to paralyze painful muscle spasms, but researchers noted its smoothing effect on skin wrinkles. In 1974, a choir singer in Minnesota was frustrated by his bookmarks sliding out of his hymnal. He knew that the 3M Company had developed a new low-tack adhesive, and while listening to a sermon in church, he came up with the idea of using that adhesive to anchor his bookmarks. A year later 3M issued free samples to residents of Boise, Idaho. Ninety percent of people who tried them said they'd buy the product. And thus was born the Post-it Note.

All these chance discoveries were capitalized on because someone was simply *curious*. Curiosity led the discoverers to not dismiss their initial findings but to keep scratching for more information, for relevance. Each of these everyday miracles was found in the search for something else. Winston Churchill once said, "Men occasionally stumble across the truth, but most of them pick themselves up and hurry off as if nothing has happened." Happy accidents happen all the time, but it requires a unique brand of curious intelligence to recognize the insights for what they're worth.

To keep my brain focused, sharp, and ready to harness all kinds of alternative data, I'm especially fond of reading nonfiction books about obscure topics: bananas, semiotics, happiness, codfish, punctuation, salt, perfume, comedy. These kinds of books are driven by their authors' curiosity and count on readers' curiosity as well. I regularly ask my writing classes to compose essays on the subject of gravel. Why such an apparently lifeless subject? To gauge their ability to fashion a narrative out of a (seemingly) dull, dry, boring topic. The class always comes alive to realize that everything, and I mean *everything*, in this world can be fascinating if you sprinkle just a little curiosity dust on it.

> "The cure for boredom is curiosity. There is no cure for curiosity."
>
> —Dorothy Parker (1893–1967), author

Commit to a Life of the Mind

Curiosity's number-one accomplice is the Internet. A limitless flow of electronic media is happy to oblige you in your life-of-the-mind quest.

Check out Stepcase Lifehack. This blog is a well-respected showcase for tips and tricks to get things done quickly using automation, increased productivity, and organization skills. Bookmark this site and other keepers—but continually edit your bookmark list so it doesn't become unwieldy. If nothing else, make a commitment to use the Internet with strategic care. Make it work for you; ask it to deliver just what you want straight to your inbox.

Subscribe to Wikipedia's "Featured Article" list. Every day, Wikipedia posts an article selected from its vast repository of entries. If you were a subscriber recently, you would have discovered that daylight saving time was first proposed by William Willett in 1907 and adopted during World War I as a way to conserve coal. You might also have been interested to find out that

Kazakhstan discontinued daylight saving time in 2005 because of alleged health risks associated with changed sleep patterns. Other daily tidbits have covered topics such as the Boy Scouts of America, Atlantic hurricanes, and the Paleolithic diet.

Subscribe to the feed at The Free Dictionary or peruse the home page. The Free Dictionary offers several daily features on its home page, including "Article of the Day," "In the News," "This Day in History," and "Today's Birthday." Recent stories have focused on the history of the Hell's Angels, the identity of the new "Seven Wonders of the World," the origin of the first cultured pearl, and the life story of one of the world's most prominent tenors.

Subscribe to the feed at Your Daily Art. Every day you'll receive an electronic facsimile of a classic work of art to contemplate, along with a few notes about the piece. If you were subscribed right now, you might have recently seen Man Ray's intriguing and playful *Le Violin d'Ingres* and Frank Weston Benson's luminous *Red and Gold*.

Subscribe to the feeds at Did You Know? and Tell Me Why. If you were a subscriber to these sites, you'd have recently learned why clouds are white, the function of the European Union, the French terms for the days of the week and the months of the year, and the history of the development of public health efforts in response to the hazards of the Industrial Revolution.

Listen to podcasts of In Our Time and Radio Open Source. Radio Open Source is a daily interview show that covers everything from politics to science, art to an exegesis of the movie *Groundhog Day*. For a history of the events and ideas that shaped the present, In Our Time is ideal. It's a weekly gathering of scholars discussing subjects as diverse as the life of Joan of Arc, theories of gravity, and what we should know about the Permian-Triassic boundary (which pushes even my threshold of curiosity).

Subscribe to word-of-the-day services. Merriam-Webster's Word of the Day delivers a vocabulary word to your e-mail inbox each morning. It includes a definition of the word, features it in a sentence, and then gives you a brief etymology.

Take advantage of no-cost online education. Regularly visit online education sites to take advantage of the extensive free tutorials offered on the Web: college course podcasts, online documentaries, foreign language lessons, auto maintenance guides, and more—all at no cost to you. Since MIT first opened two thousand of its courses to the world on the Internet, dozens of other schools, including Yale, University of California at Berkeley, and Notre Dame have followed suit using podcasts and videos. DailyLit.com sends literature in five-minute readable chunks right to your e-mail inbox.

"Only barbarians are not curious about where they come from, how they came to be where they are, where they appear to be going, whether they wish to go there, and if so, why, and if not, why not."

—Isaiah Berlin (1909–1997),
philosopher

Read the *New York Times* every Sunday. Revel in some of the best writing and most astute thinking around—or rail against the overrated writing and biased thinking. Your choice!

Hypomania: Curiosity Gone Wild

Hypomania is a term that's been applied to people who choose to load a lot—a whole lot—onto their plates. It's an odd term, even counterintuitive, since *hypo* means *less*. Actually, the word refers to a milder form of clinical, debilitating mania. Hypomanics are restless, eager people, consumed with confident curiosity, according to a *New York Times* story from 2005 called "Hypomanic? Absolutely. But Oh So Productive!" by Benedict Carey. Hypomania may, in fact, be related to manic depression. Though it's often associated with professional accomplishment and bursts of creative and focused work, a hypomaniac's grandiosity sets the stage for a severe crash. For some, their fevered, scavenging curiosity may overwhelm any excess rumination: new projects beckon before the old ones can be mourned. Hypomania is a vigorous mind gone off the deep end. Laurence McKinney, as described in the *Times* story, is a polymath who lives near Boston. He described hypomania thusly: "I'm not so much smarter than other people as faster. I swing more often, I make errors, but I make them faster. That's how I sometimes describe it. If you can focus this energy, you can do great things with it. If not, well, I think it can be difficult."

"On my epitaph I want it written, 'He was curious to the end.'"

—Tom Peters,
speaker and author

NEURO NUGGET

Every thought we have is an event that exists physically in the neurological pathways of our brain. The more often we repeat a certain thought, the more robust the particular pathway needed for that thought becomes. And interestingly, the more we repeat a certain thought pattern, the more readily that neural pathway fires in the future. Neuroscientists call this increase of ease in neural firing *kindling,* and we can leverage this physiological mechanism to increase our individual curiosity.

We can get a good glimpse of this process by looking at the neurology behind a phobia. Human beings are not born with phobias. Phobias are created—they begin either with an unpleasant experience (a very rough airplane flight), or a compelling story told to us about an unpleasant experience (seeing TV coverage of a plane crash), or listening to the story of an individual who has the particular phobia (someone who is very afraid of flying on planes). The neural pathway required for the thought "flying is dangerous" has been energized and fired. If that thought pattern is repeated frequently, and no countervailing pattern is fired ("flying is safer than driving," for instance) then the kindling effect allows that pathway to fire more easily and frequently in the future, resulting in a full-blown primitive "fight or flight" response, which can be experienced as a panic attack and seen by others as a phobic reaction. This neural kindling tendency can give rise to phobias, or it can be leveraged to create something useful, like curiosity. When you ask yourself how to enhance curiosity, you fire the neural pathway of that question as well as firing the general neural pathway of seeking newness.

A "Schmattering" of Activities

"You're always so curious," a friend once told me. "You get involved in a real 'schmattering' of activities." Yes, but it's fun. An *autotelic* activity (from the Greek root *auto*, meaning *self*, and *telos*, meaning *goal*) is one that we engage in simply for the pleasure we derive from it. No ulterior motive exists—no hope for future gain—and no "reason" to do it other than that it brings us happiness and a sense of satisfaction. Csikszentmihalyi, author of *Flow: The Psychology of Optimal Experience*, would say that Einstein's physics studies were an autotelic activity, because Einstein undertook the study of physics as a hobby. Extrinsic rewards, such as the desire to earn good grades or to secure a better job, are actually poor incentive for study, because the motivation is coming from the outside. Only when you pursue your interests for your pleasure alone—when the ultimate reward comes from inside you—will you have the drive and the patience to master a skill as thoroughly as Einstein mastered physics, Mozart music, or Disney animation. Of course, those men were all experts/specialists, but the point about autotelic activities is no less relevant to those among us who identify as generalists.

The truth about learning lessons is that they're never learned; they must be relearned every day. In *Walden*, Thoreau describes a Chinese inscription he discovered on a bathtub: "Renew thyself completely each day." Do it again . . . and again. Feed your soul with continual curiosity—daily. Do not think of this as quotidian tedium; it is *the way forward*. Practice daily curiosity renewal using kaizen. Today's to-do list should include tasks that bring you one small step closer to realizing your cross-training objectives.

Kaizen helps you develop a talent for life. And it gets easier as you get older, because living more intentionally is the biggest gift that growing older bestows upon us. Allow kaizen to sometimes sneak up on you. Go for long walks in the country. Whenever I walk, sing, chop vegetables, shower, drive, or talk to myself, thoughts and ideas sometimes rain down on me so fast I can't capture them all in memory. So wherever I go, I've taken to carrying a notebook with me to jot down those ruminations—though I concede this is least effective while driving and especially awkward in the shower.

Plastic and Enthusiastic

When the rub and press of daily responsibilities begin to overwhelm you, you may be tempted to backslide on your commitment to a life of the mind. This is the cycle of all things, so don't resist it; instead, acknowledge it. You'll need to overcome "vigor mortis" in order to regain your enthusiasm. Change your locale; see a movie; peruse a magazine; read a book; take a nap; lift some weights. Something's pinching you—probably a pinching of possibilities. You will regain your enthusiasm, just as surely as it will flag again. Simply acknowledge it. And make one small kaizen step in the direction of committing to curiosity, because I want you to be *hemorrhaging* possibilities for your life.

"Is there not a certain satisfaction," Einstein once wrote, "in the fact that natural limits are set to the life of the individual, so that at its conclusion it may appear as a work of art?" When our time is near, will we note with satisfaction the many years we spent in curiosity, reveling each day in joyous tests of our abilities? Or will we have to face the dismal truth that for most of our lives we oscillated nervously between anxiety and boredom? I firmly believe

> "I have no special talents.
> I am only passionately curious."
>
> —Albert Einstein (1879–1955)

that most people would very much like to live a more multifaceted, self-empowered, curiosity-encrusted life, but assume it's simply not possible in the rat race involved in making a living and raising a family. It's about devoting yourself to renewal, in ways big and small, remembering that the key is kaizen employed in service of your Triumph in Twenty.

> *"The important thing is not to stop questioning. Never lose a holy curiosity."*
>
> —Albert Einstein (1879–1955)

"Give Me Life": Falstaff

The world needs curious, wide-ranging Renaissance people as well as single-focus experts. The world needs *everyone's* contribution. For experts we are perhaps especially grateful—we want them as our florists and furnace-repair people and bridge builders, for instance. But this book demonstrates that those very experts, as well as those of us who never achieve that lofty status, can strengthen our minds, our hearts, and our careers by doing a little strategic cross-training—girded by curiosity as the hallmark trait. We must commit to reinventing ourselves as polymorphous polymaths. I'd be flattered to be called an intellectual gadfly or an intellectual grazer, or one of those terms I'm trying to resurrect: dilettante, jack-of-all-trades, or my coinages, desultorian or versatilist or superficialist. *Curiosity specialist* works, too.

> *"I live each day as if it were my last. Life in all its moments is so full of glory . . . the staggering glory of being alive."*
>
> —Helen Keller (1880–1968)

EXERCISES

To rev up our curiosity muscle, let's give it a little workout, so it's strong enough to prop open the doorway to our brain.

1. Batch o' Questions

At work, you encounter a new idea, a new theory, a new proposal, a new person. Rather than accepting the new person or thing at face value, dig deeper. Seek subtext. Devise a list of curiosity-based questions you can ask yourself to peel back the onion, because there's always more going on than meets the eye. To prime the pump, here are a few sample questions:

What's the history involved here?
Who's really in charge?
What's the motivation?
What's really going on?
What's the payoff?
Why is he the way he is?
What are the interrelationships?

2. My Favorite Martian

Channel Richard Feynman, who would love this exercise. Experience curiosity as if you were a Martian who's just landed on planet Earth. For ten minutes, sitting or standing in just one place, create a question about everything your eye falls on. Your questions can be about not just tangible things, but also behavior, attitudes—literally anything. Sitting at my keyboard, I created questions such as "How was the familiar QWERTY keyboard developed?" and "What kind of people design typefaces? Is typography considered 'art'?" and, glancing out the window, "Why can grass turn yellow and still revive later, yet houseplants cannot?"

3. Of Course, a Course

When was the last time you were intentionally curious about something you're not normally interested in? Obtain a course catalog from your local university. Assume you have to enroll in three courses. Which three are most appealing? Can you find something interesting about most offerings?

4. Meeting of the Minds

The late Steve Allen, Renaissance man, forged the notion of a dinner party to which were invited an eclectic group of dinner guests. Their mandates were to (a) ensure the dinner was an intellectual success and (b) not throw dinner rolls. Resurrect Allen's idea. Or establish a "salon" as practiced in Proust's day—a gathering for intellectual, creative, and spiritual generation and retrieval. Katharine Graham was for several decades the social czarina of Georgetown, Washington's posh neighborhood where many of its power brokers live. Few turned down an invitation to one of her cerebral soirees.

5

IMPERATIVE #2:
THE INDIVIDUALITY IMPERATIVE
To Thine Own Self Be True—Or Not

There will be only one of you for all time.
Fearlessly be yourself.

—Anonymous

Award-winning film director and comedian Mike Nichols has been called a millipede with a foot in everything, connected to everyone. "Mike is so stimulated and interested and attracted by the world—sort of in wonder to the world," says actress Natalie Portman. "He fills up his seconds. He reads everything, tastes everything, experiences everything so fully. It seems inevitable that that type of experience would diminish over the course of one's life, because one gets desensitized to the beauty and strangeness of the world. But you look at Mike, and you realize it's not an inevitability at all." Nichols seems to be immune from world-weariness. His individual style often involves synthesizing humor with social satire. Indeed, he is a savvy cultural critic who stands just off the playing field, keeping a low public profile, and observing the folly of our culture with fresh eyes. Nichols told *Vanity Fair* writer Sam Kashner, "There's nothing better than discovering, to your own astonishment, what you're meant to do. It's like falling in love."

Famed acting coach Stella Adler (1901–1992) took a multidisciplinary approach to her work. Her currency was individuality. She exhorted her students to use the individuality of their imaginations to enrich their roles, and urged them to grow as human beings by studying nature, art, and history. Adler believed that the more her students knew, the more choices they would have. Her mantra: "Your talent is in your choices."

Actor John Malkovich, best known for the films *Dangerous Liaisons* and *Being John Malkovich*, is so thoroughly rigorous in pursuit of his multiple interests that he's almost over the top. A recent profile of Malkovich in the *New York Times Magazine*, written by Lynn Hirschberg, portrays him as an actor, expatriate, clothing designer, director, and "a man still game to try anything." Hirschberg depicts Malkovich as "constitutionally repelled by anything simplistic or ordinary . . . He has no attraction to the mainstream in anything, from home decoration to clothes to movies." A perfect example of the actor's unconventional approach to life: during a stint performing on Broadway, when he was footloose between the matinee and evening shows, he would work a shift at the flower shop in the nearby Marriott and get paid in flowers. A design aesthete, Malkovich planned his home down to the last coffee mug and light switch. He seems to seek, and find, spiritual nirvana in details that he designs himself. "I'd be a political person if politics was about solving problems," says the actor. "But politics diminishes and devalues the meaning of intellectual curiosity. The only thing I'm truly interested in for very long is the stories we tell each other." Director Stephen Frears describes Malkovich as "very funny, very smart, and . . . extremely scary in that whispery seductive way." Following where your passions lead you provides boundless opportunities to explore your many "selves." Malkovich himself says, "I get to shed my skin every few years. When you're immersed in something, you can become a new person."

"As long as you are trying to be something other than what you actually are, your mind wears itself out."

—Jiddu Krishnamurti (1895–1986), author and philosopher

"Let your freak flag fly." It's both a Jimi Hendrix lyric and a manifesto for individualism. (Be mindful of where, when, and how high you fly it, of course—but do fly it.) Welcome to our second imperative, individuality. We Americans may pay lip service to individualism, but the fact is, nearly everyone is a milquetoast conformist. Sadly, most people are handicapped in the expression of their fullest selves. "I am not eccentric," insisted Dame Edith Sitwell. "It's just that I am more alive than most people."

On one level, it's true that there's nothing new under the sun; on a more meaningful level, however, this is not the case. That's because there never has been—and never will be—anyone who sees, thinks, or responds exactly the way you do. Whether you're revolutionizing neuroscience or creating a scrapbook, you must put your difference forward if you intend to make a difference. Even if your gifts are basically the same as mine (good with words, kind to animals, patient with children), we each express those gifts in an individualistically one-of-a-kind way.

Theologian Frederick Buechner said, "It is important to tell at least from time to time the secret of who we truly and fully are. Otherwise we run the risk of losing track of who we truly and fully are and come to accept instead the highly

"If a man does not keep pace with his companions, perhaps he hears a different drummer. Let him step to the music however measured or far away."

—Henry David Thoreau (1817–1862)

edited version which we put forth in the hope that the world will find it more appealing than the real thing." It's essential that each individual discovers his or her own unique gift (or *ichor*, as the Greeks called it) and then expresses it wholeheartedly. Ichor is the ethereal fluid that was said to have taken the place of blood in the veins of the mythological gods. It symbolizes the singular and unmatchable contribution that we mortals are capable of making in the world. We each have a gift to share with humanity; our job is to strive toward the particular brand of excellence that is distinct to us, based on the expression of our talents. Aristotle considered *eudaimonic well-being* (from the Greek *eu*, meaning *good*, and *daimon*, meaning *spirit* or *deity*) to be the noblest goal in life. In his time, the Greeks believed that each child was blessed at birth with a personal daimon that embodied the highest possible expression of his or her nature.

Deliver Your Goods

Aristotle said, "All men, by nature, desire to know." I'd add that all men and women should desire to know *themselves* and what makes them unique among all of humanity. It's up to each of us to determine our own ichor, since it's not exactly tattooed on our foreheads at birth. Here's what the writer John Updike had to say about ichor: "Until I've secreted a certain amount of my ichor, my essence, I haven't earned the right to enjoy the rest of the hours of the day. So I've built it into my biological budget, and to call it a pleasure is in a way to understate it. It's become a need, a necessity, this wish to deliver your goods."

"There is only one success—to be able to spend your life in your own way."

—Christopher Morley (1890–1957), journalist, novelist, and poet

In *The Life and Work of Martha Graham* by Agnes De Mille, the celebrated ballet dancer and choreographer Martha Graham (1893–1991) is quoted saying, "There's a vitality, a life force, an energy, a quickening, that is translated through you into action, and because there is only one of you in all time, this expression is unique." If you're not true to yourself, that betrayal could become your tragic flaw or, as the Greeks called it, *hamartia*. It's disquieting that most of us have trouble identifying our gifts, likely because they come so easily to us. We take our unique talents for granted or, worse, discount them, when we should be cultivating and celebrating them. Churchill comes to mind as a prime example of a Renaissance man who seemed to revel in his individualism. He was often feisty, sometimes brusque, utterly unique, and not in the least derivative.

The relationship between ichor and the fine art of becoming a Renaissance person is this: you need to discover and understand your ichor in order to intelligently select activities that will complement and strengthen it. For example, if your gift centers around working with children as an elementary school reading teacher, you may want to design a cross-training curriculum for yourself that complements your calling as a teacher. Even if some of the activities you choose appear to be unrelated to your calling as a reading teacher—such as practicing tai chi or studying biophysics or learning to play the cello—they will encourage you to see familiar things in distinctive ways. You may find that you'd like to incorporate the meditative aspect of tai chi into your phonics lessons. From your studies in biophysics, you could pick up a scientific principle about the neurochemical way the brain comprehends language—clearly relevant to a reading teacher's curriculum. And studying the cello might spark an insight to try more rhythmic reading drills with your students.

> *"What each must seek in his life never was on land or sea. It is something out of his own unique potentiality for experience, something that never has been and never could have been experienced by anyone else."*
>
> —Joseph Campbell (1904–1987), author and mythology scholar

Rollin' Like a River

This chapter is best tackled in two phases. The first phase is to identify those activities that ease you into a state of flow. To pinpoint those activities, we first need to examine what it means to be "in the flow." You've likely experienced this feeling or state of being before, when you've been involved in a task or project where you were so completely engrossed and totally focused that you might not even have noticed the passage of time. When you're in the midst of flow you have an inner sense of clarity and serenity—you know what needs to be done and how to do it; you may lose yourself in activity, forgetting about everyday problems or worries. You are intrinsically motivated to participate in activities that generate flow, taking part not because someone is telling you to, but because the pleasure you derive from these endeavors—whether it's gardening, writing, running, singing, exploring museums, or any others of the countless possibilities—is the reward in itself.

The second phase involves creating and exploring tributaries—searching out complementary interests to the activities you've just identified. In other words, we're looking to create more flow in your life by expanding on the number of areas in which it's likely to be found. As in a color wheel, complementary activities are likely to be those that are similar, even though they may not, at first, appear to have any particular connection. That's the essence of identifying a web of cross-training energy.

> "When you are completely absorbed or caught up in something, you become oblivious of things around you, or the passage of time. It is this absorption in what you are doing that frees your unconscious and releases your creative imagination."
>
> —Rollo May (1909–1994), existential psychologist

For example, if you ordinarily lose yourself in needlework, you may find that you also experience flow when you participate in other activities with no obvious connection, such as playing chess or volunteering at a soup kitchen. The key is that the secondary activities you choose to explore (chess, for instance) sharpen skills (such as thinking several moves ahead) that you may never have thought were applicable to the primary activity (needlework, where you need to be mindful of the piece's future application and how all its parts will come together). This process will result in a cross-training mosaic that's unique to you.

It must be noted that serendipity is central to the lives of many cross-trainers. We welcome "happy accidents" as gifts from the universe. Way leads to way, it is said, and that sums up how one thing leads to another, especially when your life is full of enriching content. Someone might discover an untapped knack for mechanics through his passion for mountain biking. One woman didn't know she had a yen for interior design until she built a cabin in the woods. These proclivities may not have made themselves known had these people set out to look for them.

The truth is that we're all coded with many more potentials than we'll ever use, but this chapter will help you expand any contracted, bunched-up notions you have about the possibilities available and achievable for you in this vast world.

"Insist on yourself; never imitate. . . . Every great man is unique."

—Ralph Waldo Emerson (1803–1882), essayist and poet

A Light Spread of Genius

The late Stephen Jay Gould (1941–2002), evolutionary biologist nonpareil, at one point set out to mend the rupture between science and the humanities. The way each of us interprets this Maginot Line is unique and reveals something quite individual about our worldview and what organizing principles we employ in our approach to challenge.

With respect to the Individuality Imperative, consider a fascinating duality Gould invoked: the contrast between the fox and the hedgehog. As you read further, think about your basic approach to life—which of the two you best relate to. The fox devises a multitude of strategies; the hedgehog focuses its energies on one effective strategy. Gould used this animal analogy to elucidate his notion of the proper relationship between science and the humanities, which is that of a "fruitful union of these two great ways of knowing." Scholars have seized on the fox/hedgehog gambit, playing a sort of ongoing academic parlor game based on it. They'll designate their colleagues as hedgehogs, for their tenacity in advocating one key idea or approach; or as foxes, for their willingness to embrace many different strategies or philosophies. For our purposes, of course, foxes are generalists, drawing on a wide variety of experiences rather than boiling everything down to a singular notion; hedgehogs are specialists, viewing the world through the lens of one defining idea. Examples of great thinkers who could be considered foxes are Shakespeare, Herodotus, Aristotle, Montaigne, Erasmus, Moliere, Goethe, Pushkin, Picasso, Balzac, and Joyce. By contrast, Dante, Plato, Lucretius, Pascal, Hegel, Dostoevsky, Nietzsche, Ibsen, and Proust would be our hedgehogs.

Taking the fox/hedgehog analogy further, Gould explained that we are all by nature inclined to "diversify and color" or to "intensify and cover." Gould suggested that foxes owe their reputation to "a light spread of real genius across many fields of study, moving on to sow some new seeds in a thoroughly different kind of field," while hedgehogs "locate one vitally important mine, where their particular and truly special gifts cannot be matched [and] then stay at the site all their lives, digging deeper and deeper."

I wonder what Gould would have made of the arguably manic regime of cross-training I champion in the Vigorous Mind program. Would he slot me as a hedgehog, sticking to one worldview—that of a liberal arts maven and a soi-disant Renaissance woman? Or would he characterize me as a wily fox, skittering from one discipline to the next—one eye always on the lookout for the next thing, never boring down deep, content to skim glossy surfaces? We unregenerate generalists are seemingly genetically incapable of digging too deep, much as we respect and admire those who do. So we're foxes, it seems. Yet maybe we're not fully foxy. Do we not subscribe to an overarching philosophy—a liberal dose of liberal arts and broad-based curiosity? Even the use of kaizen suggests one singular perspective, one course of action. How I wish Gould himself were here to discuss this. What a lively tête-à-tête that would surely be.

The fox-and-hedgehog analogy is a model for how the sciences and humanities should interact with each other, and it's essentially congruent with my recommendation to blend your work life as a specialist with a generalist modus operandi in your personal life. Each "way" is essential to human wholeness, even as generalists and specialists remain at loggerheads—as are foxes and hedgehogs—as are the arts and sciences. Ah, the eternal tension—it shall ever be thus. Consequently, I propose that you fashion your individual brand of cross-training around this eternal tension. Do you find yourself pursuing the arts to the exclusion of the sciences, or vice versa? Do you find yourself as a fox in some settings and a hedgehog in others? In either case, purposely try sampling the other way, in the name of building brain cells.

A Mind That Sparkles and Crackles

Still, when the chips go down *in extremis*—when you're under stress, in other words—you will default to your essential self, whether that "self" is a fox, hedgehog, generalist, specialist, artist, or scientist. Gould, of course, was usually described as a scientist. Yet, as a writer, he was also a humanist. So he had a foot in both canoes—as should we all. Ultimately, after all the back-and-forth and pro and con, the fox/hedgehog argument must be settled only as a squishy blend of both sets of binaries. How you resolve it reveals much about the individuality of your intellectual architecture—and it's this kind of insightful self-knowledge that will be a priceless byproduct of your cross-training.

Be a "Versatilist"

There is no single way to grow in intellectual imagination, to interact with life. We each weave our tapestries in our own ways, even when we're trying to emulate someone. Such is the dogged nature of individuality. Those of us looking to experientially boost our cognitive vigor are eager to avoid being typecast as anything less than Renaissance people. We resist borders. We are sui generis. We are idiopathic idiosyncrasies in human form. This is to be encouraged; indeed, the Individuality Imperative encourages you in a paradox: to be fully who you are, as well as to be fully who you're not, as you explore the world outside your normal parameters.

A nifty example of curious individuals forging their own intellectual paths is that of the University of Michigan's Knight-Wallace Fellows—professional journalists chosen to receive a plump stipend of $55,000. The lagniappe is a once-in-a-lifetime opportunity to reimmerse themselves in college life, this time with some wisdom under their belts. What a bouquet: this fellowship program is a sabbatical year of study and reflection designed to broaden the participants' perspectives, nurture intellectual growth, and inspire personal transformation. The lucky recipients are given the chance to devise their own individual plan of study, with the freedom to choose from the full range of the university's classes arrayed before them like a candy store. Fellows may decide to pursue interests that are directly related to their journalistic beat, or choose something that's utterly different and seemingly unrelated—or they may structure a program that's some sort of hybrid, which is the most common and strongly recommended pattern. To wit, a few recent amalgamations: A cartoonist who combined gross anatomy in the medical school with lithography in the art school; a science writer who designed and built a mechanical fish; a city hall reporter fascinated by China who found himself covering it three weeks after his last intensive Mandarin class; a feature writer who applied creative writing techniques to a series that won a Pulitzer Prize the next year; and a sportswriter who studied Asian affairs and international business and became a Far East bureau chief.

In another example of largesse in the name of interdisciplinarity, real estate mogul Mort Zuckerman has put up $10 million to underwrite, for each of the next five years, an interdisciplinary postgraduate Harvard education for twenty-five exceptional students. Among them are MBA candidates studying government at the Kennedy School and aspiring doctors studying law. The goal of Zuckerman's cross-training generosity is to develop broadly knowledgeable leaders.

The Magic of Music

Way leads to way. You might think that the top dog at a pharmaceutical powerhouse would want his scientists to be all science, all the time. But former Eli Lilly and Company CEO Randall Tobias sang a different tune. Tobias didn't want his scientists typecast as one-note wonders, noting that, "There's data available to demonstrate that people in the fields of mathematics and science have a higher-than-average predisposition toward music. So, if a firm wants to recruit world-class scientists to work at its Indianapolis research labs, those scientists are probably going to ask about a lot more than the company's vacation schedule and 401(k) plan."

"I see it in a lot of the people who work here," agrees Cathy Cormier, a cancer researcher and doctoral candidate at the Cold Spring Harbor Laboratory on Long Island. Cormier, who is herself an accomplished pianist and oboist, counts violinists, flutists, saxophonists, and singers among her fellow scientists. The musical inclination of the lab's doctoral candidates has prompted discussions of starting their own woodwind quintet, with Cormier on oboe. What do these multitalented colleagues seem to have in common? "An analytical ability that they apply to both science and music," Cormier told *Newsday*. "And creativity is part of it, because you need creativity to be a scientist."

Diana Dabby worked as a concert pianist to pay her way through engineering school and is today an assistant professor of electrical engineering and music at Olin College of Engineering in Needham, Massachusetts. "What attracted me to each [field] was a very rich language. There was always a mystery about it," she explained to the *Seattle Times*. "You can never fathom all of it, so you can continue to grow. And each has a very rich set of symbols."

Virtual reality pioneer Jaron Lanier has an aptitude for music as well as for computer science. He writes and records music in a variety of styles and genres, and he also plays the piano and a number of rare and unusual instruments. Lanier released the classical music album *Instruments of Change* in 1994 and is currently working on the music album *Proof of Consciousness*.

Parallel interests in science or math and music are more prevalent than mere chance would suggest, according to Kathleen Rountree's article "A Tribute to Music Students Who Pursued Other Careers" in *American Music Teacher* magazine. It's not uncommon to see college students choosing to dual-major in math and music. That particular combination occurs commonly enough that it almost seems to be linked. The unyielding dictates of a measure of music, circumscribed by numbers, creates a rhythm that somehow conforms to the algorithms of science and math. Does a predilection for one have something to do with the other?

NEURO NUGGET

According to neuroscientists, there is some research that indicates an overlap in the parts of the brain where language and math abilities lie. Scientific evidence also suggests that this particular area of the brain develops differently in children who learn tonal languages compared with development in children who learn nontonal languages. Tonal patterns vary widely across languages. English speakers typically emphasize one syllable within each word. But in French, for example, no such emphasis is used when speaking. Turkish features a high pitch on the last syllable. Change of pitch is used in some African languages for grammatical purposes, such as indicating past tense. Because of the complexity of tonal languages and the kinds of neurological changes that occur as these languages are learned, specific developments in the language center of the brain can also predispose a child to more easily acquire math skills. (Of course, this is only a predisposition and can be counteracted by other biological and environmental factors.) So children who learn a tonal language early in life may have an advantage for learning math later on in life. And, interestingly, that same area of the brain is also involved in processing musical skills.

It might be said that Alan Greenspan, former chairman of the Board of Governors of the Federal Reserve System, once played the economy like a fiddle. It's a lesser-known fact that he actually played the clarinet when he majored in music at the prestigious Juilliard School. Those who write about the jazz years of Greenspan's life characterize him as a "good section player"—solid and dependable—but imply that he wasn't much of a star. It was about this same time that, according to his biographer, Greenspan began to exhibit "latent and long-repressed accounting tendencies."

As an early-in-life musician, Greenspan is in good company. Albert Einstein, who's been called a "genius among geniuses," was known to pick up a violin. Einstein's name, of course, is linked to the most important scientific discoveries of all time, including the big bang theory, nuclear fission, quantum physics, and electronics. Perhaps we can thank his mother, who insisted that he learn to play the violin in childhood. Be inspired by the fascinating individuality expressed by these high-achieving cross-trainers. Their various endeavors seem to feed each other. Yes, music and science seem to wind up on the same dance card often, but your own dance card may be filled with an idiosyncratic mix of activities. I'm a big fan of music; I think it enhances everything else in your life. But remember, there is no one-size-fits-all prescription for creating a vigorous mind. You choose a palette of activities that compel you. That's the message of this chapter.

One final high-level example of a high achiever who cut her teeth on the discipline of music is former secretary of state Condoleeza Rice. In fact, Rice is a prototype cross-training Renaissance woman. Her mother was a pianist who envisioned her child's future as a professional musician, even deriving her daughter's name from the musical term *con dolcezza*, meaning *with sweetness*. Growing up, Rice studied French and participated in figure skating as well as ballet, but by her teens, she was committed to a future as a concert pianist. But about her musical aspirations, she told the *National Review*, "I structured my life to be a concert musician. That was all I wanted to do. And it fell apart on me." She instead launched her career in the field of international relations. Rice stands out in Washington for her high degree of both individualism and achievement.

A Divine Heterodoxy

Feeling centered about who you are and what you're here on earth to do—that's the real work of life. And it's hard, ongoing work. You'd think it might be simpler, since each of us is born with all we need to feel valued and unique. That's factory-standard equipment. But the grinding wheel of life slowly chips away at our self-esteem, bit by sorry bit. "We arrive in this world with birthright gifts—then we spend the first half of our lives abandoning them or letting others disabuse us of them," writes Parker Palmer in his book *Let Your Life Speak*. "As young people, we are surrounded by expectations that may have little to do with who we really are, expectations held by people who are not trying to discern our selfhood but to fit us into slots. We are disabused of our original giftedness in the first half of our lives. Then—if we are awake, aware, and able to admit our loss—we spend the second half trying to recover and reclaim the gift we once possessed." Dancer Isadora Duncan (1877–1927) observed that most women waste some twenty-five to thirty years of their lives before they break through the actual and conventional lies they tell themselves—especially when it comes to what they need to make themselves happy. That is a keenly perceived observation that makes me wince with its sad truth.

That erosion that we're all prey to—call it *identity entropy*—is every bit as tenacious as we need to be with our countervailing force: kaizen. Our daily job is to regain today what yesterday tore away from us—to regain the feeling of being a swan. You remember the story: Raised among ducklings, a beautiful young swan was considered an outsider—an ugly duckling—with its long, graceful neck. Having never seen another creature resembling it, the swan believed itself to be inferior when, in fact, it was intended to be a glorious swan all along.

Shakespeare dashed off a pretty good line about individuality when he wrote, "To thine own self be true." Bestselling author and motivational speaker Laurence Boldt put it another way in his book *Zen and the Art of Making a Living*: "The highest order of duty to self is to follow your bliss." He goes on to say that the highest order of duty to society is to make your fullest contribution to its well-being. These duties—your duty to self and your duty to society—intersect in your life's work. "Love is not a category, a compartment of life separate from work," Boldt wrote. "It is pervasive. Work is the form into which we pour this living substance of love." Freud declared the basic requirements of human existence to be love and work. A genuine life's work breaks down any barriers we might impose to separate the two. Freud was indeed right—love and work are the basic stuff of human life. Our task, according to Boldt, is to tap into "the eternal ocean of bliss and somehow express that energy in the world of form and time. While engaged in life's work, we can be said to be practicing artists—motivated not by external rewards, but by the intrinsic joys of self-expression and service to humanity." That's what I mean by fashioning your life as a divine heterodoxy: an immaculately unorthodox approach that succeeds at the level of both self and society.

Your Inborn Architecture

As you cogitate on your individual version of a vigorous mind, remember the classic distinction between two extreme character types created by the Greeks and then philosophized upon by Friedrich Nietzsche—Apollonian and Dionysian—that ideally long to be unified.

In the philosophy of Nietzsche, Apollo represents beauty, adherence to boundaries, individuality, celebration of appearance/illusion, human beings as artists, self-control, perfection, exhaustion of possibilities, and creation. Apollonians display an abundance of critical and rational powers. Friends and colleagues would describe them as partial to reason, clarity, harmony, and restraint.

Dionysus represents intoxication, celebration of nature, instinct, orgiastic passion, dissolution of all boundaries, excess, and destruction. You're Dionysian if you display an abundance of creative and intuitive powers. If you worship at the altar of Dionysus you may be considered recklessly uninhibited, unrestrained, undisciplined, and even frenzied. If you are Dionysian, my friend, party on.

Playwright Peter Shaffer once commented, "There is in me a continuous tension between what I suppose I could call the Apollonian and the Dionysian sides of interpreting life. . . . I just feel that there is a constant debate going on between the violence of instinct on the one hand and the desire in my mind for order and restraint." Along these lines, the writer Edward Wilson asked, "Can the opposed Apollonian and Dionysian impulses, cool reason against passionate abandonment, which drive the mood swings of the arts and criticism, be reconciled? The answer depends on the existence or nonexistence of an inborn human nature. The evidence accumulated to date leaves little room for doubt. Human nature exists, and it is both deep and highly structured."

"Trust yourself. Think for yourself. Act for yourself. Speak for yourself. Be yourself. Imitation is suicide."

—Marva Collins, educator

Two additional and congruent mythological dichotomies are sometimes designated as "representatives of mankind": Prometheus and Epimetheus. Prometheus exemplifies forethought and is described as ingenious and clever; his brother Epimetheus typifies hindsight and is considered foolish.

Your unique human nature may be bounded by one of these states. Exploring these dichotomies can be quite helpful to a budding cross-trainer—helpful because it's fascinating to study the extreme states of human nature. Embrace your own unique mix of the two character types, just as you will with the generalist/specialist, fox/hedgehog, and art/science pairs. All these dualities long to be united, it is said, because that unification leads to a whole and complete person: a polymath, Renaissance person, *Uomo Universale*.

I strongly recommend selecting cross-training activities that draw from opposing spheres, aiming for a fusion of your Apollonian and Dionysian sides in particular. If by nature you're more Apollonian than Dionysian, make sure you're not avoiding the latent Dionysian facet of your nature. You may be a software tester by trade, but perhaps a little tango on the side would give expression to your inner Dionysian. If your default mode is partying, painting, and pandemonium, may I offer you a side dish of Euclidian geometry? This "unity" is central to the idea of cross-training your brain. I think you'll be surprised by how much you'll get into the groove when you express a side of yourself that perhaps you've never even acknowledged.

Individual Imagination

While we're on the topic of dichotomies and dualities, let's pause for a moment and consider overachievers versus underachievers. An overachiever is someone who performs better than expected, not because of innate ability or talent, but rather due to determination and hard work. How can you not admire an overachiever? Think of the schoolkids from the 1988 movie *Stand and Deliver*, based on a true story, in which dedicated math teacher Jaime Escalante inspires his at-risk students— gang members, no-hopers—in a tough Hispanic neighborhood to learn calcu-

> *"I cannot give you the formula for success, but I can give you the formula for failure, which is: try to please everybody."*
>
> —Herbert Bayard Swope (1882–1958), journalist

lus, of all things, to build their self-esteem. Against all expectations, they become some of the country's top algebra and calculus students, performing so well that they're actually accused of cheating.

Here's the rub: If you're born reasonably smart and otherwise advantaged, it's very difficult to overachieve. You're forever toiling under the yoke of underachievement, fearful that you're not living up to your potential, probably because you're not. An underachiever is someone who performs below expectations, given a surfeit of innate intelligence or other advantages. This is the person who's truly not realizing his or her potential. Underachiever case in point: Sydney Carton, hero of Charles Dickens's *A Tale of Two Cities*, is a young barrister of outstanding natural gifts, but is "incapable of their directed exercise" through lack of willpower and self-discipline. This haunts me, because I see myself all too well in Sydney Carton. However, despite everything, Dickens put this immortal line in the mouth of ol' Syd: "It is a far, far better thing that I do, than I have ever done; it is a far, far better rest that I go to than I have ever known."

> *"I want freedom for the full expression of my personality."*
>
> —Mahatma Gandhi (1869–1948)

Identifying Your Identity:
What Color Is Your Bumbershoot?

In order to further your ideas about fashioning a fully individualistic Vigorous Mind program, it makes sense to assess your "type." (Citing our Curiosity Imperative, it is also just plain interesting to try to peer into your own cogs and circuitry to figure out what makes you the way you are). A number of personality assessment tools have been devised to do just that. Understand that the following exegesis is a simplification of these concepts, a quick once-over designed in part to spur you to further reading. Part of the fun is fulminating against these assessment instruments; the other part of the fun is being made uncomfortable by them, as if they know you better than you know yourself. In either case, evaluate yourself against the three models sketched out below. See anybody you know in there?

DISC

DISC is a popular, four-quadrant behavioral model that helps individuals determine their personality type according to four dimensions: Dominance (D), Influence (I), Steadiness (S), and Conscientiousness (C). Which behavioral traits most accurately describe you?

Dominance. People who have high D scores are active in dealing with problems and challenges and are described as demanding, forceful, egocentric, strong-willed, driven, determined, ambitious, aggressive, and pioneering. By contrast, individuals with low D scores want to do more research before committing to a decision; they're considered conservative, low-key, cooperative, calculating, undemanding, cautious, mild, agreeable, modest, and peaceful.

Influence. Individuals with high I scores influence others through talking and activity and tend to be emotional. They're characterized as convincing, magnetic, political, enthusiastic, persuasive, warm, demonstrative, trusting, and optimistic. By comparison, people with low I scores use data and facts, rather than feelings, to influence others. They'd be described as reflective, factual, calculating, skeptical, logical, suspicious, matter-of-fact, pessimistic, and critical.

Steadiness. Those who score high on the S assessment crave a steady pace and a feeling of security; they don't like sudden change. These individuals are said to be calm, relaxed, patient, possessive, predictable, deliberate, stable, consistent, and tend to be unemotional and poker-faced. People with low S scores like change and variety. They're restless, demonstrative, impatient, eager, even impulsive.

Conscientious. People with high C scores adhere to rules, regulations, and structure. They like to do quality work and do it right the first time. These individuals are careful, cautious, exacting, neat, systematic, diplomatic, accurate, tactful. On the other hand, people with low C scores challenge the rules and want independence; they're depicted as self-willed, stubborn, opinionated, unsystematic, arbitrary, and careless with details.

Now let's apply this. If you're a high D, you jump right into the middle of a challenge. You're a good candidate for the (admittedly daunting) agenda outlined in this book. Because you're forceful and aggressive about getting what you're after, once you commit to a discipline of kaizen, you'll achieve exactly what you want out of this endeavor—and out of life, overall.

> *"The highest courage is to dare to appear to be what one is."*
>
> —John Lancaster Spalding (1840–1916), Catholic bishop

If you're a high I, social ability and emotionality count in a big way for you. These happen not to be two characteristics that are imperative to success in this campaign to better your brain, but no matter—they won't impede your progress, either.

If you're a high S, you're steady, seek security, and dislike change. This book's cross-training challenge will represent a "stretch" goal for you, since it's not second nature. People with high S scores are perhaps better suited to becoming life's specialists—which is fine. We need you doing what you do best.

Finally, if you're a high C, you like all the edges to line up just right. Sloppiness and inexactitude don't cut it with you. The necessarily imprecise edges that are a given in a curriculum of skipping, scanning, and skating across the surface of life's vast amusement park may make you crazy, but this may also be just the ticket for you to loosen up a little. In Chapter 9, we'll discuss just this concept, called wabi-sabi.

"People do not have to become something they are not. They need to learn only who and what they really are."

—Eknath Easwaran (1910–1999), author and translator

Once you've identified your primary personality type according to DISC, ask yourself if you're giving yourself the best chance to overachieve within that type. Then ask yourself which of the other quadrants contain traits you admire. For instance, Jean identifies herself as high Dominance. She's okay with that and wants to become an even stronger D, but, noting her almost total lack of identification with the traits in the Influence quadrant, she now sees in a semi-empirical way that she could become a better-rounded person by selectively developing some activities or behaviors associated with Influence. Thus, she's now enrolled in a networking class and realizes that maybe her low-I, high-D appraisal wasn't so much inborn as fear-based. She'd always been afraid to be very social or emotional, and now she's realizing that it's time to develop a more complete range of her individuality, including the repressed, latent parts.

Let's now turn to another personality assessment tool, the Keirsey Temperament Sorter.

The Keirsey Temperament Sorter

Psychologist and author David Keirsey has developed a self-assessed questionnaire designed to help people better understand their own personalities. The Keirsey Temperament Sorter links human behavior to four fundamental temperaments (Artisans, Guardians, Idealists, Rationals) as described here:

Artisans are observant and pragmatic, impulsive and adaptable, bold and unconventional. They believe that variety is what seasons life, and so they seek stimulation, setting off on quests others might consider difficult or impossible. As such, Artisans are ideal candidates for brain cross-training.

Guardians are practical and hardworking, dependable and responsible, dutiful and cooperative. People of this temperament are the glue of our civilization, protecting and nurturing our cherished institutions, and as concerned citizens they naturally value membership in community and service organizations.

Idealists are introspective and intuitive, cooperative and diplomatic, inspiring and optimistic. They focus on personal growth and are concerned with finding their own identity.

Rationals are pragmatic and goal-oriented, independent and inquisitive, skeptical and analytical. Genuine knowledge-seekers, they're always searching for the fundamental principles (the whys) that underlie what we see in the world around us—making them ideally suited for the perspectives outlined in this book.

I'm guessing that you immediately relate to one of the four Keirsey types above. It's likely that a second category also reminds you of yourself. I suggest, in the name of the Individuality Imperative, that you tease out some threads from your lesser-dominant categories to buttress your major strengths. But we're not done yet. Take a look at one last personality test.

The Enneagram

Created in 1968 by Bolivian-born Oscar Ichazo, the Enneagram of Personality identifies connections among nine different personality types (*enneagram* is derived from the Greek words *ennea*, meaning *nine*, and *grammos*, meaning *written*). According to this model, nine numbered points on an enneagram figure correspond to the nine personality types and the relationships among them.

Type One: Reformers, Critics, Perfectionists. Type Ones are focused on personal integrity; they can be wise, discerning, and inspiring in their quest for the truth. They also tend to dissociate themselves from their flaws or what they believe are flaws (such as negative emotions) and can become hypocritical of themselves and hypercritical of others, seeking the illusion of virtue to hide their own vices. The greatest fear of Ones is to be flawed; their ultimate goal is perfection. This desire for perfection, along with the drive for self-betterment, strike me as traits that would be valuable in anyone embarking on a journey toward a more well-rounded life.

Type Two: Helpers, Givers, Caretakers. Type Twos, at their best, are compassionate, thoughtful, and astonishingly generous, but they can also be particularly prone to clinginess and manipulation. Above all, Twos want to be loved and needed and fear being unworthy of love. With this ever-present urge to be helpful, a Two may be representative of a newborn Renaissance person who has found a new angle from which to attack life and is eager to share it with everybody.

Type Three: Achievers, Performers, Succeeders. Type Threes are highly adaptable and variable. Some Threes walk the world with confidence and unstinting authenticity; others wear a series of public masks, acting in a way they think will bring them approval, thereby losing track of their true selves. Threes are motivated by the need to succeed and to be seen as successful. Confident and changeable, Type Threes are not likely to tolerate mental malnutrition, so they're ideal candidates for cognitive cross-training.

Type Four: Romantics, Individualists, Artists. Type Fours are driven by the desire to understand themselves and to find their place in the world. They fear having no identity or personal significance. Fours embrace individualism and are often profoundly creative and intuitive; however, they have a habit of withdrawing and looking inward, searching inside themselves for something they never find and creating a spiral of depression. Their individuality, coupled with the need to know themselves, make Type Fours likely to undertake an ambitious self-improvement program such as this one.

Type Five: Observers, Thinkers, Investigators. Type Fives are motivated by the desire to understand the world around them; they crave capability and knowledgeability above all else. Believing they are worth only what they contribute, Fives watch with keen eyes and speak only when they can shake the world with their observations. Some Fives, fearing incompetency or uselessness, withdraw from the world, fending off social contact with abrasive cynicism. Type Fives have an inner drive for mastery and a thirst for knowledge that makes them well suited to embracing kaizen and resisting brain entropy.

Type Six: Loyalists, Devil's Advocates, Defenders. Type Sixes long for stability. Although they are unwavering in their loyalty and responsibility, they can be slow to trust again if betrayed. Sixes are particularly prone to fearful thinking and emotional anxiety; they tend to react to their fears either by avoiding fearful situations or by confronting them in a counterphobic manner. Given their resistance to change and tendency to anxiety, Type Sixes aren't primary candidates to embark on a mission to defy the current trend in favor of specialization. Of course, given this book's contrarian spirit of going against the grain to vigor up your brain, Type Sixes are welcome to accompany us on our journey.

Type Seven: Enthusiasts, Adventurers, Sensationalists. Type Sevens are adventurous and active, with all the energy and enthusiasm of the Puer Aeternus—the eternal boy, epitomized by Peter Pan. At their best they embrace life for its varied joys and wonders and truly live in the moment; at their worst, they dash frantically from one new experience to another, too scared of disappointment to actually enjoy themselves. Type Sevens represent a virtual prototype for a need-to-know-and-do-everything Renaissance person. Type Seven's "deadly sin" is gluttony, not in the sense of overeating, but more along the lines of sampling everything the world has to offer (breadth), rather than taking time for richer experience (depth). The Enneagram sure nailed me. I'm a true-to-form Type Seven (with a hearty dollop of Type Five in the mix), the most proudly gluttonous person you could ever know.

Type Eight: Leaders, Protectors, Challengers. Type Eights value their own strength and desire to be powerful and in control. Natural leaders, they can be either friendly and charitable or dictatorially manipulative, ruthless, and willing to destroy anything in their way. Eights are concerned with self-preservation; they seek control over their own lives and destinies and fear being harmed or controlled by others. Type Eights may be a bit too conservative to fully embrace all the potentialities of a multifaceted polymath/versatilist, although they're smart and would likely agree on the benefits of a cross-training program.

Type Nine: Mediators, Peacemakers, Preservationists. Type Nines are ruled by their empathy. At their best they're perceptive, receptive, gentle, calming, and at peace with the world; however, they tend to dissociate from conflicts and indifferently go along with others' wishes. They fear the conflict caused by their ability to simultaneously understand opposing points of view and seek peace of mind above all else. Nines are especially prone to dissociation and passive-aggressive behavior, preferring to act via inaction. Because they aren't typically self-involved, Type Nines are probably not ideal candidates to join our generalist crusade. Nines tend to go with the flow—and right now, the flow is toward specialization.

> *"Thoroughly to know oneself is above all art, for it is the highest art."*
>
> —Theologia Germanica

Now that you have had yourself revealed to yourself (probably not for the first time), what are you supposed to do with this information? In other words, how is it relevant to our thesis of taking a much more considered approach to your free time as a way to combat the midlife "Mean Reds," as Holly Golightly (in *Breakfast at Tiffany's*) memorably termed it?

It's not about simply recognizing your unique batch of character quirks. It's how you're able to *reconstitute* your particular batch of quirky traits that I'm interested in—how you can create your own individualistic tossed salad of new potentials. For example, let's say you're a

> *"I am large; I contain multitudes."*
>
> —Walt Whitman (1819–1892)

low C, high S on DISC, with a bit of the Artisan peeking through on the Keirsey, combined with a Two/Three/Six mix struggling to gain fuller expression on the Enneagram. How can you leverage all that to become the best cross-trainer you can be? The key is to pay more attention to what you're not than what you are. I fully believe that none of us is capable of changing our true, innate personality types. Identifying ourselves within these various personality sorters is thus a bit of a parlor game. But the real action happens when you apply kaizen to tease forth a little of the energy in the descriptions that don't much apply to you. That's where the growth is. It's always frustrated me that once identified with a label—even when the label is rather fascinating in the way self-knowledge usually is—that label tends to create a door that seems to close on the question hanging in the air: how do I become a better, more complex person if I'm stuck within the bounds of my "type"? Again, the key is to spend more time with the categories you're *not*, and then select some Triumph in Twenty activities to bolster those areas. Sample from the other teams' playbooks, in other words. That brings our Individuality Imperative to life. So if you're a hard-charging, impatient go-getter with latent artistic tendencies, the way to build your brain and battle the blahs is to get in touch with your nurturing, protective, loyal, linear side, perhaps by volunteering with special-needs children or serving on the board of directors of a not-for-profit with a mission of feeding the hungry in your city. If you're resistant—and you may well be, since these activities aren't second nature to you—invoke the magic of kaizen to help ease your way into it, bit by bit.

"All men should strive to learn before they die What they are running from, and to, and why."

—James Thurber (1894–1961), humorist and cartoonist

Dare to Be a Swashbuckler

No payday can equal the feeling of contentment that comes from being the person you're meant to be, whether or not you buy into any of the personality indicators we've discussed here. In fact, don't settle for just being who you are. Go full tilt and be *de trop*—be the over-the-top version of who you are.

Author Marcus Buckingham has an interesting idea to consider: play to your strengths, rather than pouring energy into fixing your weaknesses. While there is merit to this proposal, I tend to disagree. If all you do your whole life is play to your strengths, you risk cutting a groove that becomes a rut. My prescription? Check out other activities. Be curious about things that are not characteristically your strengths. You'll likely find that you have more strengths than you ever imagined. Doing so will, paradoxically, make your strengths even stronger.

Gotta Love the Office

A friend recently startled me with a wonderfully individualistic bit of insight. You know the axiom that no one, on their deathbed, ever regretted not having spent more time at the office? Turns out that a brush with breast cancer had scared this woman into a premature glimpse of her own mortality—but, surprisingly, her reaction to it was not to dial back on work. She cowboy'd it up. She realized that while she'd spent years focusing on family obligations, socializing, and traveling, she had not been contributing to society through her work. It was time to get back to work with a vengeance. These days, she's hale and hearty and expressing her ichor with gusto, and she has the published books to show for it.

Follow Your Bliss

We'll return to Stephen Jay Gould for the last word on individuality: "In our increasingly complex and confusing world, we need all the help we can

get from each distinct domain of our
emotional and intellectual being." Gould
advocates that we should each "quilt a
diverse collection of separate patches into
a beautiful and integrated coat of many
colors." He takes a good-natured jibe at
academe and its search for a "final
theory," bestowing upon that would-be
theory the acronym TOE, or "theory of everything."

*"There is nothing with which
every man is so afraid as getting to
know how enormously much he is
capable of doing and becoming."*

—Søren Kierkegaard (1813–1855),
philosopher and theologian

Now, I don't pretend that vigoring up your mind counts as a bona fide
TOE, but it is all-inclusive; it does argue for a sort of underlying unity; it's
just wry enough, with its hint of a wink; and it's just grandiose enough for
us nonacademic science wannabes. At any rate, I think Gould would be in
our corner, along with that megaindividualist Feynman, urging us on with a
smile.

EXERCISES

To help sharpen the focus on the parameters of your own individuality, try your hand at the following exercises, all designed to provide more self-awareness.

1. Here Comes Trouble

How would your best friend describe your personal style? Ask three people who know you, in different contexts (from work, home, or church, for instance), to finish this sentence about you: "Here comes _____."

2. Next Time

If you could have five alternate careers, what would they be? Why are you drawn to these particular careers?

3. Gesundheit

Spend one of your Triumph in Twenty sessions pondering which birthright gifts, or ichor, you may be ignoring.

4. Critical Thinking

What is your "type" according to the Keirsey Temperament Sorter, DISC, the Enneagram of Personality, or other comparable psychometric personality tests? If you think these tests have merit, in what context should they be applied? (A critical evaluation of the various personality assessments on the market would make a terrific area of study for anyone with Renaissance person tendencies.) If you believe these tests are credible, why do you think so? If you believe they carry about as much weight as a horoscope, why do you believe that?

6

IMPERATIVE #3:
THE SELECTIVITY IMPERATIVE

Be Selective but Open-Minded— There *Is* Enough Time

> Time is a created thing.
> To say "I don't have time" is to say "I don't want to."
>
> —*Lao Tzu*

Dennis Hensley is a professor of English and writing at Taylor University in Fort Wayne, Indiana. He's published 44 books; 3,000 newspaper and magazine articles; and several songs, short stories, and scripts. Married for more than thirty-two years, he and his wife have two grown children. Hensley served in Vietnam for almost two years and managed to read more than 125 books; see eighty-five movies; travel to Thailand and Taiwan; keep a daily journal; study the Vietnamese language; earn a brown belt in tae kwon do; and write devotions, articles, and comedy pieces—all while he was serving in the military. "There *are* enough hours in the day to do whatever you want to do, but you've got to have discipline," he says in his book *How to Manage Your Time*. Hensley thinks of a twenty-four-hour day in segments. "If you work eight hours, sleep eight hours, and do whatever you want for six hours, you would still have two hours to work on a special goal or project, like writing a book or fixing up an old car." He estimates that within eight months, his plan will yield 480 hours of headway toward a goal—that's the equivalent of three work-months. Additionally, Hensley eschews cell phones and environmental clutter. I draw the line at a cell phone; for me it's a highly useful tool. But banishing clutter around the house and office? You bet.

Hensley is a goal setter, but his distinction between tasks and goals frustrates me. "Tasks are not goals," he says. "Stay focused on goals, not busywork. Your goals are what will advance you in life, whereas your tasks are what will eat up your life." The problem is, life is made up of tasks—endless, endless tasks. If Hensley's not doing them, who is? My guess is, it's his wife—and I'll bet she hasn't written as many books as he has. I'm thinking of chores such as doing laundry, taking out the trash, raking leaves, cleaning the house, paying bills, wrapping gifts, taking the car in for maintenance. The solution to the chronic tension between tasks and goals is our friend kaizen. Triumph in Twenty will guide you in making incremental progress toward your goals, even while you continue that never-ending dance with the task devil.

Saving himself from complete Pollyanna virtuousness, Hensley approves of the occasional nap, though he pooh-poohs daydreaming (Scrooge!). Still, I endorse his larger point about looking back on today and realizing with a sinking heart that although I was no sloth—active as I was with tasks, errands, and busywork—I made no headway on my life's goals. That is not a good feeling.

This brings us to our next imperative, selectivity. For our purposes, I'm defining and interpreting selectivity in two rather distinct ways: first, the selective use of your time (i.e., time allocation); second, the selective choices made in terms of activities pursued (i.e., effort allocation). The allied concepts of time allocation and effort allocation waltz together nicely. The glue that joins these two ideas is kaizen and Triumph in Twenty. Small increments of time (Triumph in Twenty) coupled with small increments of effort (kaizen) is the formula for Renaissance achievement. Pair the right activity with the right time (along with the right attitude), and the daunting prospect of becoming a Renaissance man or woman becomes amazingly manageable.

Paradoxically, with all the busyness we're engulfed by, stretches of unsettling boredom, wistfulness, emptiness, even depression occasionally overtake us. Why? It may seem hard to believe, but we're not busy enough. That's a bold claim, I know, but I hope by now I've made the daunting prospect of becoming a cross-training desultorian appealing and accessible.

We want to have it all—to know everyone, be everywhere, learn everything. We want to have our cake and eat it, too. In fact, we want a bakery full of cakes, and we want to be the bakers. But even for those of us who are endlessly avaricious for life's bounty, the reality is that we need to exercise some modicum of selectivity. We need a soupçon of structure, a dab of direction, a flourish of focus so we can pursue our intentions without getting hopelessly sidetracked. We require some chronological choreography, if you will.

I'm talking about making what we'll call *effort-allocation decisions*. Effort allocation breaks out two ways. First, we'll want to consider how many areas of interest are reasonable to pursue at any one time (don't worry—no ceilings will be imposed). Then we'll take time management into consideration. This chapter addresses the number-one objection

> *"The worst part about being self-employed is that you have to work eighteen hours a day. The best part is that you get to pick which eighteen."*
>
> —Anonymous

(the "yeah, but") that is sure to arise whenever I hint at enriching your life in the epic way I'm prescribing—the plaintive wail, the clichéd cry, the inevitable lament: "I don't have the time!" The thing is, there's more time than you ever imagined. Time, you must realize, is a created thing. You must begin to feel this truth in your bones.

When it comes to managing your time, don't be led into false binary thinking. Life is not an either-or proposition. Consider these false binaries: I can take a walk *or* I can help my son with his homework. I can properly maintain the house *or* I can keep up on current events. I can hold an elected office *or* I can be a good parent. I can go back to school to study history *or* I can get in shape physically. I can study marine biology *or* I can serve on the board of the opera. Without doubt there are tradeoffs involved—let's not be naive—but you don't want to do *nothing* simply because you're afraid that doing more than one thing isn't possible. The examples listed here aren't all-or-nothing, either-or, black-or-white binaries. Things can be combined, blended, made to be complementary. You can talk with your son about his homework while you're walking together. You can wash dishes while you're listening to Terry Gross. You get the idea. Some people may call this multi-tasking. I prefer "complementarity."

Life as a Geyser

You'll recall that I've referred to Renaissance people as water bugs that can skim across a pond and never sink below the surface, never become engulfed by the water, never get overwhelmed by their circumstances. Water bugs are masters of making tension work for them—they're light on their feet and never stay in one place long enough to sink, allowing the surface tension of the water to keep them afloat. They're able to skate across the water and cover lots of territory in a desirable, useful, productive way—it's their evolutionary asset, in fact. That's natural selection at work.

I'd guess that most people (and maybe even most other bugs) think water bugs are especially nifty little creatures. No one frowns upon them because they're not diving down deep into the water or doing anything other than what they were born to do. They've adapted to their world in the way that is best for them; they've evolved to use the surface tension of the water to their benefit. They love tension; they count on it. Likewise, vigorous activity skimmers of the human variety learn to thrive on the tension in their world—the tension that exists between desirable alternatives.

Tension is a good energy, not a force to be avoided. It's another of those words (such as *dilettante* and *jack-of-all-trades*) that gets consistently bad press when, in fact, there would never be any forward progress in the world without it. For instance, here's a high-quality tension to struggle against:

READER/CUSTOMER CARE SURVEY

HEFG

We care about your opinions! Please take a moment to fill out our online Reader Survey at **http://survey.hcibooks.com.**
As a **"THANK YOU"** you will receive a **VALUABLE INSTANT COUPON** towards future book purchases
as well as a **SPECIAL GIFT** available only online! Or, you may mail this card back to us.

(PLEASE PRINT IN ALL CAPS)

First Name _____ MI. _____ Last Name _____

Address _____ City _____

State _____ Zip _____ Email _____

1. Gender
☐ Female   ☐ Male

2. Age
☐ 8 or younger   ☐ 13-16
☐ 9-12   ☐ 17-20   ☐ 21-30
☐ 31+

3. Did you receive this book as a gift?
☐ Yes   ☐ No

4. Annual Household Income
☐ under $25,000
☐ $25,000 - $34,999
☐ $35,000 - $49,999
☐ $50,000 - $74,999
☐ over $75,000

5. What are the ages of the children living in your house?
☐ 0 - 14   ☐ 15+

6. Marital Status
☐ Single
☐ Married
☐ Divorced
☐ Widowed

7. How did you find out about the book?
(please choose one)
☐ Recommendation
☐ Store Display
☐ Online
☐ Catalog/Mailing
☐ Interview/Review

8. Where do you usually buy books?
(please choose one)
☐ Bookstore
☐ Online
☐ Book Club/Mail Order
☐ Price Club (Sam's Club, Costco's, etc.)
☐ Retail Store (Target, Wal-Mart, etc.)

9. What subject do you enjoy reading about the most?
(please choose one)
☐ Parenting/Family
☐ Relationships
☐ Recovery/Addictions
☐ Health/Nutrition
☐ Christianity
☐ Spirituality/Inspiration
☐ Business Self-help
☐ Women's Issues
☐ Sports

10. What attracts you most to a book?
(please choose one)
☐ Title
☐ Cover Design
☐ Author
☐ Content

TAPE IN MIDDLE; DO NOT STAPLE

BUSINESS REPLY MAIL
FIRST-CLASS MAIL PERMIT NO 45 DEERFIELD BEACH, FL

POSTAGE WILL BE PAID BY ADDRESSEE

Health Communications, Inc.
3201 SW 15th Street
Deerfield Beach FL 33442-9875

FOLD HERE

Comments

will you work on perennial plantings for the next few weeks or draft your book on sorbets or mount an effort around historic preservation in your neighborhood? Whatever you choose to do, some degree of tension will always be involved because you can't be doing one while you're doing the others, especially if you've chosen to engage with just one area of concentration at a time. And that's fine, because that tension serves as a catalyst—an extra boost that keeps you in motion, since you know that more good stuff is always waiting around the corner.

Successful brain trainers, past and present, have managed the neat trick of being selective at the same time they're inclusive and comprehensive about the things they're interested in. Generally, this feat is accomplished by employing a sequential pattern of activities. In other words, these individuals will concentrate on pottery for a few days or weeks; next, they'll turn their attention to kayaking for the summer; then, they'll return to their easel for their pen-and-ink drawing.

Again, I want to emphasize that whatever you select to do as part of your cross-training, there is no judgment. I am not prescribing any single "must-do" activity—unless you consider kaizen an object of study (which you could). You can choose to do whatever it is you want to do, and you can elect to juggle multiple activities simultaneously, or focus on just one thing at a time. I'd like to see you select topics that are contrary to what you do professionally, in true cross-training fashion, but that's your call. If you draw a blank when you sit down to map out your Vigorous Mind program, pick up a batch of magazines at any newsstand and you'll hit upon a wealth of ideas. Here's another unexpectedly fun source of wide-ranging activities: a Boy Scout handbook, where ideas for more than 100 merit badges are listed—everything from atomic energy to bugling to insect study to cinematography to Indian lore

"Guard well your spare moments. They are like uncut diamonds. Discard them and their value will never be known. Improve them and they will become the brightest gems in a useful life."

—Ralph Waldo Emerson (1803–1882), essayist and poet

to crime prevention to salesmanship to plumbing. And while we're praising Boy Scouts, I'd like to salute James Calderwood, from Chevy Chase, Maryland, an Eagle Scout who's earned all 121 Boy Scout merit badges, from American business to woodwork. To display all the badges he's earned, he's fashioned his own extra-wide sash by stitching three together. Calderwood clearly has the impulse to become a well-rounded icon of the liberal arts—an übergeneralist, a cross-trained Renaissance man, and a guy who knows how to effectively harness the nooks and crannies of his days.

Cognitive Catalysts

Michael Maurer is a man with a keen sense of the value of time. Maurer follows his own North Star, which is made up of a dozen things he likes and does well. He creates sensationally successful businesses (a commercial real estate venture, a movie production company, an investment firm) by following his gut and his heart. Both his personal life and his professional life revolve around his passions. He's a deep-sea photographer of minuscule ocean creatures, *New York Times* crossword puzzle constructor, gardener, woodworker, and mountain climber (a few years ago, he summited Mt. Kilimanjaro, the highest peak in Africa). "Interesting things to do catch my eye all the time," he understates. "One thing naturally leads to another. Plus, my friends all know I like interesting stuff. They turn me on to new things all the time. I climbed Kilimanjaro on a dare."

While Maurer's many passions are each affirming on their own merit, they also feed back to his primary occupation as a businessman. Woodworking teaches him about concentration and precision. Crosswords teach him about relationships and pop culture. Mountain climbing teaches him about the nature of business: there are always obstacles; preparation means everything; attitude counts. This is precisely the kind of innovation and insight that can result from cross-training your brain. Despite his generous nature, Maurer's interpersonal style is crisp; he wastes almost no time on small talk, which transmits the message that he values his time and uses it carefully. His is a tough act to emulate, but he serves as a prototype of an individual who has strategically structured his time to include all the elements he insists on being present in his life.

When I think of Sherlock Holmes, I think of him as the human version of a Swiss Army knife: he can do a lot of cool things, but he has some significant shortfalls. The creation of Sir Arthur Conan Doyle, Holmes is a fictional London-based detective—who also happens to be a classic dabbling dilettante. He is as famous for his intellectual prowess as for his coolly astute powers of reasoning and Columbo-like observations. When it comes to solving crime, Holmes describes himself and his habits as "Bohemian." Modern readers of the Sherlock Holmes stories might be surprised to find that he was an occasional user (sometimes habitual, when lacking in stimulating cases) of both cocaine and morphine. Dr. Watson, his confidante and biographer, describes this as the detective's "only vice," and later weaned Holmes off drug use. Holmes seems to have been completely in touch with, if not his time-allocation skills, at least his effort-allocation skills. According to this list in which Watson wryly assesses Holmes's abilities, Holmes wasn't bashful about his shortcomings:

Knowledge of Literature—Nil

Knowledge of Philosophy—Nil

Knowledge of Astronomy—Nil

Knowledge of Politics—Feeble

Knowledge of Botany—Variable. Well up in belladonna, opium and poisons generally. Knows nothing of practical gardening.

Knowledge of Geology—Practical, but limited. Tells at a glance different soils from each other. After walks, has shown me splashes upon his trousers, and told me by their colour and consistence in what part of London he had received them.

Knowledge of Chemistry—Profound

Knowledge of Anatomy—Accurate, but unsystematic

Knowledge of Sensational Literature—Immense. He appears to know every
detail of every horror perpetrated in the century.

Plays the violin well.

Is an expert singlestick player, boxer and swordsman.

Has a good practical knowledge of British law.

How to Select: Some Tips

It is both invigorating and intimidating to a curious mind to survey the
sheer mass of written sources available on every interest and topic. The question is, how do you separate the wheat from the chaff, the gold from the
dross? Cross-trainers are adept skimmers who know how and when to gloss
over reading material—it's a skill every up-and-coming cross-trainer needs
to master. If you're looking to wrest the most impact from your hours and
minutes, you may want to institute some of these time-management tips:

• When it comes to written material, keep your eye out for what journalists call the "nut graf." The nut graf is a sentence or paragraph near
  the top of the piece that summarizes what the article is about, helping
  the reader make a stop-reading or continue-reading decision. The
  Readers' Bill of Rights grants you license to abandon any article or
  book whenever you wish—you shouldn't robotically persist in reading
  just because you feel some obligation to finish. Of course, this doesn't
  mean you should pass on reading an article just because the subject
  doesn't immediately grab you. Sometimes authors take a while to
  warm to their topic. I must admit that I've had some of my most
  enjoyable reading experiences despite the fact that the nut graf didn't
  seem terribly promising. For instance, I recently read an article about
  some guy who arranged to have a suit of clothes custom-made for

himself. No particular intersection with my life there, yet the story turned out to be interesting, well-written, insightful, and therefore enriching.

- Maintain a list of your favorite writers. When they come out with something new, you can be pretty well assured that it'll be a read worth your time. Many online book vendors can alert you to new offerings by your designated favorite authors.

- If you feel your attention flagging while you're reading an article or book, scan just the first sentence of the next few paragraphs. Perhaps the author will have introduced a fresh topic or taken a new tack, thereby providing you with enough traction to stick with the piece. Jump to a new part and start over at that point if you aren't getting anything out of the segment you're reading.

- Set up an aggregator on your computer that serves up your favorite blogs right into your e-mail inbox, to reduce time you might otherwise spend surfing the Web.

- If you're reading nonfiction, learn to parse the table of contents. There's no rule stating that you must read a nonnarrative book straight through. Perhaps one chapter title jumps out at you above others. Often, too, a book's introduction or first chapter entices you into reading further.

I am advocating a ruthless attitude about what we let into our world and what we keep out. It's high praise to have your life described as "well edited," but at the same time, you need to be forever open to new authors, new ideas, offbeat articles—this is the essence of the Curiosity Imperative that's at the heart of this book's message. That's the trick: negotiating the tension between unfettered curiosity and disciplined gatekeeping.

> *"I value my time. I choose to use it wisely and do not let others steal it from me."*
>
> —Paula Peisner Coxe, author

Divide and Conquer

You may be surprised to find that there is more than enough time to do everything you choose to do. For example, Beth drew up a list of thirty-five areas of interest that were meaningful enough for her to want to tackle with the rest of her life. She plunked five of them on a list for the current year, five more for the next year, and so forth. Within seven years, she will have addressed all of her original areas of interest. Of course, her list will require modification as she goes along. She might lose steam on growing orchids and realize she wants to spend more time than she anticipated on piano. She might even determine that five subjects per year is too ambitious and thin her list accordingly. The point is that thirty-five subjects may seem like a lot, but that number becomes manageable when you divide and conquer. This strategy is, of course, another expression of our friend kaizen. In any case, this systematic approach will free you from the tyranny of unexamined options later in your life.

Complementarity

It's possible that you'll feel overwhelmed by the range of potential activities available to you—such is the munificent nature of our great, big, complicated world. We've already discussed how to call on the quiet, simple wisdom of kaizen to bypass the mental blockade that confronts us when we're faced with overwhelm. Another powerful tool I'd like to recommend is *complementarity*, in which you hitch two coordinated activities together in order to reach your desired level of expertise faster—it's a great time-saver. The best way to hitch a ride on the back of complementarity is to choose a nonphysical pursuit that's primarily a mind builder, and combine it with a physical activity that's primarily a body builder. (Yes, this book's title refers to a vigorous *mind*. But a vigorous body correlates superbly well with a vigorous mind.) For example, you might want to engage in a six-month immersion in comedy writing, coupled with a six-month immersion in skateboarding.

There will likely be incidents and accidents and anecdotes and observations arising from your skateboarding forays that can liven up your comedy writing. Presto! That's complementarity. An obstetrician I know was able to make the unlikely leap from yo-yoing to her surgical practice when she began learning about yo-yos with her two teenage sons. One day she noticed something that made her pause: the tension on a yo-yo string reminded her of the tension on the sutures she used while doing laparoscopic hysterectomies. Her surgical thread was prone to knotting; certain yo-yo techniques were applicable to the problem. Voila! Surgical problem solved, thanks to a children's toy. This is a perfect example of creating a linkage from an entirely unrelated field back to your primary endeavor. It's also an example of the splendid combination of a physical pursuit (yo-yoing) and a cognitive pursuit (surgery).

The reason that mind-body combinations are so powerful is that physical activities release the brain from its grip on your conscious mind—and this can be a big relief, a welcome respite from having to be relentlessly ourselves. Physicality establishes a much-needed congruence between mind and body, given that so many of us have more active brains than bodies in this Information Age.

NEURO NUGGET

It seems that working out builds more than just muscles. Scientists theorize that exercise improves memory by ramping up the creation of new brain cells. The more physically fit you are, the better you'll perform on word-memory tasks. "Physical exercise might be a very effective way to ameliorate age-related memory decline," summarizes Scott Small, a neurologist at Columbia University. Researchers have long known that people who have physically active and intellectually challenging lives are less likely to develop dementia than those who do not. Fighting mental malnutrition by cross-training your brain is itself protective.

You'll find you experience insights, epiphanies, and brainstorms while you're moving. During exercise, you'll even remember things you didn't realize had slipped your mind. So while you're ice skating, you might finally understand exactly how to change the oil in your car the way it was demonstrated in your auto repair class. While hiking, you may think of the ideal turn of phrase for an essay you're writing. You'll begin to perceive meta-level connections between skating and oil changing—subtleties that never would have occurred to you before. You'll compare and contrast, perceive parallels, generate metaphors, and above all, become a more accomplished skater for having mastered the oil change technique. Perhaps these correlates may be about balance, positioning, and muscle control; patience and practice; or the interplay of interrelated parts. It turns out that the Tao of skating isn't all that dissimilar from the Tao of car maintenance. The particular Eureka! moments (the Germans call them *Aha-erlebnis*) will be different for everybody, but they will arise.

For argument's sake, let's say you're not the athletic or outdoorsy sort—you would no sooner get up on ice skates than fly to the moon. How can *you* harness the timesaving power of complementarity? Fortunately, the principle still holds. Think of a general concept or broad area and spin off two related activities from that concept. Let's say you choose the outdoors. You could spin off camping and outdoor cooking to create your particular portfolio of complementary pursuits; pair photography with arboreal studies; enhance your study of ancient textiles with visits to related history museums. The mind-body diametric may not be as extreme, but each activity still feeds nicely off the other.

That schism between the arts and sciences provides another model for complementarity—simply select an activity from each of these sprawling domains. Our friend Stephen Jay Gould referred frequently to the traditional taxonomy of the arts and sciences. Gould, a paleontologist, fed his vigorous mind with the passive delights of reading, the ambulatory pleasures of architecture appreciation, and a serious participation in choral singing.

In terms of time management, Butler University president Bobby Fong told me he alternates between solitary and social activities—what he calls "cyclical syncopation." Every Saturday morning he spends an hour playing the piano. Sometimes he sorts through his baseball card collection when he gets the whim. Then it's off to meetings or social activities. Fong is a voracious reader and the world's foremost authority on the poetry of Oscar Wilde. His wife says he has the vision of a poet and the soul of an accountant. I say he has the time management skills of a pro.

High-Brow, Low-Brow Pendulum

Generalists are gluttons, and not only do we have the temerity to be proud of it, we also have the gall to greed for even more. We've trained our pendulums to swing so widely that we embrace even those things commonly disparaged as "beneath us." We have designs on a vigorous mind, and that implies a vibrant open-mindedness. If something is said to be "beneath us," as contrarians, we're instinctively drawn to it. Long live philistinism.

As we exercise our prerogative of selectivity, coupled with complementarity, let's not overlook so-called nonintellectual pursuits. I could be referring only to TV, maligned stepchild of our cultural landscape. There's plenty of fare for the mind on TV, but it takes a little effort to pluck what's worthwhile from the flood of pap. TV newsman Eric Sevareid (1912–1992) correctly noted, "[Most people] will make plans, go to trouble and expense, when they buy a book or reserve a seat in a theater. They will not study the week's offerings of music on TV, though, and schedule themselves to be present. They want to come home, eat dinner, twist the dial, and find something agreeable ready, accommodating to their schedule." But you *can* make television work for you. Scan the weekly program guide on Sunday and circle the shows you're interested in watching or recording for later viewing. This keeps you from drifting into mindless sieges of watching whatever's on. On the other hand, shoot, you can just have some fun with *Seinfeld* reruns.

Television is our culture's reliable fall guy for wasted time. Time management gurus will invariably advise you to scale back the amount of time you spend watching TV, assuming that you're idling away your evenings in front of the tube, zoning out in front of a witless, laugh-tracked sitcom. And maybe you are. (If you are, cut it out.) Some savvy observers have advanced the fascinating thesis that even bad TV can be good for your brain, but I'd nonetheless argue that you should limit your TV watching to the best shows available—and *you* get to pick which shows are the best, not some critic. Perhaps an analysis of scripts from *The Simpsons* is one of your designated Vigorous Mind activities—that's absolutely valid and it's a legitimate way to sneak more TV into your life. Sometimes, I'll tape a show, then watch two-thirds of it before turning it off. I'll then make several guesses as to how the scriptwriter will wrap up and resolve the situation he's constructed for himself. Then I compare my ending to his. I find this to be a stimulating way to enjoy the "wasted time" TV represents. After all, if you're truly enjoying wasting your time, it's not wasted time. "This wasted time I have found by constant experience to be as indispensable as sleep," said John Adams, our second president and founding father, who managed to get a good bit accomplished in his life even without the stimulus of *Will & Grace* reruns.

The Spirit of the Calendar

Another time management tool to consider: your humble calendar. Let's say you've committed to making swimming one of your priorities for the next twelve months. To make this resolution stick, you've got to unpack it—move it out of the abstract and into the concrete here-and-now—so that swimming is no longer a concept, but rather a line-item in your weekly schedule. Your calendar is one of the most powerful yet underused and underappreciated tools in your arsenal. Maybe you think you're already too tethered to your calendar—that it's a ball and chain. On the contrary, calendars are transcendent tools. I believe that you need to tether yourself even more closely to your calendar, because to be disciplined is to be free. In the end, it's going to become the symbol of your chosen aspirations, the manifestation of your will.

Now, I'm not suggesting you schedule yourself so tightly that every minute is booked. Life as it's lived isn't complicit in that kind of extreme-style scheduling; the unexpected is the norm in our daily lives. What I am suggesting is for you to note in your calendar that every Monday and Wednesday, from 7:00 to 7:20 PM, you activate Triumph in Twenty and take a kaizen step toward whatever goal you've chosen for yourself. Then honor that commitment, just as you would a doctor's appointment booked at that time. We move heaven and earth to make our medical appointments, don't we? That's the very same reverence and respect we need to dedicate to our own cross-training. Taking baby steps, committing just twenty minutes of your time each day, is entirely doable—you just need to do it.

The calendar is your ally, not your enemy. It can actually "create" time by helping you find moments throughout your day where you can squeeze in your Renaissance activities. Much of the magic of time management is due to the spirit with which you approach your planning. For instance, if you always keep a notebook with you, you can noodle the makings of a haiku while you're cooling your heels in the checkout lane at the Piggly Wiggly. You just bought yourself five minutes that otherwise would have been wasted. Or perhaps you're able to listen to foreign-language tapes while you're commuting in the car or on the subway. You just bought yourself twenty-five minutes of time you'd written off as wasted. Even if you simply commit yourself to thinking about haiku or Spanish verbs for the few minutes you're waiting in line at the bank, you reclaim some time. Purposeful thinking is an excellent (and underused) kaizen activity. These are examples where so-called multitasking can work. However, dear reader, do not be misled—you'll soon see that I am no fan of multitasking, for I'm certain that it works only in limited circumstances and only when you're the sort of person who can make it work. Not everybody can. Generally speaking, multitasking is surprisingly *counterproductive*.

Multitasking: What's Really Going On?

NEURO NUGGET

According to neuroscientist Sandra Aamodt, whether or not you're able to multitask depends to a great extent on how you originally learned to do a particular activity. If you initially learned to make jewelry while you were listening to music, you should always be able to make jewelry while listening to music. If you learned to make jewelry in silence, playing music will fracture your concentration. That's because the brain is very much a contextual instrument—meaning the way it functions is contingent on what else is going on at the time.

Go ahead and make like a honeybee, flitting from flower to flower, sampling all the adventures the world has to offer—but beware of multitasking. People who boast about doing more than one thing at a time claim to be multitasking, but what they're actually doing is toggling inefficiently between tasks, losing momentum each time they turn from one to the next. Leonardo da Vinci was said, perhaps apocryphally, to have taken notes with one hand while drawing with the other. But even if we were all ambidextrous, the human brain is not constructed to undertake two tasks in the very same moment. As powerful as it is, the brain is just not capable of thinking two thoughts at once. It may feel like that's what you're doing sometimes, but that's simply a reflection of how quickly your brain can jump from one thought to the next; you're still thinking just one thought in each instant. And the problem is that you lose momentum each time your brain pops from one thought or task to another. Visualize this vignette, as a hyped-up paragon of multitasking: Bill is researching an article on fluoride, delivering a speech on traffic patterns, and studying Sanskrit—all at the same time. Imagine the result.

NEURO NUGGET

Research has shown what consummate common sense dictates: We perform better and more effectively when we perform tasks successively, rather than trying to do them all at once. "We've identified a kind of bottleneck in the prefrontal cortex of the brain that forces people to address problems one after the other, even if they're doing it so fast it feels simultaneous," says Rene Marois, Ph.D., associate professor of psychology and neuroscience at Vanderbilt University, commenting for the science journal Neuron. "Results are always worse when you multitask, but in some areas they're especially compromised," agrees Russell Poldrack, Ph.D., associate professor of psychology at UCLA. If you're trying to grasp a new skill, you make it much more difficult on yourself if you attempt to do two things at once. "Our research shows that if you try to master something while splitting your attention, brain activity switches regions—from memory building to short-term habit making," Poldrack adds.

My advice is to multitask only when you're not engaged with something on a deep cognitive level. You can compile your grocery list while waiting in line at the bank, because neither activity likely requires much brainpower. You can fold laundry and listen to vocabulary-building tapes at the same time. But listening to music while you read may be too much stimulation. And talking on your phone while driving is a bad idea: formulating thoughts and translating them into cogent sentences is mental work; do not mix it with driving, which also requires mental power.

NEURO NUGGET

To get another perspective on multitasking, I spoke with neuroscientist Samuel Wang of Princeton University, author of *Welcome to Your Brain: Why You Lose Your Car Keys but Never Forget How to Drive and Other Puzzles of Everyday Life*. I asked him the following: Is multitasking a myth? I can listen to *Car Talk* and fold laundry at the same time, but I can't give a speech and talk to a client at the same time—and both examples could be said to be multitasking. So it must depend on what the tasks are and what burden they place on the brain, right?

His reply: Different tasks make different demands on our brains. To pick a low-level example, we can walk and talk at the same time because the brain centers that control walking, which include motor cortex and midbrain structures, are not involved in generating language or other higher cognitive functions. In the case of your example, language is generated and processed in specialized centers of the brain: Broca's area and Wernicke's area. Two tasks that relied on language capacity would compete with one another. This is where the brain's executive processes come in; the brain can switch between tasks with effort and a delay.

It's important to note that switching between tasks is associated with inefficiency and an increased error rate. So unless one of the tasks is an easy one, like making tea or folding clothes, it's not a good idea to try doing two things at once.

So multitasking really only works when one of the tasks does not command too much of your mental energy, such as vacuuming the carpet, scrubbing the floor, or folding the laundry. In addition to the obvious safety concerns associated with fractionating your concentration while you're operating heavy machinery, it's insulting to the people who get in the path of your spastic splintering. Multitasking is absolutely counter to the Zen principle of mindfulness, which calls for complete absorption in the task at hand, even if that task is as simple as vacuuming, scrubbing, or folding. Mindfulness is a technique whereby you're intentionally aware of your thoughts and actions in the present moment, activating no judgment. Multitasking is a technique in which you're activating nothing *but* judgment: "I ought to be doing something else right now."

Any activity done mindfully is a form of meditation, and mindfulness is possible practically all the time. This helps tremendously in letting go of the disdain we have for busywork, to which we devote so much of our time. Sure, I wish I could be creative all the time, but the truth is that I'm dealing with busywork—chopping vegetables or shampooing my hair or emptying the dishwasher—probably 80 percent of my waking hours. The corollary truth is that I probably couldn't withstand the pressure to be creative 80 percent of the time. Creativity is intense, and it requires the yin/yang counterpart of busywork, when the conscious mind can idle a bit. Ironically, while you're in the moment with dusting or carpooling or standing in line at the dry cleaner's, your subconscious mind is nibbling away at the issues on your mind. So as it turns out, busywork really isn't really wasted time after all. Earlier I suggested that you might choose to think about haiku or your Spanish language studies in those spare moments, but you can also dedicate that downtime to thinking, planning, meditating, or just zoning out. Your choice. It's all good.

When people describe themselves as "multitaskers," I believe what they're trying to communicate is that they're very important and therefore very busy with lots of tasks that need to be accomplished. Rather than spend thirty minutes on one of many tasks, in thirty increments of one minute each, better to devote thirty straight minutes to the task—which you'll probably get done in twenty minutes, since you have allowed for the magic known as momentum to kick in and help you along. Remember, every time you break from one task to work on another, you shoot momentum in the foot. And please note that I'm not talking about taking periodic breaks that you need to refresh your mind, body, and spirit. Those kinds of breaks—grabbing a bite to eat, taking a quick walk around the block, making a phone call—truly can be energizing. They enhance the power of momentum, which is the potent chemical behind kaizen.

Why does momentum work? Without going into the physics behind it, suffice it to say that it requires effort to start something, to get over that hump of inertia, but it is comparatively easy to *keep* that something going once you've started. Momentum is also akin to flow—you don't want to break the spell once you've got that groove going. Even if you've allocated just twenty minutes a day, three times a week, in pursuit of your interests, don't allow interruptions to stop your momentum. Get out of your own way.

Another benefit of harnessing the power of momentum is that you can accomplish more in a day. Once you banish the counterproductive notion of multitasking and instead catch the wave of momentum, you'll get that thirty-minute task done in twenty minutes, leaving you with ten minutes of time you just "created." No one ever became a Renaissance person by multitasking. The way to pursue your cross-training is through kaizen: focused attention on an activity of your choice, at the rate of ten or twenty minutes a few times a week. You may be engaged with portraiture, antiques, and artisanal cheese making each week, but you're certainly not doing them all in the same moment. As business consultant Stephen Covey has said, "The main thing is to keep the main thing the main thing."

Kairos and Chronos

Kairos and *chronos* are ancient Greek words designating time. Chronos refers to the continuous flux of time, while kairos points to unique moments in the temporal process—moments in which something unique can happen or be accomplished. Of the two, kairos is the more powerful notion. Chronos just keeps chugging along, whereas kairos is akin to timing, or doing something at just the right moment. One can express the differences by saying that chronos brings out the quantitative, calculable, repetitive elements of the temporal process, while kairos emphasizes the qualitative, experiential, unique element. We Americans tend to get our knickers in a knot over chronos, when it's kairos that's much more potent. Kairos is represented by the kind of strategic thinking about time that we're undertaking in this chapter.

I asked an executive friend to reveal any time-management tips he used. I figured he'd drop a juicy secret or two; after all, for decades now, he's balanced a platterful of interests on top of a full career on top of family obligations. "I can offer no time management tips that a sensible person hasn't already thought of," he said, "and I never found a need for a regimen—family and profession always came first. A rough metaphor is that my interests are constantly soaking into the interstices of my life." I am floored by the simple wisdom of that expression: *allowing your interests to soak into the interstices of your life*. Years ago, I spent some time with columnist George Will while he was in town for a speaking engagement, and I noted with awe how he wasted not one minute. Without being the least bit breathless or harried, he productively used every minute of his time, especially those random interstitial moments that must accumulate to an hour or two every day. For instance, he signed books during the random minutes after lunch and before his speech began.

Fit Management

What George Will did so well, so subconsciously even, was "fit management." Allowing your life's interests to soak into the interstices of your life is a good way to begin to think about "fit." We all want to be fit. Physical fitness—we know about that. Fitness in terms of our time and energy is another matter. The idea is to set up an equivalence between a task you need or want to do and the available window of opportunity. If you have ten minutes between appointments, you have time to do something productive. Checking your phone for messages is an ideal use of small scraps of time, as is returning calls that you're pretty sure will be quick hits. The point is, what you want to do with that ten minutes is a task that requires only ten minutes.

I'm never without a magazine, a chapbook of poetry, or a blank notebook to capture musings. What you probably don't want to do with ten unaccounted-for minutes is go scuba diving or begin painting your backyard fence. These are obviously large projects; ten minutes would barely allow you time to gather the required gear.

Energy Management

According to time management advisor David Allen, most of the stress we experience doesn't come from having too much to do. It comes from *not keeping agreements we've made with ourselves*. That just scares me with its searing correctness.

It is not my intent to overwhelm you with an exhausting laundry list of "things you must do in order to become a Renaissance person." Balderdash. "You must learn to fence and master ancient Greek and take up sailing and Indian cooking. . . ." Arrgh! That has about as much appeal as a drudge job, so enervating that I want to plop on the couch like a slug at the prospect of so much sanctimonious self-improvement.

The minute you realize you can have what you want in this life, you run smack into the paralysis of freedom. The writer Laura Jacobs put it this way: "Some people are wired, it seems, to 'have it all'—they have that kind of energy, an ambition that revs them up, keeps them going. Other people, like me for instance, are overwhelmed just thinking about having it all—it means we'd have to 'do it all,' and there just aren't the hours in the day. I think one of the great challenges for women today, with all the choices available to us, is to make our choices, find our own balance, and then not be thrown off by the different choices other women make." Touché. Don't allow yourself to be thrown off by the choices other people make, and certainly don't approach your cross-training as a Sisyphean struggle. Rather, just take ten or twenty minutes each day and dedicate that time to expanding and enriching your mind. Do what you wish, in increments as tiny as you choose. Don't make it complicated. Because here's the point: it's not really about time management at all. The concept of time is so malleable that it's an almost meaningless currency. A more accurate currency is our *energy*. We all operate on an energy budget. It's a more evolved way of looking at our primary finite resource. Each of us has only so much energy throughout the course of the day, and we need to think about its rhythm and use it to our advantage. We each notice times of the day when our energy is peaking and other times when we're off-peak—the trick is to match the activity we have in mind to our level of energy. For instance, stenciling the walls in your den would require a lot less physical energy than training for a triathlon, but more than reading *Don Quixote*. Reading *Don Quixote* requires a lot more mental energy than watching reruns of *MASH* on television. And anything may require more energy than you have at eleven o'clock on a weeknight.

When you're scheduling your days, don't make commitments to tasks or projects without some thought about your expected energy level at that time of day. If you've got yourself booked to take the next step toward creating this summer's State Fair exhibit on Wednesday night at 9:30—a time when your energy is waning—you have not set yourself up for success. You need to dedicate yourself to that project at a time when your energy level is matched to the task. Perhaps 9:30 PM is an optimal time for that, if it doesn't require all that much psychic energy, or maybe you typically experience a peak of energy at that time. In terms of energy management, the first thing to do is find out where, how, and when your energy ebbs and flows. Maybe there's an hour before work when you're fresh and snappy, yet you spend that time slowly browsing through the newspaper while you drink three cups of coffee. (Stay with me here, because I know many of you are running around getting kids off to school and don't so much as glance at a newspaper or a sip a single cup of coffee.) Perhaps you occasionally (some of us, routinely) stay up late watching TV. What you need is an "energy audit": assess at which points in the day you could tighten things up and at which points you prefer to decompress. (And always leave room for fun, for daydreaming, for spontaneity. No drones permitted.)

Most people need routines—structured, preplanned blocks of time—to remain disciplined in pursuit of their goals. Others chafe at such rigidity. If you fall in the latter camp, you'll want to ask yourself at the end of each week if you were able to spontaneously engage in your Triumph in Twenty sessions, and you'll need to give yourself an honest answer. Remember, kaizen in concert with Triumph in Twenty creates brief and manageable periods of focus on something that you have identified as being of great interest to you. I recommend that you develop a new perspective on your calendar and begin to see it as a friend and ally. The calendar doesn't represent rigidity; it represents your life in miniature. The way we spend our days is the way we spend our lives.

It *is* possible to carve time out of hectic schedules filled with day jobs and family responsibilities, even if you aren't the kind of person who can live on four hours of sleep. (Time is a created thing, remember?) By the way, I would never advise anyone to cut sleep time for any reason. I have always been crazed by so-called expert advice recommending you get up an hour earlier every day to write your novel or exercise or meditate or whatever it is you're after. As far as I'm concerned, sleep time is sacred and off-limits.

What's false, debilitating, and even paralyzing is the notion that you can't do something because you "don't have the time." We look at busy people and wonder, "How do they do it all?" Well, they don't "do it all" every day. They don't get overwhelmed by their simultaneous desires to write comic essays, train sled dogs, sculpt busts, and play the mandolin. Today, they may have the opportunity (or more accurately, *make* the opportunity) to jot down the beginnings of a poem—twenty minutes or less. Then the penchant for poetry may wane for weeks or even months, as another aspect of their cross-training comes to the fore. The point is, most activity is done in jags. Additionally, busy people edit their environment well, allowing in little that is beside the point to them, and then they see to it that their odd moments are productive.

Balance Management

We spend a great deal of time and energy paying homage to the notion of balance in our lives. The Holy Grail is finding a happy medium between personal and professional concerns. Of course, this is understandable—especially for parents of young children. I'm an advocate of balance, all right: I'm all about the unfashionable "well-rounded person" with an interest in the liberal arts. That's a balanced attack if ever I heard one. But it is highly ironic that our society stresses the value of balance, given another of our cherished obsessions: specialization, which is the antithesis of balance. So we're receiving a mixed message. The balance I'm advocating for might be called metabalance: it exists beyond the customary notion of balance at the level of personal and professional demands. My notion of balance exists at the brain level, as an effective means of thwarting midlife stagnation.

More Time- and Energy-Management Thoughts, Evaluated

There's no shortage of ideas and devices claiming to help you better handle your time. Some of them are themselves time wasters. Let's evaluate a batch of common time-management nostrums against the rigors of the way real life is really lived.

E-mail. I'll grant you, e-mail can be disruptive if you have activated the alarm that alerts you to incoming messages. But overall, I'm grateful for e-mail. It's how I manage my business. It's my lifeline, my oxygen. It's saved me inestimable amounts of time previously spent on returning phone calls. I'm happy to be addicted to it and think it's one of the easier features of our lives to manage. (I say this even given the scourge of spam.) The accepted wisdom is to limit the time you spend checking and sending e-mail, designating two times a day as e-mail time. I think that's great if your job and your nature are set up that way. If you feel you have to be responsive to e-mail within minutes, then you will want to be attuned to every nuance of e-mail fluctuation. If you don't need to be quite that quick to respond, then don't be. (Frankly, unless you work as an emergency medical technician, there's probably no reason to rile up your adrenaline for every incoming message.) I evaluate my level of e-mail urgency on a daily basis. If I'm crashing on a deadline, I turn the entire program off. If I'm expecting an important message,

I leave it on, in high-alert mode. I actively manage it, in other words, rather than passively succumbing to it. Consider the tradeoffs e-mail presents. You will lose momentum but gain responsiveness by having your e-mail program open all day. You will lose reactivity but gain productivity if you close your program. You choose.

Delegation. How about buying some time—literally? Paying someone to perform certain routine chores—mowing the lawn, cleaning the house, running everyday errands—could give you the extra time you need to knuckle down to your aspirations. Keep in mind, however, that the tradeoff for delegating these so-called make-work activities is that you eliminate opportunities for your subconscious to tackle whatever's going on in the back of your mind. I'm actually a fan of errand running since it gets me out into the bustle of commerce and culture that feeds my energy and ultimately my work. Errand running activates thoughts, ideas, inspiration, and the joy of discovering new places and people.

Flextime. Requesting flextime at work is another good idea—as long as you're conscientious about using the time you've freed up. It's amazing how "found" time can slip through your fingers. People who go part-time often end up working full-time hours. Slippage happens. Beware.

Planning. I'm a big fan of time spent planning. You might think of planning as nonproductive busywork—and it can be, if you find yourself battling "paralysis by analysis." Generally speaking, though, the more time you spend in planning, the better your results will be. (Of course, there's an upper limit to this, such as if you're using planning as an excuse to not take action.) Ten to twenty minutes spent planning what tomorrow is going to look like will buy you back that time first thing in the morning when you're able to jump right in and not scramble around trying to figure out where you were when you left off. I never pause in the midst of any project without making a WILO, or "where I left off," notation. This enables me to jump right back into the project without fumbling around, shuffling papers, trying to recall what I was doing when I knocked off yesterday.

Sequencing. Think like a film director. They shoot the scenes in their movies out of order, in an effort to use time and resources most effectively. You may be able to employ this strategy in some of your activities that don't require following an exact sequence.

Superhumanness. Let go of your insistence on being everything to everyone. Psychologist Abraham Maslow noted that human beings have only a few true "needs": food, shelter, safety, love, and an opportunity for self-actualization, or self-fulfillment. In other words, you do not have to fill everyone's lunchbox every morning.

Decimating. I've read about a so-called 10 percent prescription. The theory is that shaving off 10 percent of one thing or adding 10 percent of another is the key to time management. Increase your productivity at work by 10 percent. Get 10 percent less sleep. Waste 10 percent less time. Eat 10 percent less. Think 10 percent faster. Delegate 10 percent more. I'm actually bothered by these suggestions. For one thing, how do you know when you've achieved a 10 percent reduction or increase? Maybe you're not supposed to obsess, but I'm data driven enough to wonder. I've already copped to my nutty need for 100 percent of my sleep, not 90 percent. We've already discussed that "wasted" time is in the eye of the beholder and is never wasted if you're having fun. If you go to bed forty-five minutes earlier every night, that cuts into the prime time of your evening. That's not acceptable, in my opinion. I could certainly stand to eat 10 percent less food; the 10 percenters got me on that one. But other than that, just say no to the 10 percent solution.

Just Do It

These "Three Ds" may help you manage your time:

1. **Do it fast.** Selectivity dictates that you need not labor over many routine tasks. In other words, be efficient.
2. **Delegate it.** Selectivity dictates that you examine your to-do list and delegate where and when it makes sense.

3. **Don't be a perfectionist.** Selectivity dictates that you ask yourself if the particular task you're facing truly requires 100 percent perfection. Don't waste perfectionism when it's not required. Is it imperative that you get every single leaf when you're raking your lawn? No. Is it imperative that you be a maniac about perfectionism when you're performing a root-canal? Yes.

Leisure Pleasure

"Leisure" does not always equal "pleasure." This is how go-getters get so much done: they avoid long spans of idle leisure, instinctively knowing that idle leisure is actually counterproductive to happiness, anyway. The road to richly satisfying experiences usually passes through the terrain of discomfort; everyone wants satisfaction, but not everyone is bulldog enough to persist through the struggle phase. If the themes of this book have spoken to you at all, I'm pretty sure you're not the type to ask nothing more of a vacation (or of retirement) than to loll interminably on a beach, soaking up the rays. The most fulfilled people I know don't sit still—they're tenacious in their pursuit of challenge, for they know that that way lies true pleasure.

A New Perspective on Time

We must restructure our relationship with time and our persistent perception of it as scarce. I say we blow it up and start over. I can't emphasize enough that time is a state of mind. If you think you have enough time, you will; if you don't, you won't. It's stunning how rethinking the concept of time can make a difference in terms of its grip on you. Time is elastic—it does indeed stretch and contract depending on what you're doing and how you feel about what you're doing. The various minutes in a day are not equivalent: some do indeed pass quickly, others slowly. Thus, time is an elastic, creatable thing.

There is always time for what's important. If your child is injured, you will find the time to attend to him or her. We always find the time to eat and to brush our teeth. No matter how busy we are, we regard certain routines as simply and irredeemably nonnegotiable. It just goes to show that what we *choose to do* gets done. Remember, Triumph in Twenty calls for just ten to twenty minutes a day, two or three days a week. It's not a lot. You can do it.

"Time is too slow for those who wait, too swift for those who fear, too long for those who grieve, too short for those who rejoice, but for those who love, time is eternity."

—Henry Van Dyke (1852–1933), author and educator

Find a New Gear, Called "Blessedly Stressed"

I am continuously amazed to find so many otherwise astute people looking for easy answers. There are none, unless you count savvy hard work as a "quick fix." I've designed the Vigorous Mind program to be as manageable as possible, but I'm going to level with you—it's not going to be a cinch; at times, it may even be a bitch. But anything worthwhile involves Sturm und Drang. That's how you find a new gear. University of Washington sociologist Pepper Schwartz says that people with robust multi-track lives are "blessedly stressed." If you want to cross-train your brain as a means of achieving gratification in both your professional and personal life, nothing will stop you—not time, not money, not any of the "yeah, buts" that disguise the fact that you simply don't have the want-to. Blessedly stressed is a blessing.

"We say we waste time, but that is impossible. We waste ourselves."

—Alice Bloch, academic, City University London

EXERCISES

Let's bring time- and energy-management theory to life. The following exercises are designed to catalyze you as you discover techniques that work best in your unique circumstances.

1. Sand in an Hourglass

Conduct a "time audit" of your day. First, block out a sheet of paper in ten-minute increments. For three days, set a timer to go off every ten minutes. Make note in just a word or two what you're doing at that moment. After three days, audit your chart. Where were you squandering time? The point is to become aware of your unconscious tendencies so that you can trim away time wasters and consolidate time-eating errands and routine life-maintenance tasks. Aim to create just twenty extra minutes in your day—enough time to tackle one of your cross-training activities.

2. Energy Ebb and Flow

Conduct an "energy audit" of your day. On the same sheet of paper as your time audit, make note of your energy levels throughout the same three days as the time audit. You will begin to see ebb-and-flow patterns: periods throughout the day when you're energized, and other times where you're enervated. At what time of day are you most productive? One week, schedule your Triumph in Twenty session during that time; the next week, try a medium-energy interval; and the third week, a low-energy interlude. Which works best for you, in the context of your other obligations?

3. No More Calendar Calamity

Using the twenty "new" minutes you've isolated in your day, note on your calendar for the next three months a twenty-minute block of time that you commit to use in pursuit of a cross-training activity. Harness the power of the calendar to stay on track.

7

IMPERATIVE #4:
THE EMPATHY IMPERATIVE
Share the Riches

I am somehow less interested in the weight and
convolutions of Einstein's brain than in the near certainty
that people of equal talent have lived and died
in cotton fields and sweatshops.

—Stephen Jay Gould (1941–2002), evolutionary biologist

Sandra Lerner is a Renaissance woman with an especially strong philan-thropic bent. The cofounder of Cisco Systems, she walked away with $85 mil-lion when her company went public in 1990. She was thirty-five years old. The self-described "nerd" then decided to embrace all of her interests, explor-ing her enthusiasms as an entrepreneur, farmer, animal rights advocate, medieval jouster, restaurateur, and preserver of rare books. Lerner is now involved in a variety of high-tech and philanthropic activities. For instance, she's invested money into the restoration of the Jane Austen family dwelling, Chawton House, making it a center for the study of English women's writing.

Benjamin and Rosamund Zander also have the empathy idea. In their book *The Art of Possibility*, the couple espouses a synthesis of their diverse professional worlds: the symphony orchestra and human psychology. They endeavor to create a heightened sense of the possible in everyone's life—fully in keeping with this chapter's theme.

Paul Robeson (1898–1976) is best remembered as an internationally acclaimed actor and singer—known for his performances in the title roles of *Othello* and *Porgy and Bess*—but he was also a true Renaissance man. Robeson was an accomplished scholar, with a law degree from Columbia Law School; athlete, earning letters in track, football, baseball, and basketball at Rutgers University; and political activist on behalf of oppressed people for nearly fifty years. The son of a runaway slave, Robeson was empathic to the highest degree, and his highly evolved social consciousness more than matched his prowess on the stage.

Art and science have been the twin engines propelling Jeff Rouse's life since he was a small boy in Chicago. Rouse was drawing seriously by the time he was five years old; next, he tackled ceramics and pottery. By high school, however, he abandoned art in favor of his parents' wishes that he study science instead. His science of choice, dentistry, turned out to be auspicious—his specialty became maxillofacial prosthodontics, which is the creation of artificial prostheses for patients needing facial reconstruction as a result of birth defects, accidents, or disease. "It was a specialty that would allow me to sculpt," Rouse explains, "and I knew that's where I needed to be." Soon he was taking classes at art school, casting figures in bronze, and in 1993, he produced his first monumental bronze work. Today, Rouse's sculptures are part of a number of private collections around the world; however, he continues to demonstrate personal empathy as he serves those who need him most—the recipients of his dental prostheses. "I've been blessed with an unusual combination of skills," he noted, "and with them comes the responsibility to relieve people's suffering."

Virtual reality developer Jaron Lanier is another paradigm of a share-the-riches imperative. As a technology pioneer, Lanier fears a future in which impoverished Third World volunteers are used as guinea pigs to test new techno-marvels until the gadgets are deemed safe—but he's lending his clout to forestall that possibility. Displaying true humanitarian impulses, Lanier has been critical of any "denatured effect," as he calls it, "which removes the scent of people." He worries that collectively created high-tech advances could be manipulated by people who bear no individual responsibility for misdeeds—the threat of a "misbehaved collective which oppresses individuals."

This chapter casts a spotlight on the Empathy Imperative, the fourth essential facet of a quality cross-training program. Being a fully evolved Renaissance person consists of much more than undertaking a passel of hobbies in your leisure time. Burying yourself in your own whims might easily imply selfishness or even degenerate into a narcissistic orientation. While we are indeed striving to create a multidimensional chord for your life—a harmonizing blend of several notes—one of those notes must be empathy. Anyone with a genuinely vigorous mind needs the capacity to share in another's feelings and to cultivate a social consciousness.

> "When one man, for whatever reason, has the opportunity to lead an extraordinary life, he has no right to keep it to himself."
>
> —Jacques Cousteau (1910–1997), French marine explorer

I encourage you to avoid isolationism as you pursue your cross-training goals. Author Robert Putnam noted the tendency toward social isolationism in his book *Bowling Alone: The Collapse and Revival of American Community*. Putnam shows how we have become increasingly disconnected from family, friends, neighbors, and our democratic structures. We belong to fewer organized groups, we are barely familiar with our neighbors, we meet with friends less frequently, we socialize with our families less often—we're even bowling alone. Luckily, building a more vigorous mind does not entail separation, segregation, or seclusion. Developing empathy requires the involvement of others.

The Vigorous Mind program is about more than simply "remodeling" yourself as a multifaceted, multitalented island of achievement. To redesign your life as a magnificent model of liberal arts achievement—existing only for your own sake—would be hollow and, ultimately, unsatisfying. The fully developed vigorous mind possesses caring, concern, and compassion for others—in other words, selflessness. Thus, the larger aim of cross-training is to seek self-improvement along many dimensions, so that we may go out into the world and share our hearts and minds with others—and so their lives, in turn, will be made better.

> *"The great gift of human beings is that we have the power of empathy."*
>
> —Meryl Streep, actress

I am inspired by Ralph Waldo Emerson's comment that in order to be a truly educated person, one must go forth into the world and contribute, rather than seclude oneself in books. It's self-renewal we're after—which, happily, holds the seeds of renewal for those around us as well. We attract what we give away: love, kindness, and peace, or fear, distrust, and tension. That's why if you're in need of joy in your life, the first question to ask yourself is not "How can I bring myself more joy?" but rather, "How much joy am I giving to others?"

"Those Who Can, Do. Those Who Can't . . ."

We must resist cognitive torpor, or the tendency toward intellectual slumber. We must wake up—not only for personal betterment, but for the betterment of those around us, our society, and civilization itself. Fortunately, a variegated lifestyle brings with it more than the usual number of opportunities to demonstrate empathy. Further, I believe our hearts are more sensitive to the suffering of others when we're engaged in a challenging quest of our own. So our chapter on empathy seeks to inspire your fascination with all the world has to offer, and then urges you to go forth and share what you've learned.

> *"A teacher affects eternity; he can never tell where his influence stops."*
>
> —Henry Adams (1802–1872), Baptist minister

This going-forth-and-sharing mind-set suggests a teaching orientation. It doesn't matter whether you teach in a formal setting, as part of an official school system, or you share your discoveries in a more informal manner. It's the spirit of empathy-based sharing that matters.

Renowned management guru Peter Drucker made famous the term *knowledge worker*, and he's credited with unknowingly ushering in the "knowledge economy." His observation: "You don't know anything unless you teach it." Accordingly, he taught American history, Japanese art, and religion—not at all the normal fare for his particular specialty of business management. To teach what you don't yet know helps you learn more than just a new set of facts; you practice the discipline of *learning to learn*. I'll grant you, it sounds risky, even fraudulent, to stand before a group of eager students who naturally assume you're fully versed, and perhaps even a certified expert, in the subject at hand. But misrepresenting yourself is not what we're talking about here. We *are* talking about how teaching your favorite subject to others brings added nuance to your own understanding, allowing you to plumb deeper levels, creating new depth and richness of perception. Learning, and then teaching others, is the backbone of the other-orientation known as empathy.

Teaching what you want to learn is a powerful yet oddly neglected learning strategy, perhaps because it's a little shameful to admit that although you're the teacher of the class, your grasp of the topic may be weak. Throwing embarrass-

> *"To teach is to learn twice over."*
>
> —Joseph Joubert (1754–1824),
> moralist and essayist

ment to the wind, I have occasionally structured continuing education programs for adult learners on topics that were of interest to me personally and about which I knew comparatively little. As a classic pedagogue, I knew I could do it, since teaching is second nature to me. I've created and taught classes in artistic empowerment, British-speak, the Great Books, and even—irony of ironies—the conceit of teaching. Although I have a strong interest in all these topics, I was not what anyone would have considered an expert at the outset. However, I'm a ferocious learner; I used the preparation for the class as my own private tutorial. Still, the *real* learning invariably takes place in the classroom, where I'm forced to defend theories out loud—to be cogent on my

feet—and explain concepts to adult students who aren't too cowed to ask prob-
ing follow-up questions, challenge assumptions, and pick apart discrepancies.

Teaching in this highly stimulating environment forces upon you a deeper
level of understanding than the more glancing comprehension that occurs
when one is simply reading about a given topic. A very appealing pressure is
present—to rise to the challenge; to not let down the class; and to empathize
with the role of students, putting myself in their position, intuiting what
they want to glean about the topic. Currently, I am noodling on the idea of
debuting a class called "Shakespeare for Those Who Never Really Understood His Work but Have Spent a Lifetime as a Fraud Pretending They Do."
I count myself among this group of shameless poseurs. Teaching a class on
this topic would force me to dig in deep and confront Shakespeare as I've
always meant to do. I have read (okay, *skimmed*) esteemed books such *Will
in the World: How Shakespeare Became Shakespeare* by Stephen Greenblatt;
The Shakespeare Wars by Ron Rosenbaum; and *Shakespeare: The Invention of
the Human* by Harold Bloom. But I'd delve a quantum level deeper and with
a great deal more intensity if I knew I'd be standing in front of a group of
astute adult learners tomorrow evening.

It is a paradox, to be sure, this idea of teaching that which you need to
learn—yet it's also a superb manifestation of the principle of articulation,
which states that the more you express a thought, the more you will perceive
it, understand it, believe it. Simple in theory, mighty in practice. Win
Wenger, author of *The Einstein Factor*, discovered that geniuses are little more
than ordinary people who have stumbled upon a technique for widening
their channels of attention. One of those channels of attention is articulation:
the more you express or articulate a given perception, the more you will perceive and understand it. "The sheer act of persistently expressing our
thoughts on some subject causes us to learn more about that subject, even
when no new information has been provided from without," says Wenger.
"What enhances our knowledge is not the addition of outside facts, but rather
our own perceptions *about* our perceptions, feeding back into our minds in
an ever-growing snowball effect."

The act of expressing our thoughts on a given topic causes us to learn more about that subject, and to calibrate what we already know—even when no new facts are part of the mix. What happens is a sort of perceptual Möbius strip as we begin to juggle existing information with new thoughts about it, in a nifty feedback loop that just keeps going. There's a saying in the educational field—"Read-Write-Teach"—that refers to sequential levels of comprehension. For example, reading about Shakespeare's use of metric scheme in his sonnets is the first level of understanding. To test your command of your topic, next try writing a cogent expository essay about the metric scheme of Shakespearean sonnets; you'll probably realize with a bit of alarm that your reach has exceeded your grasp. Eventually, teach the bard's rhyme scheme to a group of bright, inquisitive, critically thinking adults. Your Achilles' heel will surface to trip you up faster than you can say "iambic pentameter." Your heretofore hidden areas of weakness will pop right up when nothing parses, nothing scans. If nothing else, the three-pronged gauntlet of "Read-Write-Teach" will make you respect and esteem good writers and good teachers. The principle of articulation will enhance your performance across the board: in your career, as well as in the pursuits you choose to undertake as part of your brain nourishment endeavor.

The principle of articulation reminds me of compound interest in an odd way. Both are powerhouse ideas, and both are all too often neglected. Demonstrating empathy toward others via teaching will allow you to experience the power of the principle of articulation; you can use it to enhance performance in virtually every field of human endeavor. Link the principle of articulation with kaizen and Triumph in Twenty, and you have a particularly potent combination. Take ten or twenty minutes to articulate (verbally or in writing) your thoughts on tree trimming, fire prevention, or childhood asthma—and you will be more secure in your knowledge, your knowledge will be better organized, you will thus be more persuasive, and you will begin to understand why you think what you think. Magic.

Cross-Trained Docs

Inspired about the intrinsic worth of the arts and humanities in a world that celebrates the practical and quotidian, let's turn to a real-life example of a profession that just may be on the cusp of transformation thanks to empathy. Physicians ought to feel a particular obligation of empathy with their patients, given the patients' vulnerability under inherently stressful circumstances. Toward that end, medical schools have begun integrating courses in reading and writing into their curricula—with interesting results.

In a story called "The Writing Cure," published in the *New York Times Magazine* in 2008, Melanie Thernstrom examines how medicine lost its way and subsequently tried to restore a sense of story. Thernstrom cites the example of physician Rita Charon, who describes a visit with a new patient. The patient in question is a thirty-six-year-old Dominican man who's complaining of back pain. Charon asks about his general health. Nothing unusual there, but the way she allows the man to talk without inhibition is unlike most doctor-patient visits. She employs no checklist of symptoms to tick off on a clipboard; she does not interrupt him as he speaks. "She listened in an analytical way as if he were a character giving a soliloquy . . . not only for the content of his narrative but for its form—its temporal course, its images, its associated subplots, its silences, where he chooses to begin in telling of himself, how he sequences symptoms with other life events. After a few minutes, he stops talking and begins to weep. I ask him why he cries. He says, 'No one has ever let me do this before.'"

Charon is the leader of the burgeoning movement that seeks to situate storytelling at the center of medicine. A fifty-something internist with a Ph.D. in literature (there's a dandy combination), she's the director of the pioneering Program in Narrative Medicine at Columbia University, which teaches literature, literary theory, and creative writing to medical students. The program's practices are rapidly being incorporated and adapted by schools across the country. Charon is a superlative example of a cross-trainer with a highly developed sense of empathy that she's sharing with the world in the guise of a teacher.

Jeff Rothenberg, forty-six, is a glass-blower and sculptor. He also happens to be a professor of obstetrics and gyne-cology. He got into art when he was seek-ing a release from the rigors of medicine. Now an accomplished artist, he's become convinced that the arts are something all doctors should pursue. The arts, he believes, open up new avenues of experi-

> "A man, to be greatly good, must imagine intensely and comprehensively; he must put himself in the place of another and of many others; the pains and pleasures of his species must become his own."
>
> —Percy Bysshe Shelley (1792–1822), poet

ence and interaction and keep burnout at bay. "By paying attention to liter-ature and the arts," he says in an Indiana University newsletter, "one can develop and nurture the skills of observation, analysis, empathy, and self-reflection. These are humanistic attributes that are essential for humane medi-cal care." As a result, Rothenberg is encouraging medical schools throughout the country to incorporate the arts into their curricula.

And increasingly, the medical profession is providing alternative course offer-ings. One is known as the literary cure. Numerous medical schools have begun integrating courses in reading and writing into their curricula. Charon is not the first to relate literature to medicine; over the past three decades, many medi-cal schools have begun to offer optional literature courses, under programs known as "literature and medicine" or "medical humanities." At Columbia, all second-year medical students are required to take a seminar in narrative medicine; other students may take additional classes such as figure-drawing classes at the Met and poetry and fiction-writing workshops—practices Charon says will create more imaginative, empathetic doctors.

Intensity Versus Extensity

In the contemporary Western world, we are well trained to become insa-tiable consumers. However, we must learn to be active and creative produc-ers as well. Consuming too much of another's media or art is choosing to live someone else's life rather than living your own. I know a woman who reads all the best novels she can get her hands on. While this is a laudable activity, I don't believe she realizes that she's using it as an excuse to avoid writing a novel of her own. The world is being deprived of her one-of-a-kind creative output. Other people may pour their energy into taking workshops in painting, sculpture, acting—you name it. Of course, this kind of initiative is commendable, but if classes are a cover for avoiding the real, rewarding effort of creating a truly original work of art, then they are actually counterproductive to the intended goal. Each of us must find our own balance when it comes to this consume/produce balance.

Ask yourself if you're consuming the fruits of someone else's creative labor as a way of avoiding getting into the game yourself as an original producer. This is one risk that cross-training can engender: consuming the creativity of others and thereby squeezing out the possibility of producing something yourself—a short story, a symphony, a backyard landscape. In an interesting way, that's the antithesis of empathy, because you're not sharing your unique talents and perspective with others. The writer and educator Vida D. Scudder said that it is through creating, not possessing, that life is revealed. When you create something of your own, designed for others to consume and enjoy as a means to enrich their own lives, you are demonstrating empathy.

It's all too easy to put off our life's real work when we've convinced ourselves that we need to read just one more book on the topic or enroll in one more workshop. When I was beginning my career as a writer, I felt a compulsion to read every book and attend every class available in the Northern Hemisphere on the topic of nonfiction writing—only then would I be qualified to call myself a writer. But this procrastination technique doesn't count as knowledge gathering. Let's call it what it is: a fear-based stall tactic. I had a client once who cloaked herself in untouchable propriety—reading to the blind, volunteering at a hospice, working at the local soup kitchen—as a means of running from her own potential. Her dream was to open a day spa, but the possibility that she could actually accomplish this goal terrified her. She literally trembled with terror. She was afraid to be called forth into her fullest potential, so she wrapped herself in unimpeachable virtue by filling her days with all these unassailably humanitarian activities. It's all in the motivation, and hers was a large-scale avoidance tactic.

The point is, do not deny the world your unique contribution. Whatever your particular Renaissance weave consists of, share it with others. That develops your empathy muscle. Pay it forward. Selfishness violates the mandate of this imperative and will impede your progress as a full-tilt Renaissance person. I fear that some readers might assume that the kind of self-development I'm advocating in this book is solely about the self. The self is just the start. Share your cognitive wealth: teach, mentor, volunteer.

"Grief can take care of itself, but to get the full value of joy you must have somebody to divide it with."

—Mark Twain (1835–1910)

Habits of the Heart

Butler University president Bobby Fong wrote this in a recent letter: "I pledge that a Butler education will engender in students not only habits of mind but also, in de Tocqueville's famous phrase, 'habits of the heart' which will enable them not only to make a living but also to make lives that are personally fulfilling precisely because they are implicated in the well-being of others."

When I'm out with friends or colleagues, I try a sneaky little tactic—I attempt to move the conversation one level higher: one increment funnier, one increment smarter, one increment more incisive. I have noted consistently how eager my seminar participants are to learn, to raise their own level of discourse, to think, to be engaged by the life of the

"Until we know what motivates the hearts and minds of men we can understand nothing outside ourselves, nor will we ever reach fulfillment as that greatest miracle of all, the human being."

—Marya Mannes (1904–1990), author and critic

mind, to emerge from intellectual dormancy. They leap at the chance for a challenge, eager to return to the life of the mind they experienced in school but have long since forsaken. You know how you want to share with your friends that little gem of a restaurant you've discovered, or a fabulous flea market in the next town over? In that same way, people who are rediscovering their best selves, after having gotten a sip of that fine wine, will most likely want to share it with others. That's empathy in action. It's actually quite natural to want to share.

> "There's no delight in owning anything unshared."
>
> —Seneca (c. 4 BC–AD 65), philosopher

I encourage you, my reader, to embark on a "returning to learning," to fend off mental malnutrition and intellectual dormancy. Lifelong learning is a way to banish the blahs—a move toward rediscovering your intellectual edge. So this book is about self-development, absolutely, but it's also about encouraging the development of other people in your orbit. Don't be self-congratulatory about your cross-training; share the bounty with others. The term *cross-pollination* works well for our purposes. Not only does it apply to cross-training your brain, but it can also refer to sharing what you've learned with others. Cross-training via kaizen combats learning lassitude. We seem to have lost our edge, and that's one reason we feel unfulfilled. The solution lies partly in taking kaizen baby steps to gradually broaden our own horizons, and partly in using our newfound knowledge to reach out to others.

As important as empathy is in building a more vigorous mind, becoming an accomplished cross-trainer requires a delicate specific gravity—toeing a careful line. In other words, do not allow yourself to become subsumed in empathy. I don't want vigorous mindedness to degenerate into one of the Panglossian "seven deadly virtues": conformity, cheerfulness, piety, chastity, sobriety, propriety/political correctness, and anal retentiveness. Don't allow your pursuit of the Renaissance life to become your blind spot because, as the writer Christa Wolff observed, "The thing about your blind spot is that you can't see it."

Social Networking and Creative Generalists

Social networking sites can be a good source for locating like-minded buddies when you embark on your Vigorous Mind quest. Facebook is great for getting "friended," and MySpace, the social-networking site that boasts 90 million members, is galvanizing its user base to get involved in public service through a contest searching for the best short video public-service announcements encouraging social activism. Better still, share the wealth of your brainwork with others on Creative Generalist (http://creative generalist.blogspot.com). It's an outpost for curious divergent thinkers, those so-called dabbling dilettantes of knowledge who are curious about everything, yet experts at nothing.

Technology is helpful in bringing people together, but it has its limits. The tools of technology are used voluntarily, and by only the self-aware. So the personal, "human" factor is key in bringing people together. Travel is also a perfect fit for people looking to develop greater empathy while, at the same time, scratching that wanderlust itch—and one need not wander far. You don't have to travel the globe to get what you're after. Just move beyond your ingrained surroundings, engage with a new set of people, listen, observe, and learn—your approach to a different environment is more important than the distance you traveled to get there.

Travel is arguably as mind-expanding as learning a new language or study-ing music—two of the biggies. "It isn't necessarily just the excursion—it's the idea behind it," says Dan Fraser, cofounder of a cultural adventure com-pany. "Just like the fascinating juxtapositions of Thailand—majestic temples next to crazy nightclubs, urban chaos surrounded by peaceful countryside, traditional Eastern values mingling with modern Western commercialism. The pollination of different experiences from high adventure to an emotional giving of oneself creates a very stimulating and cerebral experience. Experi-ential adventures foster empathy and facilitate discovery."

Be Cognitively Buff

"I want our students learning art and music and science and poetry," said President Barack Obama in a crowd-pleasing line. I certainly perked up when I heard those words, recognizing a reference to bestowing our cultural riches from one generation to the next.

Art, it seems, offers up a particular power to transcend the mundane, making us all more human, more attuned to the pulse of humanity. Larry Salander is an art collector and that rarest of rare breeds: an aesthete with no formal art education—not even a college degree. Salander built his art empire on an intensity of will and an inborn talent for understanding and empathizing with the artistic temperament. "He is a very unusual combination of street vitality and aesthetic refinement," says Leon Wieseltier, the literary editor of *The New Republic* and a close friend of Salander's. Speaking to *New York* magazine, Wieseltier calls Salander "a street kid who's read Ruskin. I don't know anybody else who so naturally recognizes the brutality of the world but lives in such a fine way." I like Salander's approach: art has the power to exalt us. "Art," he says, "is the human attempt to make one plus one equal more than two." I could say the same for empathy.

> *"Some people think only intellect counts: knowing how to solve problems, knowing how to get by, knowing how to identify an advantage and seize it. But the functions of intellect are insufficient without courage, love, friendship, compassion and empathy."*
>
> —Dean Koontz, author

Let's Hear It for the Guys

A Prairie Home Companion radio-show host Garrison Keillor, writing in *The Book of Guys*, seems to be seeking some empathy for guys trying hard to become multifaceted versatilists:

> Years ago, manhood was an opportunity for achievement, and now it is a problem to be overcome. Plato, St. Francis, Michelangelo, Mozart, Leonardo da Vinci,

Vince Lombardi, Van Gogh—you don't find guys of that caliber today, and if there are any, they are not painting the ceiling of the Sistine Chapel or composing *Don Giovanni*. They are trying to be Mr. O.K. All-Rite, the man who can bake a cherry pie, go play basketball, come home, make melon balls and whip up a great soufflé, converse easily about intimate matters, participate in recreational weeping, laugh, hug, be vulnerable, be passionate in a skillful way, and the next day go off and lift them bales into that barge and tote it. A guy who women consider Acceptable. Being all-rite is a dismal way to spend your life, and guys are not equipped for it anyway. We are lovers and artists and adventurers, meant to be noble, free-ranging, and foolish, like dogs, not competing for a stamp of approval, Friend of Womanhood.

EXERCISES

Empathy is usually considered an inborn, innate human emotion. We see it in young children, who often react with great empathy to another child's distress. Still, even as adults, there are ways to apply some conscious vigor to your empathy gene. Let's try a few.

1. Empathy and the Dating Game

Mahatma Gandhi is famous for declaring, "You must be the change you wish to see in the world." This quote reminds me of an exercise I once did, an exercise with overtones of both empathy and empowerment. I was instructed to write down every characteristic and quality I sought in a husband. Then I was told to forget about snaring a husband. I was to go forth and become all those things myself. Whether you're coupled or not, ask yourself to what extent are you going forth in the world to represent your finest qualities?

2. Flexing the Empathy Muscle

Using your twenty-minute block of Triumph in Twenty time, sit down and free-write steadily for five minutes (composing continuously and without self-editing), writing from a good friend's point of view. Next, free-write again for five minutes from someone else's point of view, someone you know only slightly whose circumstances are markedly unlike your own. A good tip is to think of an actor or actress you admire and how they might "become" this person by getting into character. In your writing, be sure to consider what these individuals' worldviews might be, what their relationships are like, their sorrows, their joys; think about whether they regard the world as a friendly or hostile place. Feel how difficult it is to walk in someone else's shoes. When you're finished, your scrawlings should not sound as though you had written them.

3. Roll Up Your Sleeves

Sign up to volunteer with an organization in your community: one that interests you—or, alternatively, one you've never heard of. Ask your fellow volunteers what prompted them to become involved with that particular cause. Is it true that compassion is born of tragedy? The following websites can help you get started:

www.volunteermatch.org
www.idealist.org
www.citycares.org
www.interaction.org
www.serviceleader.org

8

IMPERATIVE #5:
THE STRETCH IMPERATIVE
Put Something on the Line

Twenty years from now you will be more disappointed by
the things you didn't do than by the ones you did do. So throw
off the bowlines. Sail away from the safe harbor. Catch the
trade winds in your sails. Explore. Dream. Discover.

—*Mark Twain (1835–1910)*

Steve Martin is stretchy. As a rubber-faced actor, he stretches himself physically, but the more meaningful stretch is his eagerness to stretch experientially. Andrew Marton, writing for the *Fort Worth Star-Telegram*, has characterized Martin as "the world's most unsung Renaissance man," and with good reason. Martin was willing to risk his initial success as a stand-up comic to delve into roles where his fan base could very likely not have followed: serious actor, novelist, playwright, musician, producer, director, essayist, and painter. It's this risk-embracing approach to these sundry endeavors that's made Martin the boldest kind of Renaissance man: he is simultaneously cerebral and zany, highbrow and lowbrow: fearless in his pursuit of his full potential. Since the '70s, his pendulum has swung in the widest of arcs as he's portrayed uptight, put-upon suburban white guys, as well as offbeat "wild and crazy" guys. A master of cognitional elasticity, he can do slapstick physical comedy; he can do edgy intellectual stuff. He made us believe in him as dim-witted, down-on-his-luck Navin in *The Jerk*, then captivated readers with the witty and urbane pieces he's written for *The New Yorker*. Martin has range, all right. "He has range" is praise often applied to actors, but Martin has distinguished himself by ranging into other fields, even while willingly putting his career success on the line.

"And the day came when the risk to remain tight in a bud was more painful than the risk it took to blossom."

—Anaïs Nin (1903–1977), author

We have now reached the fifth of our seven Vigorous Mind imperatives. The Stretch Imperative will show you how to extend your reach beyond, above, and even below where you ever thought you could possibly go. But there's more to it. Stretching, for our purposes, refers to getting in the face of your fears and anxieties and self-doubts. It's about going beyond what you habitually do, even going beyond new things that you're willing to try—going far enough that you *put something at risk*. You put something on the line. Steve Martin, for instance, put his career at risk. There are not many standup comics writing for *The New Yorker*. There are not many standup comics playing straight dramatic roles in movies. Martin was willing to stretch into these domains, and of course he's succeeded brilliantly. Stretching thus refers to getting past the very human impulse to play it safe, to be conservative, to practice self-preservation.

As you read this chapter, think about what you're willing to risk to build the kind of brain you ultimately want. Think about what you're willing to risk when there's something meaningful at stake: it may be money; it may be professional reputation; it may be ignominy; it may be fear; it may be embarrassment, loss of face, derision, ridicule. The payoff, and it's immeasurable, is not having to cope with regrets later in life. No what ifs, no woulda/shoulda/couldas. Just an immense sense of satisfaction that you went for it.

You're not going to become your fullest self by playing small. To structure a vigorous mind for yourself, you have to be truly madly deeply vigorous about it. You may want to think of stretching as curiosity writ large. Our Curiosity Imperative, you'll recall, refers to a questing outlook on life. The Stretching Imperative kicks in when you allow curiosity to put you in a little jeopardy. You know you're stretching when you've got some skin in the game: something's riding on the outcome. Now—for those of you I may be scaring, note that in our specialist-worshiping world, you are almost automatically taking a risk, simply by throwing in your lot with generalists. The world often labels generalists as scattered, hyperactive, unfocused—especially if you wish to implement your generalist impulses in the workplace (more on that in Chapter 12).

I like Eugenia Zukerman because she, like Steve Martin, stretches into realms you wouldn't expect. The *Boston Globe* has called Zukerman "an international triple threat," referring to her published novels, television commentary, and world-class stature as one of the finest flutists of our time. Think about it: a classy symphonic musician who also works in TV news—high culture juxtaposed against a much more populist medium. Clearly, she's risking her professional reputation in one of the most highbrow endeavors imaginable to consort with those in television—an enterprise Newton Minow famously termed "a vast wasteland." American classical music lovers know Zukerman as the longtime arts correspondent for CBS News's *Sunday Morning;* what they may not know is that she has also coauthored *Coping with Prednisone,* a medical self-help book she wrote with her sister, Julie Ingelfinger, who is a physician. The book grew out of Zukerman's own experiences: in 1995 she was diagnosed with a rare, incurable lung disease; her main treatment was the use of the medication prednisone, and the book tells how she suffered with the side effects of the drug and overcame some of them—all the while maintaining a busy concert and recording schedule, given the ongoing demand for her performances throughout North America and Europe. Zukerman also speaks frequently about the importance and necessity of the arts in schools and in the lives of people everywhere. To me, though, her most salient personal attribute has been her willingness to risk scorn, failure, and professional standing to take a chance on expanding her capabilities far beyond the flute and delving into television, writing, and arts advocacy.

Although he's an unlikely Renaissance man, Ben Stein may have the most diverse career of anyone now on the national scene. He has a résumé beyond belief: besides having one of the most distinctively recognizable voices on television, Stein is an actor, humorist, financial whiz, lawyer, economist, columnist, presidential speechwriter, bestselling author, and an expert on bringing meaning to both life and work—not to mention being Ferris Bueller's teacher. He's as well known in America's boardrooms as he is in its dormitories and fraternity houses. After graduating from college (valedictorian at Yale Law, no less) he worked as a lawyer, teacher, and speechwriter for Presidents Nixon and Ford. He wrote columns for the *Wall Street Journal*, eventually moving to Hollywood ("You're selling out," I'm sure his critics crowed) to become a novelist, TV sitcom writer, and movie scriptwriter, amassing an amazing seventeen books along the way. Most of these works are about Hollywood and mass culture, but some are self-help resources, and others cover finance. Stein has taught law and economics at Pepperdine Law School and has served as an expert witness in many securities law cases. In 1986, with zero professional training, he became an instant cult hero for his role as the droning, stupefying economics teacher in the movie *Ferris Bueller's Day Off*; his deadpan scene is frequently referred to as one of the funniest scenes in American film history. Stein's movie debut led to recurring roles on television and morphed into his long-running hit quiz show *Win Ben Stein's Money*. His latest book is called *How to Ruin Your Life*, although his life is anything but ruination. I'd call Stein's life primo modeling for our Stretch Imperative. With everything at stake, he risked not being welcomed back with credibility to his former roles as an academic, lawyer, and economist as he went toiling in a diametrically different vineyard: showbiz. Imagine returning to the boardroom after having played the fool in a teen comedy: most button-down types do not have the chutzpah or versatility to pull this off. Stein, though, seems to possess a rare magic, because he has by no means renounced his more staid and straitlaced life for showbiz; he seems to toggle happily between the two worlds.

Known for an ardent intellectual curiosity that led him in multiple directions, the late Michael Crichton, much like Stein, also risked being labeled a sellout to "the dark side" known as popular entertainment.

> *"Change and growth take place when a person has risked himself and dares to become involved with experimenting with his own life."*
>
> —Herbert Otto, psychologist

Imagine the scorn and incredulity he must have faced for abandoning a serious career in medicine or medical research to "go Hollywood." In addition to being a trained physician, Crichton was also a computer game designer, nonfiction author, novelist, screenwriter, director, and producer. He was best known for his TV shows, techno-thriller novels (selling more than 150 million copies worldwide), and movies. He was the creator and executive producer of the popular television drama *ER*, and many of his futuristic novels have medical or scientific underpinnings, reflecting his medical training and science background. Crichton was also the author of a book about computer programming. He said that learning to program a computer is liberation: "In my experience, you assert control over a computer—show it who's the boss—by making it do something unique. . . . If you devote a couple of hours to programming a new machine, you'll feel better about it ever afterward." Crichton was not one to be content with what surely would have been a more than adequate medical career; he forsook a conventional practice of medicine, risking ridicule and a stable financial outlook for the risk-filled vagaries of an artistic life. His gamble paid off big, of course.

The twinning of Crichton's talents—a scientifically trained mind paired with powerful creative leanings—is both unique and vital. "The ongoing fragmentation of knowledge and resulting chaos in philosophy are not reflections of the real world but artifacts of scholarship," writes Edward Wilson in his book *Consilience*. Wilson maintains that the greatest enterprise of the mind has always been and always will be the attempted linkage of the sciences and humanities. This is much more than a parlor game for elite aesthetes.

Learning all we can about the world around us is practical to our very wel-
fare. It's estimated that half the legislation coming before the U.S. Congress
contains important scientific and technological components. As Wilson has
observed:

> Most of the issues that vex humanity daily—ethnic conflict, arms escalation,
> overpopulation, abortion, environment, endemic poverty, to cite several most
> persistently before us—cannot be solved without integrating knowledge from the
> natural sciences with that of the social sciences and humanities. . . . [T]he vast
> majority of our political leaders are trained exclusively in the social sciences and
> humanities, and have little or no knowledge of the natural sciences. The same is
> true of the public intellectuals, the columnists, the media interrogators, and
> think-tank gurus. The best of their analyses are careful and responsible, and some-
> times correct, but the substantive base of their wisdom is fragmented and lop-
> sided. A balanced perspective cannot be acquired by studying disciplines in pieces
> but through pursuit of the consilience among them. Intellectually it rings true,
> and it gratifies impulses that rise from the admirable side of human nature. To the
> extent that the gaps between the great branches of learning can be narrowed,
> diversity and depth of knowledge will increase. Consilience gives purpose to intel-
> lect. It promises that order, not chaos, lies beyond the horizon.

A Literal Cross-Train for Your Brain

Just as our bodies need physical activity to stay strong and nimble, so do
our brains need exercise to stay in shape. Otherwise we risk a bad case of
brain malaise. We all know that arteriosclerosis refers to a hardening or narrowing of the arteries. Similarly, psychosclerosis is a hardening or narrowing
of the attitude. Psychosclerosis is the inability to perceive possibilities even
when they're all around you—a shutting off of the mind, spirit, and heart.
Symptoms? A dwindling of the desire to dream, visualize, perceive. Psychosclerosis is not inevitable—that's where kaizen comes into play. And,
wouldn't you know it, a workout routine for your brain should parallel the

program you might follow for physical conditioning, including cardiovascular work, strength training, and stretching:

- Brain cardio. Try some rote memorization to keep your brain active and agile—rehearse and then recall song lyrics, mathematical formulas, vocabulary.

- Brain strength training. Strengthen your mind by tackling material that's difficult to comprehend—astrophysics, cryptology, or any topic that will challenge your understanding.

- Brain stretching. Reach beyond your comfort zone and try something completely new—learn a foreign language or test your skill at logic-based puzzles or brain teasers.

If you're just now embarking on your cross-training program, these kinds of mental exercises could mean calling upon the side of your brain that you're less accustomed to using. The right-brain versus left-brain dichotomy is well-documented. Professor Roger Sperry was honored with the 1981 Nobel Prize for his breakthrough research, which found that there appear to be two modes of thinking, verbal and nonverbal, represented more or less separately in the left and right hemispheres of the brain. Ordinarily, the left hemisphere of the cerebral cortex processes logical, analytical thinking, while the right hemisphere processes imaginative, big-picture thinking. Some researchers are moving beyond a rigid left-brain, right-brain segmentation, claiming that it's too simplistic. Whatever the case, modern society typically tends to discriminate against the area in our brains that harbors our creative mojo. Our culture ordinarily rewards and remunerates linear thinking over artistic thinking. Unfortunately, rationality, business sense, and structured thought are given more credibility than fluid, desultory, or expressive thought. That built-in bias makes it all the more important to exercise your creative side, since it's likely to have been neglected. Note that I said to *exercise* your creative side—don't default to it entirely. I have known many free-spirited artists who sabotaged themselves by giving the back of their hand to the business end of their enterprise, with its emphasis on cash flow, debits, credits, invoices, and accounts receivable. The result was predictable: soon, those artists were out of business. But it's a myth that artists can't be financially successful. It's particularly gratifying to observe truly creative, talented artists who have taken the time to tend to the business end of their enterprises. Still, few parents stand up and cheer when their children announce an intention to move to Soho to become an abstract artist or play guitar in a rock band or write blank verse. Parents think: starving artist, no job security, a life on the tenuous margins of respectable society. (One author—quite a successful one, in fact—admits, "I'm still trying to find a way to tell my parents I'm a writer.") On the other hand, announce one's intentions to become a doctor, accountant, or teacher, and chances are parents will exhale with relief, thinking: financial comfort, job security, a respectable life among decent members of society.

"Life is either a daring adventure or it is nothing."

—Helen Keller (1880–1968)

You Gotta Be in It to Win It

Let's talk about fear. If you're feeling paralyzed by fear, self-doubt, anxiety, pessimism, or any other sabotage that runs counter to a stretching mentality, create a "Life List." For every year from now through the rest of your life, list a handful of topics you intend to explore that year. Don't forget to include the things you're now doing that you plan to continue. Some of the activities you'll list will persist indefinitely; others you'll be content to let go once you've satisfied your curiosity. In any case, a Life List allows you to take in all your plans at one swoop and thus confront your anxieties all at once. If you're like most people, your list will be long. You'll appraise it and be struck by overwhelm. Experience the overwhelm, and then expel it. How? Kaizen. Break that Life List down into manageable chunks (say, five topic areas a year, as mentioned in Chapter 6) and suddenly it's not quite so scary.

However many topics you generate, spread them more or less evenly through-out the future years. Look for natural synergies, such as landscape photogra-phy and digital photography.

In another modest example of staring down intimidation, I recently decided I needed to learn more about science. So I bought a subscription to a science magazine. Sure, some of it (okay, a lot of it) is over my head, but I intend to persist until I've developed a groove for it—a comfort that I can read a science magazine and not feel like a gate-crasher. You have to be willing to stretch past feelings of insecurity, tres-passing, and being an imposter to get what you want, to intrude into certain territories without any authority, license, or credential.

"Far better to dare mighty things, to win glorious triumphs, even though checkered by failure, than to take rank with those poor spirits who neither enjoy much nor suffer much, because they live in the gray twilight that knows not victory nor defeat."

—Theodore Roosevelt (1858–1919)

Cultivate an Undisciplined Curiosity

Howard Gardner is an eminent psychologist and originator of the theory of multiple intelligences. His claim is that IQ tests simply don't reflect the way human intelligence really works; instead, each of us possesses strengths and weaknesses across multiple intelligence dimensions. Gardner posited seven dimensions of intelligence: visual/spatial, musical, verbal/linguistic, logical/mathematical, interpersonal, intrapersonal, and bodily/kinesthetic. That groundbreaking contribution to psychology would have stood alone as the culmination of a lifetime's work. But Gardner wanted to go beyond rest-ing on his laurels. Since he first identified his multiple-intelligence theory, he has gone on to identify additional dimensions of intelligence, including facets he calls naturalist and existentialist. I have to admire Gardner for insisting on stretching his ideas to innovative extremes, even as he was cautioned against jeopardizing his reputation by investigating uncharted areas. He took a substantial risk with his professional prominence—put it on the line, in fact. Those wagers don't always pay off—let's not be naive—but his did. He slayed the impulse to play it conservative.

"Only those who risk going too far can possibly find out how far one can go."

—T. S. Eliot (1888–1965)

I like to think Gardner paved the way for his thought process by keeping himself intellectually limber and thus open to new ideas and new connections between existing ideas. At Harvard, which he referred to as an "elysian field for the mind," he took more courses than anyone he knew, from Chinese painting to the history of economic thought. Concerning his own learning style, his explication appears in a paper called *One Way of Making a Social Scientist*:

I always had a wide and relatively undisciplined curiosity. As a child I liked to read books, newspapers, magazines, even encyclopedias. I particularly cherished biographies. Today, I read far more than is advisable. This kind of searchlight curiosity is probably more appropriate for social science than the laser-like focus needed by molecular biologists and particle physicists. It also may explain why I have not hesitated to investigate new areas *even when cautioned not to do so*. I am eager to learn about things that have not yet been described and analyzed and to share my tentative syntheses with others. I see myself primarily as a describer and synthesizer. I have always been an independent person, unwilling to accept orthodoxy. My choices reflect my idiosyncratic configuration of intellectual strengths and weaknesses.

In his own words, Gardner is an independent and iconoclastic personality. I salute his choices and, especially, his intrepid willingness to stretch.

More, More, More

We only *think* we want a simpler life. We've been told we should crave simplicity. But what we really want is more. Bonnie Fuller is the former editor of magazines including *Glamour, Marie Claire, US Weekly,* and *Cosmopolitan.*

Her autobiography, entitled *The Joys of Much Too Much*, extols the virtues of complexity—even turmoil—over simplicity and tranquility. Fuller negotiates both a hectic career as a media executive and a busy home life as the mother of four children. She's been characterized as a boss from hell, a perfectionist multitasker, even a tyrant and the Cruella de Vil of the magazine industry. Fuller has said she was "an unremarkable teenager" with bad clothes and worse hair—the "geeky girl in the front row with her hand up." The other girls teased her about her eager demeanor and lack of fashion sense. These days, Fuller says, she enjoys her multitasking, hard-driving, always-crunched-for-time life and sees nothing wrong with taking a business call with one hand while she pushes her son on a swing with the other. And she believes a lot of women feel the same way.

"Fortune favors the audacious."

—Desiderius Erasmus
(c. 1466–1536), theologian

Consider how Fuller has stretched to get what she wanted. She risked affiliation with the tabloid called *Star* (known for a history of skewering celebrities) before relaunching it as a glossy magazine. Tabloids, as we all know, are the whipping boys of journalism. Now debuting an online venture—a rather risky enterprise given her relative lack of experience in that forum—Fuller is embracing the stretch. "I like the idea of blue sky," she said. "It will be fun to make something brand new."

Although I don't necessarily admire her style or agree with all her choices, something Fuller said in *The Joys of Much Too Much* speaks strongly to me: "A jam-packed, maxed-out, full-to-the-very-top existence is the secret to an insanely happy life, no matter what these odes to simplicity say." I do admire her reach, her stretch, her desire to live wide, her choice to just say no to no.

A poignant Japanese concept called *shibui*, meaning simplicity devoid of unnecessary elements, is relevant to this

"And if you take a risk and fail? Well, there is nothing like calamity for refreshing the moment."

—Anonymous

discussion. It's thoroughly applicable to art, especially, but it's precisely what we're *not* after here. One of our current cultural trends calls for celebrating simplicity, and I certainly encourage that at the level of household clutter. But vigorously minded generalists prefer a life overflowing with unnecessary elements—because, in a weird way, the unnecessary is necessary.

Ten Pounds of Life in a Five-Pound Sack

You don't necessarily need to risk your career to cultivate a cross-trained brain, but like the individuals profiled in this chapter, you do need to stretch until it hurts at least a little. Start small: the bounty of the ages is waiting patiently for you to discover it—all you have to do is pick up a library card or make the most of your Internet connection. But you've got to risk something—a little money; a bout of *longueurs* now and then; twenty minutes of your time three days a week—if you can fairly expect to grow from your cross-training. Risk a little, gain a lot. That's as close to a free lunch as you'll ever get. And the process will be immensely satisfying.

The April 2008 issue of the *American Journal of Psychiatry* cites research showing that, in addition to a happy marriage and a sense of purpose, one of the most important factors in a happy retirement is learning how to play again. "Play" is defined as engaging in activities that are highly gratifying, lack any economic significance, cause no social harm, and do not necessarily lead to praise or recognition from others. The researchers were most surprised by the finding that happiness in retirement depended neither on being free from physical disability nor on having a large income. Instead, the answers to two questions were most important: "What are your most enjoyable activities?" and "What gives your life a sense of purpose?" Developing a highly flexible and vigorous brain qualifies on both counts. This sort of joy represents the ultimate benefit of stretching in the direction of a cross-trained brain.

Intellectual Ecology

In his article published in MIT's May 2005 *Technology Review* titled "Whither the Renaissance Man?" Michael Hawley encourages us to stretch ourselves in proportion to the scope of information available to us. Hawley advocates bringing together ideas and cultures in fresh ways and with unprecedented intensity. "From Ethernet to Internet to World Wide Web to Google, from silicon biology to nanoscience, worlds of ideas have collided," he writes. "Just as a 16th-century Renaissance man felt empowered by a bundle of books in his saddlebag, a 21st-century Renaissance woman with a laptop feels she has the entire store of human knowledge at her fingertips." But a sad irony persists: while we're experiencing a massive widening of knowledge, our educational system is churning out ever more narrowly focused graduates. Hawley laments that college has become less an exploration and more of a forced march—even the run-up to higher education has become a gauntlet of preparatory crash courses, aptitude tests, campus visits, and interviews. But will the enriched, expansive pool of online knowledge promote more specialization, or will it promote more sharing among fields? That's the big question, and that's also the big risk: that our fast-growing base of knowledge will foment even more specialization rather than breeding versatilists who can maneuver with ease within this knowledge base and make sense of it by putting it in a broader perspective and perceiving linkages. "Such an intense global mix of cultures, ideas, and innovations, all apparently a mouse click away, would seem to demand broad educational perspectives," writes Hawley. "Yet most schools persist in turning out laser-focused young professionals. To make a dent in a particular field, a person has to devote a good chunk of his or her lifetime just to getting to the starting line. This doesn't favor the jack-of-all-trades." So you're putting something quite meaningful on the line when you commit to being a Renaissance person: you're competing in the world of work with specialists who are held in higher favor.

> "If you don't risk anything, you risk even more."
>
> —Erica Jong, author

Renaissance man Ben Franklin knew how important it was to stretch his mind—and he even knew how to do it. When he was just twenty-one years old, Franklin created the Junto, a collective of artisans and tradesmen who hoped to improve themselves while improving their community. A noted polymath, Franklin was a leading author, printer, satirist, political theorist, politician, scientist, inventor, civic activist, statesman, diplomat, and as an early proponent of colonial unity, he was one of the founding fathers of the United States. As a scientist, he was a major figure in the Enlightenment and in the history of physics for his discoveries and theories regarding electricity. He invented the lightning rod, bifocals, the Franklin stove, a carriage odometer, and a musical instrument. He formed both the first public lending library in America and first fire department in Pennsylvania. Franklin compiled a list of thirteen moral values (waste nothing; practice moderation; aspire to justice, cleanliness, and tranquility; among others) and kept a scorecard to grade himself on how well he realized these goals. He simply wanted to be a better person and to lead a better life, and seemed to intuitively know that part of that meant elasticizing his brain. Although Franklin clearly stretched his intellectual boundaries to their limits, I ask myself what he risked by being such an accomplished polymath; what was at stake for him? I can think of nothing, frankly, which makes my point that so much has changed about our perception of what constitutes a contributing member of society. Being a polymath two hundred years ago was commendable and praiseworthy; today you're considered an outlier, a contrarian, a superficialist—even a crackpot.

"Nobody said getting your face on money was easy," writes Hawley in his Renaissance man article. "In today's complex world, perhaps it's simply not possible for someone to lead a creative life that contributes so seminally and so powerfully across so many areas. Yet we need to be concerned with our intellectual ecology. Will the enriched pool of online knowledge promote more specialization, or will it promote more sharing among fields? The answer is up for grabs." Our best bet is to immerse ourselves left, right, and center in more and different areas of growth—to stretch. Ben Franklin himself said it best: "When you're finished changing, you're finished."

Long Live Gluttony

Obsession is usually associated with one endeavor, whether it's bird-watching, orchid collecting, violin making—whatever. World-class cross-trainers, on the other hand, are obsessed with practically *everything*. This is both our curse and our blessing. Nonetheless, we're intent on stretching ourselves until we feel the pinch. In his book *The World Is Flat*, columnist Thomas Friedman of the *New York Times* calls for maximum flexibility and freethinking. Simply put, being flexible makes you better at what you do. That should be encouragement to break free from the rut of your attenuated specialty and seek input from anywhere and everywhere else. Friedman refers to "free thinkers" as those who are willing to reject their beliefs in the face of new evidence. Specialists, I must believe, could use a dose of freethinking, to augment their boxed-in existence.

> *"If you're never scared or embarrassed or hurt, it means you never take any chances."*
>
> —Julia Sorel, author

Debrah Farentino is a Hollywood actress who's starred in several TV series, including *NYPD Blue, JAG,* and *CSI: Miami.* As she recalls in *Medianews*, "I had lunch with my agent and told him, 'I'm going to go be a scientist.' He's like, 'Yeah, right.'" Well, she did indeed return to school, eventually earning a degree in molecular biology. Kudos to Debrah! It is a surprising, ambitious, counterintuitive, mind-expanding accomplishment. She risked her career momentum in the name of personal growth and satisfaction. Actors, in my experience, are cross-trainers by instinct. Actor Raymond Michael Fox says, "Education is important [in the theater]. As much as you can learn about anything—about science, literature, sports, as well-rounded as you can be as a person—that's going to help you as an actor. As richly as you live your life, that's the best thing you can bring to the stage."

Be a "Polymathlete"

Reinvention is what baby boomers do better than anyone, and now they're redefining retirement just as they've redefined every other aspect of life. Rebelling against any shard of their lives that's unlived, boomers are scratching creative itches, signing up to learn about drawing, dance, piano, poetry, acting, and other arts—and not just for idle amusement. According to Ronald Manheimer, executive director of the North Carolina Center for Creative Retirement, this kind of mastery-level learning enriches older students' quality of life, attitude, and health. After careers spent in the business world, these lifelong learners must be thrilled with the joy of discovery as they explore their creativity during their retirement, perhaps for the first time in their lives.

> "I'm very brave generally, only today I happen to have a headache."
>
> —Tweedledum in Lewis Carroll's
> *Through the Looking-Glass*

Shakespeare's Hamlet is literature's most prominent avatar of inaction. He fusses and frets and fumes, but he never really *does* anything. Life is not a dress rehearsal. Many of us have assumed there would always be time for mulligans and do overs. But now, right now, is the time to learn to speak Italian, blow glass, or join a choir. No one should have to wait until retirement to engage with his or her fullest self. *Now* is the time to enhance the quality of your life by stretching yourself further than you thought possible. If all you do is stew about taking up your paints and easel "one of these days," you've just added one more item on your mental to-do list, which plays out as one more stressor in your life. Thinking about taking action without *taking* action creates stress. Poet, playwright, and philosopher Rabindranath Tagore (1861–1941) phrased it thusly: "I have spent my days stringing and unstringing my instrument while the song I came to sing remains unsung."

Shore Huggers Versus Pouncers

If you wait for the perfect moment to do something, you'll never do anything. If you're going to build a more vigorous mind, you must adopt a go-for-it attitude. All glory comes from daring to begin. Simply begin. There is magic in action. Do not wait for all circumstances to be ideal before you launch your program. Good things come to those who act. Actress Demi Moore summed it up crisply: "I have a career, a marriage, and children, and I am an independent woman. I don't have any magic. I have these things because I worked to create them." I would add that she was willing to stretch herself to get everything she wanted into her life. A willingness to stretch *creates* stretch.

People who are in the habit of stretching their mental hamstrings don't allow themselves to get bogged down in convoluted preparations. There's an element of "jump and the net will appear." These people have a sense for how much planning is too much, how much analysis is too much. It nets out to "the power of the pounce." To borrow an expression from business consultant and author Stephen Covey, "don't oversharpen your saw." I'll admit that I was once a chronic oversharpener. I'd buy all the equipment—pencils, notebooks, computers; I'd do oodles of research—read books, take classes, scour the Web; I'd prepare my environment—fresh paint, rearranged furniture, organized files; I'd network with colleagues—lunches, coffees, e-mails. I had the sharpest saw within a hundred-mile radius, but wasn't using it to cut anything.

A good friend once needled me, saying that I was just sitting back and waiting for Hollywood to come to me. He was right, and he actually changed my life by that one stinging barb. So when it comes to flexing yourself into a fuller, more vigorous life, stop putting your plans on hold until you lose weight, get your money straight, or finish raising your children. Whenever you feel a stirring to start stirring, that's the moment to take action.

The Power of the Next Action Step

If we're going to create elastic lives that stretch to accommodate big goals, we have to place special emphasis on kaizen. As we've seen, the act of thinking can be a legitimate act of kaizen. But don't handicap your kaizen with excessive thought. Too much thinking could be hazardous to your cross-training choices, and to your happiness. Bright people often resist kaizen the most and procrastinate when it comes to taking that next action step. Their intellectual acuity gives them the capability to conjure lurid scenarios about all the negative consequences that might occur if something isn't done perfectly. (Nonprocrastinators, it is said, aren't quite creative enough to be aware of all the things that could go wrong.) The solution to avoiding kaizen is, of course, kaizen. Right now, decide on the single very next action required to move forward toward a goal. Notice what happens to your energy—you will invariably feel the pressure lighten.

Kaizen works because stretching to reach that next step requires necessary risk, mental clarity, personal accountability, and enhanced productivity, which, ultimately, lead to self-empowerment and greater life satisfaction. Kaizen is really nothing more than radical common sense. When you think about it, not implementing kaizen requires as much energy as implementing it. For instance, shelving the next book on your reading list takes as much psychic energy as reading the book. Putting off practicing that cello sonata you promised yourself to learn weighs on you more heavily than sitting down for twenty minutes to learn a few measures.

A recent study reveals that when people make decisions based on instinct, they end up happier than those who make decisions based on careful analysis. Choose to trust yourself, and to trust your ability to choose. Staying in action is the key. Our ability to thrive will atrophy unless we stretch ourselves beyond our accustomed rounds. We'll stiffen and grow brittle emotionally, professionally, and spiritually. The world needs more doers and fewer sideliners. In his book *True Success*, Tom Morris says, "We need more actors, more participants, more catalysts, performers, agents of change, movers and shakers, doers, givers, contributors, and initiators."

It's the Chutzpah!

If you're fearful of stretching yourself into areas that are unfamiliar and therefore stressful, you should know that fear can be your ally. A Japanese therapy called Morita propounds that we should all be scared to death—and then go forward and do what we have to do nonetheless. In America we support a giant drug industry designed to try to make people feel good all the time. But the truth is that being happy and anxiety-free all the time isn't useful or adaptive, especially not when you've embarked on a scheme to ratchet up your life with

"I believe that anyone can conquer fear by doing the things he fears to do."

—Eleanor Roosevelt (1884–1962)

cross-training. Anxiety reflects our desires. If you're anxious about starting guitar lessons or renovating your bathroom or hiking the Appalachian Trail or building a gazebo—great. Be anxious, be tense, be fearful, and then march straight ahead and plunge in. That continual cycle of fear/action, fear/action, fear/action is how accomplished people live and thrive.

As a college student at North Texas State University, Bill Moyers had the chutzpah to write Lyndon Johnson a letter offering him aid in an election campaign. The young Moyers wanted to help get out the vote in Texas. That act of initiative propelled him into public life. In

"Getting started, keeping going, getting started again—in art and in life, it seems to me this is the essential rhythm."

—Seamus Heaney, poet

a surprisingly short time Moyers was press secretary for the president of the United States, and then a network news commentator, and then perhaps the biggest force ever to hit public broadcasting in this country. For years, Bill Moyers has been in a position to accomplish immense good. And it all began with a letter from out of the blue. It all started with initiative. Action. Stretching. The benefits of stretching can be enormous in every aspect of your life.

*"Of all sad words of tongue
or pen, the saddest are these:
it might have been."*

—John Greenleaf Whittier
(1807–1892), poet

Playwright Suzan-Lori Parks says that the most important life lesson she's learned is this: instead of waiting for the perfect opportunity, she'd work toward a realization that every opportunity is perfect, each moment holds the seeds for growth. Difficulty creates the opportunity for self-reflection and compassion. "I learned that if we embrace what's happening, we are also embracing what is possible—and a road opens up for God to meet us halfway."

Gret and Regret

If you don't begin to stretch into your potential self today, you'll wind up at the end of your life disappointed. Very disappointed. By committing to the Stretch Imperative, you will be practicing regret minimization. Dorothy Gaiter and John Brecher, wine columnists for the *Wall Street Journal*, have popularized "Open That Bottle Night." No wine is too precious for today. What are you waiting for? The perfect opportunity? Today is perfect. You don't know that you've got tomorrow. There are no guarantees. So I would similarly propose a Wear That Jewelry Day, Wear That Dress Day, Wear That Fancy French Perfume Day, Use the Good Dishes Day, and—above all—Act on Your Vigorous Mind Impulse Day.

I frequently ask audiences to imagine themselves at the end of their lives and then tick off three things they're disappointed they didn't tackle. Woodworking, Emily Dickinson, child psychology, or whatever first comes to mind—these are quite likely the projects they need to address immediately. Then, I ask the audience to again imagine they're at the end of their lives, but this time, I instruct them to tick off three things they're glad they did during the course of their lives, which generates a much different answer-set as well as a sense of gratification. The point of the exercise is to end regret. I don't want anyone to become a victim of *saudade*—a Portuguese word meaning nostalgia for something that never was.

Speak with your grandparents, older neighbors, friends' parents. Pull up a chair and ask them to level with you. Look them in the eye and ask them what they most regret about their lives. I bet they'll talk about the chances they did not take, the lover they did not pursue, the new job that would have meant too much risk, the stretch that seemed too intimidating. Next, scan the biographies of men and women whose lives you admire. Why did these individuals earn your respect? I can with sure-fire assurance tell you that those people earned your respect because they lived their lives full-out, knowing it was the only one they had.

"It is not so much what we have done amiss, as what we have left undone, that will trouble us, looking back."

—Ellen Wood (1814–1887),
English playwright and journalist

Bulk Up

"Time is the only real wealth we're given," writes Barbara Sher in her book *I Could Do Anything If Only I Knew What It Was*. "But it's half-gone before we understand that. When it comes to time, children are unknowing millionaires. Old people know a lot about time and will tell you freely that their greatest regrets were the things they didn't do. You don't have to be very old to know what they're talking about. Look back at your adolescence and ask yourself, what do you regret most? Do you regret the things you did, or the ones you didn't have the courage to do? Do you regret the dances you went to, even when you were awkward and uncertain and felt like a fool? Or do you regret the ones you avoided so you wouldn't feel like a fool?"

"When I am an old woman I shall wear purple / With a red hat which doesn't go, and doesn't suit me." Sue Ellen Cooper, upon turning fifty-four, found, for the first time in her life, she didn't need to please people or live up to their expectations. Word of her resulting sartorial boldness spread, and Cooper's emblematic red hat grew into the Red Hat Society. Although I agree with the spirit of the Red Hat Society, I'm afraid I find the me-too wearing of purple clothing a rather modest expression of radicalism, given that it's yet another version of the conformity they're supposed to be rebelling against. Still, if it represents a stretch for the Red Hatters, that's all that matters.

Forget "Simplify"—Complexify!

Jean Houston is a prominent leader in the study of spirituality and ritual processes who has famously worked with both Margaret Mead and Hillary Clinton. She writes, "People tell me that I am uniquely blessed with opportunities. And yet, when I examine others' lives, I find that too often they are walking blind and deaf through a garden of possibilities—some of which are whistling, 'yoo hoo, over here! Hey, dummy, listen! There's a new road for you to take, a fresh role for you to master. C'mon, pay attention!' And through it all, they sleepwalk, mumbling, 'nothing ever happens. Nothing ever happens.' Only when the opportunity for a larger life throws itself directly across their paths do they stumble into possibility. I have lived mythically because I have caught the fleeting glimpse of opportunity from the corner of my eye, said yes to risk, and sought out adventure."

Forgive cliché, but the fruit truly is way out on the ends of those doggone branches. And the biggest, juiciest fruit—the optimal modus operandi—combines generalist wishes with specialist realities. The humanities with the sciences. The right brain with the left brain. Breadth with depth. It's not a zero-sum game: we can be both generalists and specialists if we make the choice. Sure, it's a stretch—a mighty one. But we must become the architects of our own evolution revolution. Be an explorer; nurture an immense intellectual curiosity; develop intense and diverse interests. Elasticize your outlook; make it pinch. You'll find that once you've crossed the Rubicon into a full-fledged life of the mind, there will be no turning back.

I'll concede that this chapter puts you under the gun a little bit. It's when we're put under pressure, however, that our true character is revealed to us. Pressure reveals the cracks in our facade. This is a good thing, because then we know where to begin our repair. In fact, the best journeys of all pit the protagonist against his or her greatest fear or rawest inner conflict. If the attempt to become a generalist in our day and age stirs up some resistance within you, I submit that's because you've got something at stake: career momentum, time pressure, fears of all kinds, professional credibility, whatever. And when something's at stake, obstacles exist. Your intention is being threatened. That's a very, very good thing. As we said earlier, that continual cycle of fear/action, fear/action, fear/action is how accomplished people live and thrive. It means you're stretching toward your fullest expression of self.

> *"Risk! Risk anything!*
> *Care no more for the opinions*
> *of others, for those voices. Do the*
> *hardest thing on earth for you.*
> *Act for yourself. Face the truth."*
>
> —Katherine Mansfield
> (1888–1923), author

EXERCISES

If you're hesitant to get started on the Stretch Imperative, ease into it with the following warm-up stretches.

1. The Wide-Open Spaces

Now it's time to take an inventory of the activities you're pursuing and where there's room to "cowboy it up." Revisit your Bliss List from Chapter 2. For each activity you're already engaged in, identify the next level within that activity. In other words, how could you stretch yourself beyond what you think you're capable of? If you're into cooking, consider entering a cook-off or submitting an entry to your state fair. Kick it up a notch! Put your pride on the line. If you're interested in computers, consider this: Chris thought she was satisfied with her computer knowledge, which consisted of mastery of rudimentary e-mail and word processing programs. At the urging of her kids, however, she signed up for a class in Excel and PowerPoint and has realized that the world of technology is useful, not necessarily daunting, and represents a life-affirming stretch for her. Where have you stretched so far in your quest for a vigorous mind?

2. Get Down off Your Toes

Identify five activities on your Bliss List that you've been tiptoeing around—thrilling things you haven't attempted for no good reason other than you've been intimidated by groundless fear, or you're simply underestimating your abilities. Maybe your list includes parasailing, horseback riding, or mountain climbing. But don't limit yourself to the physical. For some of us, starting psychotherapy, returning to school, or initiating an intimate relationship could represent the kind of daunting stretch that is vital to maximizing a cross-training adventure.

3. Don't Be Listless

Get serious about building a Life List that ranges from the easily doable to the frankly frightening. Then parcel it out over the next few years, as described earlier in this chapter.

4. Curl Up with a Good Book

Read Joe Kita's book *Another Shot: How I Relived My Life in Less Than a Year*. It's about going back and redoing his past to correct for the things he regretted not doing. Then read Po Bronson's book *What Should I Do with My Life?* which represents a modern, secular take on the classic question about personal identity. Asking yourself what you should be doing with your life aspires to end the conflict between who you are and what you do. Answering the question is the way to protect yourself from being lathed into someone you're not. That word—*lathed*—just slays me. A lathe is a machine that holds a chunk of wood motionless while another tool grinds it down into a predetermined shape. Could anyone possibly miss the power of that metaphor for our lives?

9

IMPERATIVE #6:
THE SPIRITUALITY IMPERATIVE
Peak Experiences and Constructing a Worldview

What people really want is far more beautiful, spiritual,
and holy than being indulgent, decadent, or preoccupied with
pleasure. It is discovering something buried deeply within
a person's heart that bears the handprint of God. It's hard to find
in a world that routinely ignores the multitude of capacities
that live within the core of every person.
Discovering those capacities may be the toughest and
scariest journey you have ever taken.

—Rod Smith, *author*

Thomas J. McFarlane has been immersed in the study and practice of
the spiritual traditions of the world for over fifteen years, and is employed
concurrently as, of all things, a registered patent agent. From a young age, he
possessed a constant curiosity about the world and a strong interest in science,
mathematics, and computers, eventually earning a degree in physics from
Stanford University, as well as advanced degrees in mathematics, philosophy,

and religion. But what fascinates me most about McFarlane is that his interest in meditation and mysticism was sufficiently profound that, after graduating from Stanford, he abandoned his plans for a career in physics and shifted his primary focus to spiritual inquiry. He devoted three years to intensive spiritual reading, reflection, and contemplation. While working days as a rather prosaic patent agent, McFarlane continued his spiritual practices and study of spiritual philosophy, simultaneously writing articles and giving talks on physics, mathematics, and philosophy. McFarlane has now earned a master's degree in philosophy and religion, all while maintaining his vocation as a patent agent. Clearly, he's been able to perceive the spiritual in unexpected places (the sciences) even while finding meaning and value in an "ordinary" government job. McFarlane thus demonstrates involvement with the rather otherworldly Spirituality Imperative in a real-world context.

We have now arrived at our penultimate sixth of seven imperatives, the intersection of spirituality and cross-training. Creating a vigorous and cross-trained life of the mind needs to be exemplified by more than a steady accretion of knowledge. The higher aim is to weave your own colorful and intricate tapestry, to share its beauty and meaning with others (as we saw in Chapter 7), and by doing so, to find meaning, belief, and satisfaction in life. It is this deeper meaning that can develop into an approach we might fairly call spiritual.

It's frequently remarked that life should be more about Being than Doing. That, to me, suggests the cultivation of a sense of well-being . . . a capacity to hold your center in the midst of the world's chaos and suffering. Yet I can imagine how howlingly contradictory "Being not Doing" must sound to you: I've been advocating Doing-Doing-Doing for eight chapters, and now suddenly I claim that cross-training is more about Being than Doing. It is indeed a contradiction (we'll talk about this kind of paradox in Chapter 11), yet it is also an acknowledgment of a necessary offset to all the Doing. Counterintuitive as it may sound, to become truly vigorous minded, you must regularly allow your vigorous attitude to drop away. Permit yourself a lengthy pause. Just as physical cross-trainers know to take a day off from training each week, so too must cognitive cross-trainers. Rest is critical. Give yourself the gift of quiet. Turn off the radio in the car. Stay in the quiet space long enough to let it begin to speak to you. "Hunches live in the quiet world," says Nancy Parker, postgraduate scholar of mythological studies. "If you're always immersed in the world of distraction, you can't build the capacity for a vigorous mind." It's about resting the psyche: to sometimes allow yourself to exist in a place of unknowing, without the armature of a five-year plan. Parker explains that spirituality doesn't typically emanate from "focused awareness," which is what the other six imperatives call for: highly directed attention. Rather, spirituality arises from what she calls "diffuse awareness," when your brain is fuzzily idling. "Value your time in the shower, getting dressed, brushing your teeth," she says. "See these times as a necessary engagement of this kind of skill." During periods of restorative rest, your body or mind integrates, absorbs, and makes sense of the activity you've been revving it up with, achieving something approaching mind/body harmony. That gentle, unforced integration is a significant component of spirituality. If you seldom stop to regroup and ask yourself how you're really doing, you're cheating yourself of another avenue to self-development: the spiritual avenue. Providing yourself with sufficient downtime also allows you to get freshly jazzed up about all the sparkling possibilities life presents. We all require that kind of motivation to keep going. So the purpose of spirituality is to provide sustenance for those of us on this arduous path.

The benefit of adding a spiritual component to your cross-training is two-pronged: First, it will make room in your life for meditation and the revitalization that often follows it. Second, and even more beneficial, you will eventually begin to mold your panoply of activities into a coherent Weltanschauung, or worldview. This is an amazing aspect of pursuing the generalist path. For example, Terry was busy pursuing Spanish, wallpapering, and the writings of Dorothy Parker. After months of having fun, learning, and growing, she began to perceive that her endeavors were extending well beyond fun, learning, and growth. Her cross-training, when she paused to really mull it over, revealed itself to consist of a numinous dimension. Specifically, she realized she was formulating a vision for herself as a teacher of liberal arts. This was a giant revelation. She had never considered herself teacher material at all. This epiphany changed her life.

As I've said elsewhere, many of us are occasionally afflicted with the blues and the blahs, a chronic world-weariness that's crept into our very marrow. This malaise prevents us from recognizing our callings and developing into all we're meant to be. A spiritual tune-up is in order. That's what the Spiritual Imperative is about.

One definition of spirituality might involve our emotional relationship with unanswerable questions. "What is the meaning of life?" immediately comes to mind as one such (unanswerable) question. Another question—one with some potential for practical answers—might be: "How can I make my life meaningful?" The way we answer these kinds of questions reflects our spiritual dimension, and this is what imbues all other activity with meaning—especially, in our case, our wide-ranging Renaissance activities. Yet you can't set out to "attain" spirituality. Spirituality is a byproduct of being in tune with your best self and your optimal role in the world. If you're born to be a generalist and you're honoring your nature by pursuing that path, you will soon begin to see that pursuit as inherently spiritual. Because it is. (Likewise if you're a specialist and pursuing that path.)

In the conformist 1950s, theologian Paul Tillich perhaps foresaw the move toward an ecumenical spirituality based on ecumenical interests. He looked around and saw "the will to be accepted by the group at any price, an unwillingness to show individual traits, [and] acceptance of a limited happiness without serious risks." He, like other social critics of the time, called for a more individualistic form of spiritual life. "We hope for nonconformists among you, for your sake, for the sake of the nation, and for the sake of humanity," he told graduating collegians. He implied that spiritual fulfillment was unique to every person. *New York Times* columnist David Brooks, writing in his book *Bobos in Paradise*, observes that Tillich's hopes did indeed come to pass. "It is now better to be thought of as unconventional than conventional; it is better to be called a nonconformist than a conformist. It is cooler to be a rebel than an obedient foot soldier." Brooks praises "individualistic pluralism" as the foundation of spiritual life. "There are varieties of happiness," he writes, "distinct moralities, and different ways to virtue. What's more, no one ever really arrives at a complete answer to the deepest questions or to faith. It is a voyage. We are forever incomplete, making choices, exploring, creating. We are protean. The proper spiritual posture, therefore, is to be open-minded about new choices and paths."

> *"Two questions are asked of us at the end of our lives:*
> *(1) What did you contribute? and*
> *(2) Did you fulfill your potential?"*
>
> —Anonymous

Harmony: The Heart of a Vigorous Mind

Endless, sometimes tiresome debate takes place about the need to achieve balance between personal and professional responsibilities in one's life. I've come to believe that it's essentially a fatuous question, since the scales aren't weighed until the end of your life—and who's adjudicating, anyway? Someone once said that happiness is like a butterfly: the more you chase it, the more it will elude you, but if you turn your attention to other things, it will come and sit softly on your shoulder. We could replace the word *happiness* with the word *balance* in that axiom. You can't chase balance, just as you can't chase happiness. What you *can* do is make good choices—choices that create an appropriate setting for both balance and happiness (not to mention spirituality) to come pay you a visit. So make sure to include some sort of spiritual component in your cross-training. I also like the suggestion in the butterfly aphorism to "turn your attention to other things." This is precisely my prescription for a better life as a cross-trainer.

It seems to me that harmony is a better goal than balance anyway. The concept of "balance" is pretty much subjective, and no one can really agree on what it looks like, so it's a moving target that becomes the source of the very stress it's supposed to relieve. Harmony, on the other hand, refers to a pleasing arrangement of parts, with pleasant connotations of spiritual peace of mind. Harmony could exist even on days when your life is unquestionably out of balance, when work takes precedence over play or vice versa. Harmony is personal, too, and therefore exempt from the critical judgments of others. Anyone who's ever given over their life for a time to a work project that provides great personal meaning and satisfaction knows that balance is pointless. I'm gratified in the extreme to have professional projects that are so important to me that I'm willing to put aside other priorities for a while. Writing a book is a good example of that. A full, rich life will occasionally look "out of balance" but could often provide a nourishing sense of harmony to the owner of that life. This is why spirituality is imperative to a Vigorous Mind program; with spirituality often comes a strong commitment to kaizen, by the way. I believe that if you cultivate a slightly more spiritual worldview, you'll more readily accept the patience necessary to activate kaizen. Slow and steady sure isn't flashy, and it does require faith, but it ultimately delivers the kind of deep-seated satisfaction that is implicit in spirituality.

Numinous Nomenclature

Acolytes of cross-training who are less than comfortable with the often-challenging nature of the Spirituality Imperative may find some helpful traction in the following three concepts: peak experiences, wabi-sabi, and Qi. Let's deconstruct them one at a time.

Take a "Peak"

You certainly don't need to structure your Vigorous Mind program around trying to do everything every day—unless that happens to be your preferred method of approaching life. What I prefer are daily peak experiences. This means that every day, I try to experience at least one instance of heightened existence, whether that experience is characterized by learning, well-being, novelty, fun, joy, awe—even fear, tension, or sadness. A peak experience is a moment out of time. It might come about as a result of taking a fencing lesson for the first time, giving yourself over to a weepy movie, or driving a stick-shift in the hills of San Francisco. The best jobs provide just this kind of stimulation, but people who are resigned to occupations that aren't especially invigorating are obligated to cultivate peak experiences during their off-hours. These out-of-the-ordinary moments lead to a deeper engagement with the world and, ultimately, much greater harmony and spiritual awareness. To me, peak experiences are as spiritual as things get, in their succulent secular way, and they're available to anybody, regardless of formal religious affiliation. (Speaking of religion and wide-ranging habits of mind, a rabbi in Missoula, Montana, presides over a pastiche of denominations within his congregation. The services he leads are by necessity hybridized. In a wonderful coinage, he calls the approach "flexidoxy." What you might call *cafeteria-style religion* results in the kind of descriptor one young woman in his congregation uses for herself: "I'm a Methodist Taoist Native American Quaker Russian Orthodox Buddhist Jew."

Note that peak experiences may be quite incompatible with balance, but a great motivator for harmony. If you're struggling every single day to attend to every single one of your obligations (friends, family, career, environment, spirituality, finances, creativity, recreation), not only will you exhaust yourself, but you will likely not be deeply enough engaged in any one of those components to generate a peak experience. By contrast, harmony is thoroughly compatible with peak experiences. The quest to cross-train your brain is, in a way, a quest to populate your work life and your free time with lots and lots of peak experiences.

However, the writer David Brooks points out that "the accumulation of spiritual peak experiences can become like the greedy person's accumulation of money. The more you get, the more you hunger for more. The life of perpetual choice is a life of perpetual longing as you are prodded by the inextinguishable desire to try the next new thing." I point out the risk associated with peak experience–lust because anyone subject to the siren call of a vigorous mind would also likely be seduced by the siren call of more/better/faster peak experiences. But a well-rounded life doesn't work that way, because spirituality represents the requisite flip side of more/better/faster.

A Perfectly Imperfect Motivation

There's another way to express that vitally important flip side of aggressive overachievement and constant Doing. As with kaizen, we have the Japanese to credit for it. The comprehensive Japanese worldview or aesthetic system known as *wabi-sabi* is the second of three spiritually useful terms in this chapter. Wabi-sabi can be loosely defined as respect for imperfection and incompleteness. It might be a slub in a silk jacket, a chip in a teacup, or a droop in an eyelid. Wabi-sabi has always struck me as sort of comfortingly spiritual, not to mention apt to our present discussion. Wabi-sabi is the beauty of rough edges, fleeting moments, and half-finished results. It is the beauty of things modest, humble, and unconventional. Embrace it, because in your quest to become fully faceted your goal will never be fully attained. Wabi-sabi can be a source of consolation when your Triumph in Twenty isn't going so well, or when the demons of time, money, and motivation get you down. This is because wabi-sabi reminds us that the journey to kindle a measure of spiritual awareness, let alone a fully vigorous mind, may well be unconventional, eccentric, messy, desultory, half-evolved, and half-nuts. Wabi-sabi reminds us that there is a method to madness. We're all soaking in wabi-sabi, and that's as it should be. When the going gets tough, the tough can turn for solace and centering to this lovely idea. The concept of wabi-sabi correlates nicely with Zen Buddhism, by the way. When I think of shorthand for Zen, I go for "mindfulness" and "acceptance of what is." I like the way that dovetails with wabi-sabi, because "what is" is invariably half-done, rough-edged, and charmingly imperfect.

Dwell in Possibilities

Our third spiritually inspired term is the Chinese concept of *Qi*, pronounced *chee*. Qi is a term for cosmic energy; the force of nature. It fuels not only human organisms but also the solar wind, the orbits of stars and planets, and magnetic fields. An athlete who taps into Qi vaults beyond ordinary limits of physicality into a constantly recharging power source. The Qi of a

wide-ranging generalist is truly a magnificent thing to ponder; since generalists consider just about the wide whole
world as our domain, our Qi must be off
the charts. You'll know you're closing in
on your bull's-eye when your whole life
feeds your Qi. That doesn't happen
easily, however, as we're about to see. It
requires occasional dips into introspec-
tion, frequently considered anathema to
flighty cross-trainers.

> *"People say that what we're all
> seeking is a meaning for life. . . .
> I think that what we're really seeking
> is an experience of being alive, so
> that our life experiences on a purely
> physical plane will have resonance
> within our innermost being and
> reality, so that we can actually feel
> the rapture of being alive."*
>
> —Joseph Campbell (1904–1987),
> author and mythology scholar

Be Introspective

"What is my role in this world?" That's one question we might do well to
ask ourselves over and over again. Otherwise, we may wind up playing somebody else's role and not even know it. Guru of mindfulness Jon Kabat-Zinn,
in his book *Wherever You Go There You Are*, relates the following story about
Buckminster Fuller, respected Renaissance man.

Fuller, the discoverer/inventor of the geodesic dome, at age thirty-two con-
templated suicide for a few hours one night at the edge of Lake Michigan, as
the story goes, after a series of business failures. Apparently everything he
had undertaken had turned to dust in spite of his incredible creativity and
imagination (which were recognized only later). However, instead of ending
his life, Fuller decided, perhaps because of his deep conviction in the underlying unity and order of the universe, to live from then on *as if* he had died
that night.

So he asked himself a question with piercing spiritual implications, one
that I pose to you as well: "What is it on this planet that needs doing that I
know something about, that probably won't happen unless I take responsibility for it?" You never know what will come of such introspections. Fuller
himself was fond of stating that what seems to be happening at the moment

is never the full story of what's really going on. He liked to point out that for the honeybee, it's the honey that's important. But for Mother Nature, it's the cross-pollination of flowers that's important. The moral is that interconnectedness is a fundamental principle of nature. Nothing is isolated. Each event connects with others. Things are constantly unfolding on different levels.

Fuller believed in an underlying architecture of nature, an architecture in which form and function were fused. He believed that nature's blueprints would make sense and would have practical relevance to our lives on many levels. Before he died, X-rays demonstrated that many viruses are structured along the same geodesic principles as those Fuller discovered by playing around with polyhedra. He didn't live long enough to see it, but a whole new field of chemistry opened up around the unpredicted discovery of soccer ball-like carbon compounds with remarkable properties. They quickly became known as buckminsterfullerenes, or buckyballs. Playing in his sandbox, following his own path, his musings led to discoveries and worlds of which he'd never dreamed. Yet he never thought of himself as special in any sense—just a regular person who liked to play with ideas.

"If you follow your bliss, you put yourself on a kind of track, which has been there all the while waiting for you, and the life that you ought to be living is the one you are living."

—Joseph Campbell (1904–1987), author and mythology scholar

It's for us to perceive the warp and woof of our own nature. Especially for the multitudes who are seeking a higher expression of their selfhood as an expression of vocation, we must identify and then follow our own threads through the tapestry of day-to-day life. When Fuller asked himself what needed doing in this world that likely wouldn't happen unless he took responsibility for it, I'm reminded of how special the contributions of desultorians and dilettantes and dabblers and generalists and "comprehensivists" are, since so few people are playing those roles these days. Take responsibility for your unusual role in this world. It's a gift.

NEURO NUGGET

Is the brain designed to help us answer epic questions like "What's the purpose of life?" Or is the brain just a powerful sorter and cataloguer, akin to a computer? According to Samuel Wang, an associate professor in the Department of Molecular Biology and Princeton Neuroscience Institute at Princeton University, it's most definitely not a computer. The brain processes information, but its ultimate goal is to help us to survive to fight another day. That means getting answers that are good enough to get us through life's various situations. One thing that brains do well is detect coincidences. For instance, if you hear rustling leaves and then see a tiger, the next time you hear leaves you might run because you are again expecting a tiger to appear. However, coincidences don't always imply a chain of causation.

A Rich Life

I'd encourage you to do whatever you have to do to chisel out regular time alone for spiritual reflection. These kinds of timeouts won't occur unless you insist on them. So use kaizen to keep you on the straight and narrow. In my experience, the replies to spiritual questions never present themselves until you're distracted by something: driving or taking a shower or daydreaming. That's okay. Simply setting aside time for the act of mediation, reflection, or posing questions about your metarole in life aerates your mind. Beyond that, spiritual reflection provides the peace of mind that revs up enthusiasm and keeps your momentum rolling, even when the idea of a vigorous mind may be losing some of its vigor.

"What we're really seeking is an experience of being alive."

—Joseph Campbell (1904–1987), author and mythology scholar

"We must all learn to let go of things that have lost their energy," says Parker, the mythology scholar. "We must let things die and feel the suffering in order to clear the way for new growth. Every death takes you deeper into life. It deepens your capacity for tolerance. The vagaries of life are a part of life. Don't cheat yourself by refusing to stop and feel the experience." That could mean discontinuing an activity you had thought would bring joy into your life. So it turns out that skeet-shooting or decoupage or the Roman Empire didn't rock your world after all? Let it go.

A Spiritual Tyro

Now, I must confess that I'm similar to comedian and political commentator Bill Maher when it comes to spirituality: it's an item that resides on my, ahem, to-do list. But I do make one significant effort: in the name of ecumenical Catholicism, I indulge in an annual retreat—my "radical sabbatical"—to the famous monastery where renowned spiritual writer Thomas Merton made his Kentucky home, the Abbey of Gethsemani. My goal for the retreat, or "realignment week," is simply to increase my spiritual bandwidth, however that plays out. My particular interpretation of spiritual retreats is to think of them as refreshments or re-invigorations of both my brain and my outlook. A retreat is a way to reengage with a *sense of possibility* in myself, my work, and my world.

Mine are silent retreats—no mumbling to myself; no *sotto voce* asides to fellow retreatants; no murmured greetings in the dining room; no polite "thanks" when someone holds a door open; no reflexive "excuse me" when I jostle someone in the chow line; no laughing when, striding briskly, I snag my jacket on the door hinge in the library and am abruptly yanked backward in a flailing, cartoonish halt.

Retreatants are assigned to monklike cells, austere but for the framed cross over the hard, narrow bed. The seven-times-daily tolling of the church bells somehow makes the silence even more forlorn. Vegetarian meals are eaten in howling wordlessness on long narrow benches. The surrounding woods are as quiet as the grave, punctuated perhaps by a glimpse of a red fox ambling through the snow. I am enchanted by all of this.

There's one problem, though. The retreats at Gethsemani are all about reduced stimuli ("less is more"), whereas most cross-trainers are stimuli junkies ("more is more"). I try to give myself over to the state of reduced stimuli, to stretch into it as a new experience, even as I resist it. The retreats are about simplification, whereas I'm about complexity—a seemingly intractable problem, given that *plerosis* (filling) rather than *kenosis* (emptying) is the instinctive spiritual practice of the typical cross-trainer. I've come to appreciate, however, that such conflict creates a rich and fruitful tension. Stretching into a new way of being is always worthwhile, as we discussed in Chapter 8. "Stillness is not inertia," reminds Parker. "It is a very active state, if you allow yourself to stop fighting against it."

"In terms of the soul's integrity, the great sacrilege is that of inadvertence, of not being alert, not awake."

—Joseph Campbell (1904–1987), author and mythology scholar

I have no expectation of accomplishing any particular work during my retreats. I set this time aside only to reexamine the nature of my work and how I'm changing with respect to it. Maybe letting go of expectation is the real magic of a retreat and of the Spiritual Imperative itself. After all, every field must lie fallow every so often to restore its nutrients. So, too, must a vigorous mind experience periodic, meditative time-outs. Spiritual reflection is absolutely crucial to the experience, serving as it does to stoke the fires of motivation and maintain faith in the challenging process. Perhaps, paradoxically, retreats feed one's cross-training impulse by turning contemplation inward and thus providing one more avenue of exploration.

Carol Frompton is an intellectually restless probate attorney who has been paying more attention to her spiritual life over the past decade or so, and who is also a devotee of periodic spiritual retreats. She's earned a degree in divinity from a theological seminary and engages in mission work in Third World countries. She uses her retreats for "contemplation and renewal," and says she's never anxious about withdrawing from the flurry of everyday life for five days at a time. Frompton is an excellent example of a dedicated cross-trainer who is not always craving stimuli. By the way, based partly on meditations performed during her retreats, she's made the decision to leave her current law firm to establish one of her own, on her own terms.

The Benedictine monks at Gethsemani, as well as those of religious orders elsewhere, have made solemn vows to pursue the spiritual path of the *via negativa*, meaning the simplification of life, which includes no ownership of anything. They engage in meditative practices that further empty consciousness. These monks chant their atonal, pleasurably melancholic psalms seven times a day, starting at 3:15 AM, at which unspeakable hour retreatants may join them as the monks shuffle into their wooden stalls, wearing their robes and short-cropped hair. The air somehow smells both crisply antiseptic and heavily ancient. All told, the experience is strongly appealing to those who are able to gain spiritual awareness and even transcendence from an uncluttering of life and mind.

Whether you choose to embark upon a spiritually motivated retreat or not, that longing for fulfillment and meaning in one's existence remains. The struggle of the faithful is to understand how hope can be valid even though it often seems to contradict our everyday experience. Your particular set of passions may absolutely provide you with faith and meaning, particularly once they yield up their deep-seated interconnections. At this point, your cross-training endeavors could conceivably come to represent a clear worldview, even a system of belief.

> *"Here is the test to find out whether your mission on earth is finished: if you're alive, it isn't."*
>
> —Richard Bach, author

Weird Failure

If you were born to be one of life's standout cross-trainers, heed that call. A call is a spiritual experience of divine appointment to a vocation, and if you choose not to heed your call—to disregard it or to pretend you're not aware of it—then, as Sufi poet Kabir said, your life will be infected with a kind of "weird failure." I believe that so many of us today are infected with listlessness, low-grade depression, and anxiety at midlife because we have denied our calling to move into full completeness—to express ourselves on every level. It's depression suffered at the level of the soul. Indeed, repression of the life force is said to be the most common reason people undertake psychotherapy. Psychologist Abraham Maslow, along with the writer Gregg Levoy, call spiritual and emotional truancy the "Jonah Complex": evading one's growth, setting low levels of aspiration, fearing what we're capable of doing, voluntary self-crippling, pseudo-stupidity, mock humility. Author Marianne Williamson made famous these words in that regard: "Our deepest fear is not that we are inadequate. Our deepest fear is that we are powerful beyond measure. It is our light, not our darkness, that most frightens us. But our playing small doesn't serve the world. There's nothing enlightened about shrinking so that other people won't feel insecure around you."

Levoy, in his book *Callings: Finding and Following an Authentic Life*, refers to life "in its fleshy and toothsome grandeur, all the spill and stomp and shout of it, all the come and go of it." What we're essentially talking about in this book is increasing one's level of satisfaction. Maybe the word *happiness* is just too sappy for us cynical Americans.

We moderns have lost the distinction between pleasures and gratifications, although the golden age Athenians were keen on the difference. The word for happiness that is distinct from sensory pleasure is *eudaimonia*; a better translation is gratification. It cannot be derived from bodily pleasure; it can be had only by activity consonant with noble purpose. And noble purpose is a terrific way to describe what we're striving for—the purpose of cross-training our brains. "Noble purpose" is also what many of us seek in our vocations; more on that in Chapter 12. You have a moral obligation to be your fullest self. If you play small, if you exist in only your puny shadow form, you have not only cheated yourself, but you have also deprived the whole world of the singular contribution that only you can offer. Most of us aren't greedy enough for all we can be and do. We're miserly with ourselves and our capabilities. And *that's* being selfish.

EXERCISES

I believe that spirituality is a skill, and I don't believe that it comes any easier to us than any other new skill. So let's get the hang of it by practicing:

1. Retreat, Renew, Return

Take twenty minutes to research a silent retreat, dedicated to nothing but your own spiritual growth. First, book the retreat far enough in the future that you can adequately plan for it. That might mean putting a couple of casseroles in the freezer for your family and arranging for transportation to soccer games. Next, if you're inclined, buddy up with a like-minded friend. Offer to watch your friend's children for the weekend of his or her retreat, and vice versa. Or engage a trusted babysitter. Once you're officially in retreat mode, get a journal and track your emotions over the course of your hideaway. Don't be surprised to note melancholy moments, as well as exuberant periods. Most people prefer not to plan an exhaustive agenda for themselves while on retreat. Listen to your inner voice and feel no pressure to produce great epiphanies.

2. The Buddy System

If you recruited a friend to also attend the retreat, when you return home, meet with your buddy and debrief each of your trips. Did the silence unnerve you? Intrigue you? What would you do differently if you went on a silent retreat again? What were the best and worst things about your experiences?

3. Glossies

Subscribe to magazines that refer to spirituality in all its many guises. *O, The Oprah Magazine* and *Mental Floss* are good starting points. The idea is to extract nutrients from all available sources. Be a filter-feeder.

4. Résumé of the Spirit

Create a spiritual curriculum vitae: a list of all the people, places, and things that have inspired you. Ask the people you've listed what career they think would work for you. You'll be surprised at how much they've intuited about you and how removed you may be from an accurate perception of yourself.

5. Small-Group Exercise

Consider any small group of friends you're a part of. First, have each person in the group write a brief description of two moments—the first, a moment when things went so well you knew you were born to be doing what you were doing; and the second, a moment when things went so poorly that you almost wished you'd never been born. Then, debrief your answer with one or more group members. Have your groupmates help each other identify the gifts they possess that made the good moment possible. Oddly, our strongest gifts are usually those we are barely aware of possessing; it often takes the eyes of others to help us see them. Then turn to the second case, the occasion when things cratered. Having been bathed with praise in the first case, people now expect to be subjected to analysis, critique, and a variety of fixes: "If I had been in your shoes, I would have …," or "Next time you are in a situation like that, why don't you … ?" Avoid that approach. Ask participants instead to help each other see how limitations and liabilities are the flip side of their gifts, how a particular weakness is the inevitable trade-off for a particular strength. Lesson: We improve not by trying to fill the potholes in our souls but by knowing them so well that we can avoid falling into them.

6. Peak Experiences

Test your level of spirituality: immediately after a peak experience (an especially good run, throwing a pot for the first time, receiving a standing ovation after a big presentation at work), jot down how you feel about yourself and your role in the world. I predict that you'll see that peak experiences lead directly to an enhanced sense of the spiritual. Compare those notes to feelings experienced during an ordinary, nonpeak experience moment in a typical day. The correlation between peak experiences and spirituality will probably be striking. If you don't notice a correlation, speculate why.

10

IMPERATIVE #7:
THE COURAGE IMPERATIVE

The Audacity to Be an Amateur

> A professional is an amateur who didn't quit.
>
> —*Richard Bach, author*

All contemporary generalists are courageous almost by definition, since they're bucking the prevailing prescription to funnel their interests and energies down to the narrowest possible point. But the story of Ronan Tynan represents particular mettle, as revealed by his backstory. Best known these days as a splendidly gifted tenor, Tynan started life in Ireland "as wild as a March hare," keen for motorcycles and horses. This, despite being born handicapped with a lower-limb disability. He was undaunted, even when at age twenty, both legs were amputated below the knee after an auto accident. Within weeks, he was running the stairs in his dorm at the prestigious Trinity College, and within twelve months, he was winning gold medals in the Paralympics. Galvanized by his medical experiences, he went on to become a physician, specializing in orthopedics. It was during his residency, at age thirty-three, that Tynan became interested in singing. He'd enjoyed music as a boy, but now threw himself into it, becoming a high-performing amateur. He won both the John McCormack Cup for Tenor Voice and the BBC talent show *Go For It* less than a year after he turned to singing in earnest. He's performed for the New York police and fire departments in the wake of 9/11, as well as at President Reagan's funeral and during the seventh-inning stretch at Yankee Stadium. Although no longer an amateur, Tynan nevertheless embodies the spirit of bold and inquisitive engagement, daring to plunge into disparate challenges and play with the big boys until the time when he became accepted as one of them. Tynan's inspiring valor as an amputee, Irish tenor, medical doctor, equestrian, and accomplished athlete has been built on the courage to persevere.

Peter K. Homer was unemployed and living in Maine when he heard the startling news that NASA was turning to America's "garage inventors" to brainstorm new technologies in anticipation of a return to the moon. NASA had opened up design contests for assorted space gadgets and gear—everything from a redesigned lunar lander to a new design for space gloves. An avid backyard tinkerer who had formerly worked jobs in the aerospace industry and as a stitcher of boat sails, Homer decided that the glove contest offered a real opportunity for him. Each time an astronaut flexes a muscle in space, he or she has to struggle against the spacesuit's resistance. Astronauts often return from space with their hands rubbed raw, sometimes bleeding. Heavy-duty gloves are essential, but comfort is also a considerable factor, so well-designed, well-made gloves are important. Powered by the one-step-at-a-time mind-set of kaizen, Homer's design ultimately won him the $200,000 first prize—a resounding victory for an audacious amateur who had the moxie to throw his hat in the ring.

Elsewhere, R. W. Apple, known to all as "Johnny," was one free-ranging individual—the type of person who lived large and was fondly described as a character. He wrote for the *New York Times* on an unusually broad scope of subjects including politics, travel, and food. Journalist Calvin Trillin observed that Apple would check into a hotel so staggeringly expensive that no other reporter would dare include it on an expense account. Apple could confidently knock out a complicated lead story at a political convention as the deadline (or the dinner hour) approached, or tell a sommelier that the wine simply wouldn't do, all while pontificating on architecture or history or opera or soccer or horticulture or civil rights. The irrepressible Apple was profiled in Timothy Crouse's *The Boys on the Bus*, which famously chronicled the reportage of the 1972 presidential campaign. "[Reporters] recognized many of their own traits in him, grotesquely magnified," wrote Crouse. "The shock of recognition frightened them. Apple was like them, only more blatant. He openly displayed the faults they tried to hide: the insecurity, the ambitiousness, the name-dropping. . . ."

For all his journalistic aplomb, Apple was widely known as an "amateur expert" on food and wine, and lectured on those as well as political, social, and historical topics on several continents. When he turned seventy, he threw a party at his favorite Paris bistro, Chez L'Ami Louis, an outing Trillin profiled in *Gourmet Magazine*: "It's my understanding that Apple has simplified what could be a terribly difficult choice by telling [the waiters] to bring everything." Apple clearly had cultivated a taste for the full buffet, both literally and figuratively. That's the spirit of the well-rounded Renaissance man. In fact, Apple once said, "I see two sides to too many things," which endears me by its honesty and its glimpse into the open-minded character of this muchmissed journalist, who died in 2006.

Let us now praise Meriwether Lewis of the adventuring duo Lewis and Clark. Without a doubt, Lewis put the vigor in vigorous mind. Thomas Jefferson picked Meriwether Lewis to lead a multidisciplinary venture across the wilderness of this continent in 1804. On one level, the venture was a de facto failure, since Jefferson's mandate was for Lewis and Clark to seek out a waterway linking the East with the Pacific Ocean. No dice, of course, but the group mushed on, their journey becoming a grand adventure of the mind and the spirit—a quest for knowledge as much as an arduous physical exploration. Imagine the courage it required to face a true wilderness as a trailblazer. All of Clark's heroism and their Indian guide Sacagewea's strength, however, frankly pale in comparison to Jefferson's vision and Lewis's staggering capability. Drawing on all his physical and mental musculature, Lewis somehow found the energy to record priceless detailed notes, drawings, and maps about heretofore uncharted flora, fauna, land forms, meteorology, and people, all the while surviving multiple day-to-day hardships and dangers. The knowledge Lewis and Clark brought back sparked the imaginations of eastern colonists, and furthered Jefferson's aims for political support in favor of westward expansion. It also fed Jefferson's gargantuan intellectual appetite. Fortune favors the bold, it is said. The Lewis and Clark expedition brought together two bold Renaissance men—Lewis and Jefferson—whose sweeping courage has changed the world.

Our seventh and final imperative is courage. Specifically, we're talking about the courage to persevere as an amateur—daring to be a dilettante, a generalist, a versatilist. The word *amateur* refers to anybody who engages in an activity for pleasure rather than for financial benefit or professional motivation. It does require a healthy measure of audacity, of intrepidity—of fearlessness. The world's standard formula for success is to put on the narrowest pair of blinders you can find and specialize in one slim thing, often to the betterment of society, but just as often to the detriment of the individual. My solution is to select a specialty for your profession, but supplement that with a platterful of complementary pursuits. Not only will you become more skilled in your profession, you will also forestall midlife burnout and discover more well-being and health than you would otherwise. So your courage will be rewarded in spades.

Courage is the mainstay of any worthy endeavor, and to embark upon a life devoted to diverse learning in a world that rewards specialization requires both mental and moral strength. The perseverance to stay one's course—particularly the kind of trendsetting, unusual, unconventional course this book is centered on—requires the courage of conviction. It also requires a kind of resolute daring to pursue autotelic activities for their intrinsic worth, in the absence of any particular extrinsic value or expectation of future gain. You need the courage to create fresh paradigms, to be regarded as a contrarian, and to stand your ground as a brassy amateur, toe-to-toe with recognized specialists. Courage is required to be in the vanguard of a new movement shattering the status quo. Our *Uomo Universale* is not just receptive to new ideas, but should also be the catalyst for them. Making new linkages, connecting ideas never before imagined, perceiving the old in a new way, simply holding one's own as an amateur—that's the best kind of cross-training. Have the courage to be a sui generis, or one-of-a-kind, cross-trainer: an amateur in the best sense of the word. Courage requires the chutzpah to claim the role of amateur when today's world doesn't exactly leap to its feet in a standing ovation at the mention of the word.

"An amateur is someone who supports himself with outside jobs which enable him to paint. A professional is someone whose wife works to enable him to paint."

—Ben Shahn (1898–1969), artist

A Bountiful Braid

Learning undertaken by individuals either on their own (which we'll cover in Chapter 11) or in an organized class is vitally important for staving off a bland and dispirited midlife. And the prognosis is excellent for this trend to pick up even more steam, thanks mainly to the Internet. A pipeline into every world under the sun, the Internet has given each of us amateurs the potential to expand our horizons and even to compete with the professionals in many fields. Today's "professional amateurs" are tearing down the distinction between experts and tinkerers. Cheaper technology has made increasingly powerful tools available to amateurs; the Internet offers unprecedented access to knowledge and enables global collaboration. Indeed, amateurs are making the experts quake in some quarters. Amateurs are increasingly able to hold themselves to professional standards, contributing significant innovations and discoveries. This revolution represents the courage of the amateur— the gutsy cross-trainer—to claim a rightful place among the specialists and experts of the world. Talk about a new

"It is necessary to any originality to have the courage to be an amateur."

—Wallace Stevens (1879–1955), poet

trend. This one has the potential to be astronomical. For Jay McNeil, it was literally that.

When Jay McNeil peered into his telescope and discovered a nebula—a developing young star—out near the Orion constellation, professional astronomers worldwide hailed the discovery. But McNeil himself is no credentialed scientist; he installs TV satellite dishes for a living. Today's backyard sky gazers, it seems, use equipment so sophisticated they can sometimes beat out well-financed observatories. Imagine the courage it required for McNeil to present his findings to full-time professional astronomy researchers. I applaud his admirable audacity. Go, Jay!

> *"I think I'm lucky.*
> *I was born with very little talent,*
> *but great drive."*
>
> —Anthony Quinn
> (1915–2001), actor

An Audacity Audit

Now it's time to conduct an "audacity audit" to see where you might be falling short on your AQ (audacity quotient).

1. **Are you audacious enough to own up to your most flamboyant weakness?** The purpose of admitting to your greatest weakness is not to correct it—contrary to popular belief—but to poke around under it and discover how its flip side represents your greatest strength. The truth is, your weakness is just a slightly twisted variant of your strength—its underbelly, so to speak. Because the ability to make connections is one of the most powerful strengths versatilists possess, I'm guessing you'll immediately be able to perceive the connection between your strength and your weakness. Then comes the blessed alchemy: endorse your weakness, and your strength immediately becomes that much stronger.

2. **Are you audacious enough to not be "too nice"?** Boy, will this one get me in trouble. But here it is: we are way too nice. We honor nice

to the exclusion of all, including competence, goal achievement, even the health of our own brains. If you're aspiring to be an audacious amateur, you can't put "nice" first. This is a not a program for the faint of heart. You have to cultivate a certain mental toughness— to stick with your kaizen and to keep the faith, especially when you experience those dark nights of the soul. Too much is at stake here. "Nice" isn't going to improve your ability as a plucky pluralist. So let go of that surfeit of nice you're carrying around like an albatross and replace it with a savage stylishness.

3. **Are you audacious enough to be full-tilt bold?** Fear is the flip side of audacity. Actually, it's worse than that. Fear is negativity itself. And fear is what's keeping you from honoring the radical perfection of kaizen. If you are fascinated by human potential generally, but a little scared of human potential when that human is you, know that fear is behind it. Don't be audacity anorexic. Don't starve yourself of your true nature. If it is truly in your nature to be a desultorian, then move heaven and earth to be that desultorian. Acknowledge fear, stare it in the eye, and then put your shoulder down and storm right past it. You have to triumph over fear if you're going to step into your full-fledged, multifaceted self. Feel fear. Be bold. Feel fear. Be bold. Lather, rinse, repeat.

4. **Are you audacious enough to be a contrarian?** Be audacious enough to disregard any advice—including this—if it simply doesn't suit you. Question everything; swallow nothing whole. Part of being an amateur is having the temerity to be the radical outsider, the rebel with the pocket protector. Give yourself permission to be a courageous contrarian, and you'll experience greater contentment because you'll respect yourself. Call it audacious

"Courage is doing what you're afraid to do. There can be no courage unless you're scared."

—Eddie Rickenbacker (1890–1973), aviator

authenticity. Exercise the prerogative that comes with that outsider status, and you will acquire the status of smart and even, just maybe, chic.

I offer no numerical rating system to make empirical something as resistant to quantification as audacity. But I know from working with clients that you are aware, deep down, if you tend to play it meek when you should be bold, reluctant when you should be valiant, docile when you should be fierce. These are substantial gulfs to bridge, of course. Use kaizen and its baby-step approach to gradually up the ante on your AQ.

Fallacious Experts

Not everyone is sanguine about the role of amateurs. We're seeing a seismic shift in the consecrated status of the historically venerated figure of "the expert." In fact, the proper, appropriate role of the uncredentialed amateur is a barnburner of an issue now. And it isn't going to fade away, any more than the Internet is going to fade away. How this will ultimately play out is a complete unknown, but it's hard to be too pessimistic about the idea of getting more people involved in sharing knowledge. What is truly frightening is the misuse of knowledge by those who are inclined toward ne'er-do-wellism. Indeed, Alexander Pope once wrote that a little knowledge is a dangerous thing. The corollary is that a *lot* of knowledge can be a dangerous thing, too. Those with a lot of knowledge—highly educated experts and specialists— have historically wreaked all kinds of havoc on our world.

Nonetheless, Andrew Keen has written a seething screed against amateurs titled *The Cult of the Amateur*. In his book, Keen states his case that today's surge of amateurs is destructive, and suggests it will bring about the death of our cultural standards and moral values. He writes, "The ranks of our cultural gatekeepers, professional critics, journalists, editors, musicians, moviemakers, and other purveyors of expert information are being disintermediated by amateur bloggers, hack reviewers, homespun moviemakers, and attic record-ing artists." He also expresses concern that true talent will not be able to rise to the fore in the presence of so much amateur rubbish. In my opinion, his arguments don't quite hold up. Our cultural gatekeepers have never been all they were cracked up to be. It's debatable, for example, that *Encyclopedia Britannica* is truly superior to Wikipedia. We've imbued the "experts" with too much authority, too much power, too much license to go unchallenged and thus risk complacency. It's the "expert fallacy." Furthermore, I see no con-vincing evidence that talented journalists, editors, musicians, or moviemak-ers are being "disintermediated" by crummy ones. Indeed, our multimedia age gives those with courageous audacity many more stages on which to play and get noticed.

Keen believes that in our highly specialized economy, professionals such as doctors, journalists, environmental scientists, clothing designers, and others have received years of training to properly do their jobs, but that the rise of the amateur will undo this natural order. Yet astronomy experts were stunned by the unheralded Jay McNeil in his ordinary backyard. So it's important to remember that being a conventional expert does not automat-ically confer the cloak of uniform excellence or infallibility.

In a world of audacious amateurs, observers fear that experts will be deposed, and therefore no one will know who we should turn to for counsel. My question is, where do you draw the line? The line between "expert profes-sional" and "highly informed amateur" has been blurred. Think of Olympic ath-letes, who are considered to be amateurs. They've reached the pinnacle of accom-plishment in their sports—not what you'd typically associate with the word *amateur*. And what of the criteria that an amateur shouldn't receive any monetary gain for his or her expertise? I believe

> *"If I have at times been able to make original contributions in the accelerator field, I cannot help feeling that to a certain extent my slightly amateur approach in physics, combined with much practical experience, was an asset."*
>
> —Simon van der Meer, physicist

that's a dubious, nebulous, loophole-filled standard. So a stark distinction between amateurs and professionals is artificial and sometimes unnecessary. As a result, the world is awakening to the presence of the so-called amateur professional.

In this book, I'm suggesting that being a noble amateur is a vehicle to make you better at your professional occupation. This is not a binary issue; it's a question of degree. You can't dismiss all amateurs as worthless (the amateur fallacy) any more than you can embrace all professionals as geniuses (the expert fallacy).

Cognitive Capacity

Let's discuss blogs—those darlings of the amateur world. Blogs are a favorite of dabbling dilettantes, as well as for all those who monitor special-interest groups. Perhaps the naysayers who decry blogs as conduits of useless information don't seriously understand blogs to be anything other than journals or vessels for tossed-off opinion, often driven by marketing or vanity. Given the tsunami of content that the Internet represents, one is absolutely obligated to become a supremely skilled editor in order to cull the wheat from the chaff. But that doesn't make blogs worthless, and it doesn't mean they're usurping traditional media (whatever that may be). In fact, one interesting contrast to note is the difference between "old media" and "new media." Old media consists of professional journalists who have studied journalism—they're experts in journalism but amateurs in whatever they're writing about. In contrast, new media is made up of individuals who aren't professionally trained journalists but who are experts in the topics they're writing about. I leave it to you to decide if one is superior to the other.

> "I can fairly be called an amateur because I do what I do, in the original sense of the word—for love, because I love it. On the other hand, I think that those of us who make our living writing history can also be called true professionals."
>
> —David McCullough, author

The upside of the amateur revolution offers abundant rewards. For those of us intent on creating more cognitive capacity for ourselves, courage is required to persist through the riptide of specialization facing us. The courage to persevere is the courage proud amateurs possess.

Amateur Hour

Speaking of amateurs, how can we overlook Wikipedia—the world's largest online encyclopedia, which is, oddly, becoming a leading online source of breaking news? (That's what Wikipedia's "Wikipedia" entry says, anyway. For you doubting Thomases, two outside sources are cited for corroboration: the *New York Times Magazine* and a study conducted at the University of Texas.) Straight from the Wikipedia source: "Wikipedia is a multilingual, Web-based, free content encyclopedia project . . . written collaboratively by volunteers from all around the world." Most entries are submitted by amateurs—some anonymous, some not—and many have been tweaked several times over. In any case, pedigree is not checked, leading some people to doubt the reliability of the source. Wikipedia puts its faith in the "wisdom of crowds"—the idea that because so many people are monitoring its entries, errors and vandalism will be weeded out, sooner rather than later. One favorite quip from Wikipedia's defenders, acknowledging its unlikely workability: "The problem with Wikipedia is that it works only in practice. In theory, it can never work."

Founded in 2001 by Jimmy Wales and Larry Sanger, Wikipedia has exploded in just a few short years to become the largest encyclopedia ever assembled. (Interestingly, Sanger left Wikipedia, believing that it should give more authority to experts; he has since created another site, Citizendium, that does just that.) Wikipedia hosts more than 8 million articles in more than 280 languages and is among the top ten most-visited sites on the Internet, according to Alexa, the Web Information Company. Although I'm not 100 percent certain of Wikipedia's accuracy 100 percent of the time, I feel likewise about almost any source—so I'm just about as comfortable as I can be with Wikipedia. And it's straightforward about challenging its users: one's critical-thinking skills are put into play with every word. Before the advent of the Internet, I think we'd gotten lazy about allowing our "experts" to have too much clout. Wikipedia and sites like it are helping challenge that complacency by encouraging contrarian thought processes and prodding us to be assertive enough to ask questions, both important aspects of the audacity quotient referenced above.

Intellectual Nomads

Once you appropriate the courage to be an amateur, the world opens up like a fan before you. You gain a subtle confidence, a certain swagger. You've made a big leap toward a more vigorous mind. Think of this: Albert Einstein wasn't working in academia when he discovered the theory of relativity. He was an outsider, an amateur. Another case in point: The literary critic Jacques Barzun is a man who possesses an amateur's delight in learning. He maintains abiding interests in opera, medicine, German civilization, science, humanities, detective fiction, Western history and civilization, education, etymology, classical music, modern art, psychiatry, baseball, history, French literature, language, ghost stories, cultural criticism . . . and on and on. Barzun's breadth of erudition is legendary. He takes genuine pleasure in learning—indeed he is the archetype of someone who holds steady the seemingly contradictory ideas of scholarly rigor and the unaffected enthusiasm of the amateur. However, Barzun is not strictly a darling of academics. According to a recent *New Yorker* article, he speaks most eloquently to fellow amateurs, such as doctors who play music and lawyers who read philosophy.

> ## NEURO NUGGET
>
> Recent recommendations made by a panel of experts reviewing a poll by the American Society on Aging stated that no "single activity, no matter how challenging, is sufficient to sustain the kind of mental acuity that virtually everyone can achieve." Using your brain to solve creative challenges is excellent practice and will help slow down the effects of aging. But we need to exercise all our mental muscles. Have you ever seen the guys in the gym with the buff upper bodies supported by little chicken legs? The same thing can happen in your brain. Just as you cross-train in your physical fitness routine (mixing cardio with strength training and flexibility) to get a balanced workout, you need to cross-train your mental fitness to exercise your brain through motor coordination, emotional understanding, memory, focus and attention, sensory processes, communication, language skills, and mental visualization.

Maverick Multidimensionality

The definition of audacity is divinely delectable: boldness or daring, especially with confident or arrogant disregard for conventional thought. Let's take a moment to absorb what sort of connotation hangs around the word. In speaking to large groups, I bring up the notion of *talent* as a counterpoint to audacity. Invariably, there's a shift in the barometric pressure within the room; this tells me I've hit a collective nerve. Pondering talent, my audience imagines artists with inborn aptitudes, businesspeople with a flair that seems innate, homemakers with instinctive faculties for warmly harboring family and friends. The crowd is especially keen on unpacking the distinction between talent and audacity, certain there is one. And they're right.

Audacity does not necessarily run parallel with talent. You can be a talented tuba player, but without some measure of audacity (promoting yourself,

> "Life well lived is the greatest art of
> all. The art of your life is not a matter
> of talent. It is a matter of mounting
> the courage to live."
>
> —Laurence G. Boldt, author

auditioning, performing publicly), you will keep the secret of your talent to yourself. The inverse is that you could be no more than a middling tuba player, but through self-promotion, fearless auditioning, and public performances, you could well become successful and acclaimed. The point is that talent alone does not propel one to the top. Audacity, mixed with a smidgen of talent, can.

Everybody knows at least one audacious person, and that person makes them vaguely uncomfortable, since that person's reality hints at truths they hate to believe exist: it's often the audacious person who succeeds wildly in life, instead of the more talented one. The audacious artist draws the attention of the media; the audacious businesswoman draws the attention of venture capitalists, as well as the attention of the media; the audacious multidisciplinarian draws the attention of everyone. Despite these truths, the talented colleague, lacking the courage to break out of his or her head space, believes that talent will triumph, and waits for the world to come a-callin'. But it seldom works that way.

Audacity has the power to confer fame, especially in our media-saturated world. Anyone who's audacious enough to persistently pitch his or her story to the media is in line for renown, name recognition, and the public's eye. And where attention goes, success often follows. There are quite possibly more talented amateur astronomers than Jay McNeil, but he had the nerve to insert himself into the professional league and report on the new star he found. Turns out *he* was the new star.

Now, I realize that most audacious multidisciplinarians aren't necessarily looking for the glare of the media spotlight. But don't insist on hiding your multiple aptitudes under a bushel basket. There's value to be had in letting others know what you're up to—you'll likely find pals and partners, and you'll help advance the cause of generalists in a world where we always get a bad rap. Take a stand, be audacious, and let your freak flag fly.

Renegades

There are so many worthy and stimulating issues competing for your time and attention that you practically need a spreadsheet to keep track of them. It requires a certain grit to stick to your kaizen, even as you're freewheeling all over creation. When someone wants to take a potshot at me and my work glorifying generalists, the critique is often, "You're all over the map." My reply? "Good! I intend to be. Thanks for noticing." It takes a certain backbone to look these close-minded types in the eye and do nothing . . . other than continue to pursue your course, of course.

In an episode of *The Simpsons* titled "Bye Bye Nerdie," Lisa discovers a pheromone produced by brainy kids, a pheromone that attracts bullies. She dubs her discovery "poindextrose" (Homer frequently refers to Bart's nerdy friend Milhouse as "Poindexter"). That's the risk your one-of-a-kind nature entails: you may well be misunderstood and even condemned. Most of us are afraid to be controversial, but the world belongs to the renegades, not to the conformists—it belongs to those of us who have the audacity to be amateurs. Remember, no one ever made an impact on the world without standing out from the crowd.

Reject Orthodoxy

One of literature's preeminent symbols of courage is the Cowardly Lion in *The Wizard of Oz*. The moral he imparts

> *"Life shrinks or expands in proportion to one's courage."*
>
> —Anaïs Nin (1903–1977), author

is that courage—the very attribute he was seeking—was his all along. Whatever we want exists already within each of us; we need only look for it in order to find it. This goes for the quest to build a vigorous mind. You already have the courage within you. Life is an all-you-can-eat buffet, and the irony is that it can take courage to partake of such an embarrassment of riches—especially as an amateur standing toe-to-toe with professionals. But it's ultimately a courageous act to claim the entire world as your bailiwick. Be audacious.

EXERCISES

Sometimes it takes courage to admit you need help. The following exercises offer you a hand in deciphering the role of courage in your Renaissance undertaking.

1. The Courage of Conviction

Take ten minutes to create a personal inventory of the most courageous things you've done in your life. You'll know they were acts of courage if you experienced anxiety followed by elation. Next, write for ten minutes in answer to these questions: How does courage generally show up in my life? How would my life be different if I were just one increment more courageous? Why do I believe so strongly about certain things? Is there anything I would die for?

2. The Power of an Example

Seek out an individual in your community whom you regard as exhibiting the courage of his or her convictions—perhaps a politician who has demonstrated political bravery by championing an unpopular cause or an activist who has persevered through untold trials to further his or her beliefs. Let this person know you're ruminating on the kind of courage required to stick with a conviction in the face of pressure. Do you agree with this person's approach? Would you conduct yourself in the same ways or not? Draft your thoughts into an essay and submit it for publication to an appropriate newspaper or magazine. By committing to your thoughts on the subject of courage, you'll experience a measure of courage yourself: you'll realize the distinction between simply "having" courage and declaring it publicly with a byline.

3. The Courage to Have No Endgame

Play the board game called The Game of Life: Twists & Turns. It's divided into Learn It, Live It, Love It, and Earn It. You decide how you'll spend your time—going to school, having kids, slumming around, traveling, whatever. There are numerous places to start the game, but there's no finish line or satisfying criteria for winning. In the same way that *Seinfeld* was a TV show "about nothing," this is a board game about aimlessness. The game's box shouts, "A thousand ways to live your life! You choose!" Interestingly, you earn as many points for scuba diving in the Great Barrier Reef or for donating a kidney to a loved one as for getting a Ph.D. The purpose of this exercise is to develop the courage to make decisive choices, even in the absence of a clear endgame.

PART THREE

We've now arrived at Part 3, the final section of our Vigorous Mind program. It's time to step back from the details provided by the seven preceding cross-training imperatives to position what we've learned in the context of life as it's actually lived. Part 3 therefore provides a big-picture point of view, specifically examining the issue of choice as it pertains to generalists.

Chapter 11 concerns itself with educational choice: formal learning versus self-education. Chapter 12 is about vocational choice, with this question at its center: how does a natural-born generalist forge a satisfying career in a world designed for specialists? Our concluding chapter covers the crucial choices we have the opportunity to make around happiness, and how to wisely maximize that oh-so-precious resource, our leisure time.

11

THE BEAUTY OF BEING
AN AUTODIDACT

I never let schooling get in the way of my education.

—*Mark Twain (1835–1910)*

At last it's time to take a big-picture look at being a big-picture generalist. Now that we've learned a little bit about each of the seven imperatives a cross-trainer will want to develop and hone, let's examine a few choices about how you might actually do so.

An autodidact (*auto* meaning *self*, *didact* meaning *taught*) is someone who's chosen to engage in learning without the benefit of a teacher or formal education. The familiar image of an autodidact has often been that of some lonely wonk who's thoroughly bereft of social skills, huddled over musty books in a library. The fact is, we should each be engaged in a personal, customized, lifelong, multidisciplinary, interdisciplinary, cross-disciplinary "doctorate program" of our own making. I am perfectly willing to stretch the definition of an autodidact (or *automath*, though what a strange word that is) to include anyone who's engaged in any personal growth program that's undertaken by choice and with a spirit of joy and curiosity—and maybe even with a song in one's heart, although that's perhaps asking a bit much even of

---

*"Every man who rises above
the common level has received two
educations: the first from his teachers;
the second, more personal and
important, from himself."*

—Edward Gibbon
(1737–1794), historian

---

saccharine. Sadly, this excludes a lot of formal degree programs in which the students trudge through joylessly, with the intent not to learn but to rustle up that sheepskin.

Multiple Modalities

For most of us, autodidacticism will be what we default to after we've had the benefit of years of formal education. You've got to graduate eventually, or at least leave school (notwithstanding the small but dedicated corps of professional aging students who seem to cleave to the bosom of many universities), but leaving the familiar and comforting embrace of school doesn't mean you should abandon your personal growth. In my opinion, the most fruitful years of learning should occur *after* you've split from formal schooling.

This book is about those autodidacts who are wide-ranging generalists in terms of their sphere of inclinations—whether this is by choice or by some inborn predisposition. Next time you meet another adult for the first time, try this: rather than automatically asking, "How are you?" instead ask, "What do you study?" Most people will likely think, "I don't study anything—thank goodness. I did all that in high school or college. I'm glad I don't have to study anymore." After a moment of sincere confusion, some people will fairly spit in disdain at the notion of studying anything. It's indeed tragic that *learning*, *study*, and *school* are considered derogatory words in the minds of so many people—though fortunately, not all.

I don't mean to suggest that all adults have let their brains go to seed. On the contrary, many are in fact returning to learning. According to Carol Aslanian, president of the Aslanian Group, an organization that studies adult student market trends, adult learners (25 years of age or older) make up more than 40 percent of undergraduate and graduate learners nationwide. Of course, these figures don't include millions more people engaged in noncredit programs or autodidacts learning via self-study. Other data indicates that more adult women than men are engaged in credit-based higher education and that regardless of age, adult's credit-based study is primarily work related. In my experience working with clients and from direct observation of others, it seems that the more education you have (at least based on degrees attained), the more you want—and what you want as you get older is typically learning via self-study.

"A lot of people are finding that they have more money, or the kids are older, and so they can do what they have always wanted to do," said Betsy Carter, editor in chief of *My Generation*, the AARP's magazine for baby boomers. According to the Hobby Industry Association, in 2001, the hobby business grew to $25.7 billion, an 11 percent increase over $23 billion in 2000. Predictably, it's the baby boomers—some 76 million strong and fairly affluent—who have fed that growth. Boomers have pursued their interests with the same enthusiasm and discipline they demonstrated with their careers and families. They take classes, buy the essential equipment, and even consecrate their most precious resource, time, to their leisure pursuits. In a recent survey by *My Generation*, 60 percent of boomers said it's important to them to be active and learn new things. Fifty-four-year-old massage therapist Kathy Jacobs takes weekly painting classes because, as she says, she wants to know everything about it—and immediately. In her words: "I wish I could know it all right now. Time is running out."

There's a misconception that the only way to achieve the status of "scholar" is to be affiliated with a university as a professor. That's simply not so. I am content to be a "scholar without portfolio," meaning a self-directed learner with no formal, ongoing ties to a university. Educator and author Parker Palmer serves as a true role model of a genuine scholar sans portfolio, because although he's chosen to work as a teacher, he's doing so without employment at any institution of higher learning. Palmer earned a Ph.D. in sociology from the University of California at Berkeley, and has written seven books and more than a hundred essays. He's also founded the Center for Courage & Renewal, which oversees the "Courage to Teach" program for K–12 educators across the country and parallel programs for people in other professions, including medicine, law, ministry, and philanthropy. Says Palmer: "Today I serve education from outside the institution . . . rather than from the inside, where I waste energy on anger instead of investing it in hope." I call that a brave and authentic choice.

It may be that you don't even realize you're a lifelong learner because, like so many others, you equate "learning" with what's taught in officially sanctioned schools. In other words, society has "schooled you up," to borrow a phrase from Ivan Illich. (Illich was a scathing social philosopher who wrote critiques of contemporary Western culture.) Historian Arnold Toynbee said that fostering intellectual independence should be the objective of education, that structured schooling should serve as a ladder to hoist children up from a passive learning role to the proper adult role of actively educating themselves. Educational activist John Taylor Gatto has been another pillar of self-learning and basher of normative education. Named New York City Teacher of the Year several times, he retired in despair in 1991, at which time he declared he that "no longer wanted to hurt kids to make a living," referring in part to the prevalence of mandated curricula and national testing. "There isn't a right way to become educated; there are as many ways as fingerprints," he wrote in a *Wall Street Journal* article at the time. "We don't need state-certified teachers to make education happen—that probably guarantees it won't." Gatto—not without his critics—has since gone on to become an articulate proponent of what he calls "unschooling," an educational model that abjures standard curricula and grading rubrics. Children learn instead through experiences and social interaction, reflecting Gatto's belief that mastering any particular body of knowledge is secondary to learning how to learn.

In any case, the future belongs to self-learners—people who see the value in learning, who want to learn, and who are willing to learn *how* to learn. Alas, the rigors of schooling have left many a scar, a point that was driven home recently when I was hired to do some communications consulting for a large corporation. I composed a raft of important memos concerning sweeping changes at the company, and duly communicated them to the workforce. Even as I carefully crafted the words, I knew in my heart that most of the messages would not even be read—let alone studied, carefully filed away, memorized, or otherwise absorbed. That kind of studious behavior is too reminiscent of school, that horrid experience that most people are grateful to find only in their rearview mirrors. During a meeting with corporate officials, I half-jokingly suggested we pull together a mild little quiz over the material in question, vital as it was to the success of the company. My cohorts were aghast that I would suggest "insulting" the employees in this way. In turn, I was aghast that we test our schoolchildren every day about material we deem important, yet allow equally important material to drift right past employees in the workforce, with no means of accountability required. I think the blame lies with the albatross of learning and schooling, whose sinister residuals haunt most of us to this day. Most of us, that is, except those who realize that the journey to adult freedom is one of self-learning.

"Why does the government regard sending citizens to school or even to college as so important that the opportunity should be furnished free by the state," asked historian James Flexner, apropos the fiscal crisis of New York City's famed Public Library, "and yet allow libraries to languish? Does education mean taking courses only? Surely self-education, once universally recognized as basic to the American spirit, remains basic to all learning."

> "[Formal] Education makes a straight-cut ditch of a free, meandering brook."
> —Henry David Thoreau (1817–1862)

Intellectual Confidence

Founded in 1980, The Learning Annex is considered the largest adult education company in North America, with a wide range of course offerings on topics as diverse as how to develop and write a winning business plan; how to write a book proposal that publishers can't refuse; how to talk to your cat; how to buy foreclosed property; making contact with lost loved ones; how to make it in comedy; Kabbalah dating; discovering your past lives; how to make your own soap; how to lower your golf score; and how to marry money. The esoteric collides with the obscure in other adult education programs, too, including courses titled Falconry School, How to Build an Airplane, Learning to Blacksmith, Simple Shoemaking, How to Create Welded Sculpture, and How to Make Teapots. The genius of The Learning Annex and similar educational programs is that they tap into the zeitgeist with portion-controlled, easily digestible one-session chunks. This approach has been derisively called "pedagogy in pellet form," but that makes me like it all the more—after all, pellets of pedagogy are the gist of this book. Another put-down-masquerading-as-quip I like is that The Learning Annex promotes "a CliffsNotes approach" to continuing education, otherwise known as "knowledge lite." I say, bring it on!

The Learning Annex also draws on our culture's endless fascination with celebrities. So mixed in with the earnest but low-profile instructors are high-profile celebrities such as Donald Trump, lecturing on money—naturally; hip-hop mogul Russell Simmons on hip-hopping to the top; and Jerry Lewis on laughter and healing. Furthermore, The Learning Annex doesn't even call classes . . . well, "classes." Instead, they're "shows," or "edutainment." That's the same approach I've taken when lecturing on cruise ships all over the world. We laugh, we learn, we dabble, we argue—then, of course, we eat.

Endeavors such as The Learning Annex are really a contemporary expression of a great American tradition. Self-betterment used to take place in lyceums, Chautauquas, and religious and political forums of all kinds. From Ben Franklin and Abraham Lincoln through Thomas Edison, Henry Ford, Eric Hoffer, and Malcolm X, people have lusted for *more*. Public libraries are certainly evidence of our thirst for knowledge, though these days the online world is where the action is. Book clubs are booming across the United States, another indication of our enduring hunger for intellectual nourishment. Several American cities have organized mass book-reading programs.

For instance, residents of Chicago and Seattle read *To Kill a Mockingbird*. Tim Swarens of the *Indianapolis Star* says the object is to promote "literacy and literature . . . to bring a city together by something other than sports. We'd like to see discussions of social issues breaking out at coffee shops and soccer fields."

Thomas Paine, Henry David Thoreau, and public intellectual Paul Goodman all exalted the free learner over the merely school taught, the perfunctory student who typically absorbs only the sanctioned curriculum. The savviest people these days are discovering themselves intellectually and using their minds for themselves—all free from the strictures of a diploma, a degree, parents, teachers, or jobs. Encouragingly, a trend is afoot that's moving Americans away from being nonintellectual (or worse yet, anti-intellectual), to becoming true autodidacts.

Live a High-Test Life

After universities were founded and after they became rigidly "academic," it was autodidacts such as Galileo who established "learned societies" outside of academia as a means of exploring new ideas and new ways of knowing. But truth be told, independent scholarship has always made those in academe a little nervous, and where misunderstanding exists, fear and loathing are usually not far behind.

It's simply a myth that serious scholarship can take place only in established, orthodox institutions, and that learning is the exclusive domain of the professoriat. We urgently need to hear the voice of the Socratic amateur—that individual who seeks to share and spread information and thought, as opposed to controlling or possessing knowledge. (Socrates did not consider himself to be a possessor of knowledge. All he'd concede was that he loved wisdom—which is what the word *philosopher* means.) The Socratic amateur isn't ashamed to be a novice or a generalist. He or she is comfortable tackling thorny problems without reducing them to schools of thought or convenient techniques.

> *"Formal education will make you a living; self-education will make you a fortune."*
>
> —Jim Rohn, entrepreneur and motivational speaker

The autodidactic idiom has been prominent throughout history. In just the twentieth century alone, for example, physicist and judo maven Moshe Feldenkrais (1904–1984) developed an autodidactic method of movement enhancement for dancers, musicians, and artists. John Boyd (1927–1997), a fighter pilot and military strategist, was an accomplished autodidact who not only revolutionized fighter aircraft design, but also developed new theories on learning and creativity. After his formal education, mythologist extraordinaire Joseph Campbell (1904–1987) came to exemplify the autodidactic method. Following completion of his master's degree, Campbell opted against a doctorate. Rather, he retreated to the woods in upstate New York and read deeply for five years. According to Campbell, this was where his real education took place—where he began to assemble his seminal views on the nature of life. Campbell felt the work he did during this phase was far more rigorous than any doctoral program could have been, and more fruitful in developing his perspectives.

To this day, it's been estimated that at least half of this nation's cache of intellectuals have exercised their choice to be independents—those who are dedicated to independent scholarship: Dwight Macdonald; Mary McCarthy; Norman Mailer; Susan Sontag; Willie Morris; John Gardner; even Pauline Kael, famed movie reviewer for *The New Yorker*. (Alex Trebek seems like he belongs on the list, too.)

Tangents and Tentacles

Alan Tough is an interesting man. He has a Ph.D., yet his research focuses to a large extent on autodidacticism. For forty years, Tough has been globally recognized as a pioneering scholar in adult learning. His work explains that adults expect the learning experience to mirror their feelings of autonomy and self-worth, and to acknowledge their life experience. He observed that most adult learning takes place outside of institutional frameworks, as we've seen, because it allows for a flexible time commitment and is available at low cost. Adult learners, Tough demonstrated, are much like the ideal "self-actualized" individual that today's humanistic psychologists hold out as the highest expression of living. The bottom line is that the supremely healthy individual is an avidly curious lifelong learner.

Let's meet a few autodidacts who would make Alan Tough proud. Consultant Mark Sanborn is a former president of the National Speakers Association and a committed devotee of self-improvement. "Leaders design their own continuing education program," he says on his website. "Almost all of our formal education was determined for us by someone else. We had little if any input into what we learned. In college, you may have had electives, but the choices were limited to the approved curriculum. As adults, we control the flow of our learning. We decide what we learn and how much. That means we need to design our own curriculum. Few people have any formal learning agenda."

Cornelius Hirschberg was a modestly successful New York salesman who wrote of the rich learning life he created for himself from the classics of Western literature. He said, "True liberal education can be achieved in the midst of the busiest adult life." Sitting on New York City subways, commuting to and from work for forty-five years, Hirschberg devoured history, language, math, philosophy, literature, astronomy, physics, and music. He estimated he had undertaken twenty thousand hours of serious reading during his working life—as much reading as required by five college degrees. "I am stuck in the city, that's all I have," he wrote. "I am stuck in business and routine and tedium. But I give up only as much as I must; for the rest I live my life at its best. . . . I shall know the keener people of the world, think the keener thoughts, and taste the keener pleasures as long as I can and as much as I can." As a way to document his experience, Hirschberg wrote a book called *The Priceless Gift* in 1960. It's currently out of print, but if you find a used copy somewhere, snap it up.

Eric Hoffer (circa 1902–1983) was a longshoreman turned writer. His parents were German immigrants, and by the age of five he could read in both German and English—although he did not attend school. When he was seven, his mother fell down a flight of stairs with Eric in her arms. He lost his sight; his mother lost her life. Inexplicably, his eyesight returned when he was fifteen years old. Fearing he'd again lose his sight, he dedicated himself to reading as much as he could for as long as his sight might hold out. His eyesight remained, but Hoffer never abandoned his habit of voracious reading. After his father died, the young Hoffer lived on skid row and worked as a migrant, following the harvests up and down the coast of California and, when possible, finagling library cards in nearby towns. Even after he found work as a longshoreman, he continued his concentrated reading, despite the often strenuous daily work of loading and unloading ships. He managed to read more books than many academics, and may well have been the best-read individual in modern times—as a self-educated man.

When Hoffer turned to writing, his work was hailed by both scholars and laymen. In a 1941 letter to Margaret Anderson, assistant to the editor of a magazine called *Common Ground*, Hoffer wrote: "My writing is done in railroad yards while waiting for a freight, in the fields while waiting for a truck." Termed a philosopher, Hoffer placed a high value on his independence from "the academy." He saw himself as one who was free to tell the truth without fear of patron, publisher, department head, or tenure committee. In avoiding the academic mainstream, he also managed to avoid the straitjacket of established thought. Hoffer's lack of a formal university education certainly contributed to his independent thought. With his ubiquitous cloth cap and dark green Filson jacket, pockets bristling with pens and notebooks, Hoffer was a true stylist. He went from homeless and uneducated indigent to notable and world-read philosopher—and recipient of the Presidential Medal of Freedom.

Hoffer's life affirms the primary axiom of independent scholarship, that mental power is far more pervasive in our society than we assume. "Every intellectual thinks that talent, that genius is a rare exception,"

"*Education is that which remains after one has forgotten everything he learned in school.*"

—Albert Einstein (1879–1955)

he said in his bestseller *The True Believer*. "It's not true. Talent and genius have been wasted on an enormous scale throughout our history." The life of the mind, as Eric Hoffer demonstrated so well, is available to everyone. All you have to do is make the choice.

The Art of Living

Academia is a place where silos are born, thrive, and multiply. The term *silo* is itself a metaphor borne of taxonomy, meaning not cylindrical barn-yard structures, but suggesting instead that each department on an organization chart stands alone, not interacting with others. Turf wars rage because turf exists to be defended. If you're a math professor, you don't want the archaeology department encroaching on your turf—it's threatening. If you're a literature professor, you don't want zoology stalking within your territory—they know nothing of what you teach. If you're an art appreciation instructor, you'd rather the music school not be dabbling in your bailiwick—it's an insult to your expertise. Granted, this sort of intrusion is unlikely to happen on purpose, since the silos of academia are so well established and ingrained. But the underlying truth is that all knowledge is ultimately interconnected.

Silos are artificial constructs. They exist because they serve a practical purpose: to organize the world so that the various subject areas can be manageably studied and taught. Unfortunately, the silos have come to be regarded as "real" in the minds of students, who may not yet have experienced the epiphany that the world is organized not in independent silos, but as interconnected webs, like Ariadne's labyrinth. For instance, history is a discipline that easily and obviously crosses over to other precincts. If you're studying World War II, how can science not come into play when you begin to talk about the atomic bomb? Literature is very much about human nature, which could be seen as impinging on the turf of psychology. Business-school classes routinely call on mathematics. Regretfully, however, this natural cross-pollination of knowledge is simply not the way we've been encouraged to think about education.

Stephen J. Gould, illustrious paleontologist, spoke on behalf of deconstructing silos because he suspected that the conceptual tools he craved might be located in another department's silo, just beyond his grasp. And he was right—he was able to achieve certain breakthroughs in paleontology only when he realized that the answers to evolution were sometimes found in the humanities department. By the way, for all his celebrated scholarship at Harvard, Gould was a friend of self-study. He urged a pal to pursue the history of science as an independent scholar, to make a pilgrimage to Darwin's home in England, and to buy antiquarian natural-history books in the shops near the British Museum. This friend, Richard Milner, eventually wrote *The Encyclopedia of Evolution* and is today a noted expert in the field.

Alan Watts (1915–1973) was another notable autodidact, best known for popularizing Asian philosophies for a Western audience. He often commented that his mission was to act as a bridge between the ancient and the modern, between East and West, and between culture and nature. Considered by some a bit of a loose cannon, he suggested the need "to go out of your mind in order to come to your senses." Since the publication of his first book, *The Spirit of Zen*, in 1936, Watts went on to write numerous books on higher consciousness, personal identity, and the nature of reality. But his interests were eclectic. He admired an enclave of Californians who fashioned a life of simple harmony around their devotion to architecture, gardening, and carpentry. Child rearing, education, law, and technology kept his mind occupied, but the finer things such as art and cuisine also beckoned to him. "Cultural renewal," he said, "comes about when highly differentiated cultures mix." Watts was popular with the American intelligentsia of the '50s and '60s, but less so with academics. Some professors sniffed that Watts was not a true scholar of Eastern philosophy, claiming he wasn't that disciplined. Alan Watts doesn't teach Eastern philosophy, they said; he teaches "Alan Watts." Watts replied, "The scholar who is interested in medals and prizes and not interested in the fun of it has amazing put-downs." Later, perhaps channeling Hunter Thompson, Watts dabbled in drug experimentation, commenting that his drug use was "like loading the Universe into a gun and firing it into your brain." He would later comment about drug use, "When you've got the message, hang up the phone."

Silo-Busters

The Gallatin School of Individualized Study is a highly unusual college within New York University that exists so undergrads and graduate students can create a multidisciplinary academic curriculum tailored to their own interests. Gallatin was created in response to the needs of a special kind of student—focused, self-disciplined, and creative. Some students were already accomplished professionals or brought with them broad life experiences, and the university recognized that they wanted to exercise more personal freedom in designing individual paths of study. You may want to pull threads from the Gallatin tapestry, as spelled out in its university bulletin: "Students design their own concentration, a program of inquiry organized around a particular theme, activity, period, or area of the world; then produce an Intellectual Autobiography." This autobiography describes the trajectory of students' interests and education and includes a plan for further study. It's also an opportunity for students to reflect on how they learn as individuals and to consider what they find academically worthwhile. They may select a particular area of concentration from among a number of organizing devices, including theme, geographic area, period, method, profession, event, person, multidisciplinary inquiry, or interdisciplinary study. These can serve as highly useful devices for vigorously minded autodidacts to use when tailoring their personal programs of inquiry.

Level the Learning Curve

People who have reached a crossroads in their life often go back to school with hopes of pursuing some noble goal—perhaps reasoning that a degree in interior design or landscape architecture from a well-respected local college is the key to launching a new and more fulfilling professional career. In fact, pursuing a program of self-directed independent study can often achieve the same objective. A little-acknowledged truth is that by returning to formal schooling, these well-intentioned people are often *avoiding* what they're really seeking. School becomes a virtuous smokescreen, a stall tactic. Yet a return to school appears so darn honorable and righteous—who could possibly speak against education, for heaven's sake? As a result, few people challenge anyone's resolve to pursue a degree. However, it might actually be a lot cheaper and more meaningful to get an internship or entry-level job in your desired field; find a mentor who will say, "Here are three things you need to know about this business . . ."; and then plunge in and start making the mistakes you're going to make anyway. No degree from any institution has yet to replace the school of hard knocks.

I can remember being moderately insecure about not having a master's of fine arts degree when I decided to pursue writing professionally. No formal training whatsoever! Likewise, I didn't have any broadcasting training prior to working in television and radio. It turns out that I was really not at any disadvantage. I have succeeded in every one of these fields as a "primitive." So being a generalist is a preemptive strike in favor of job security in a world where new technology can quickly make specialists obsolete. Do *not* let lack of audacity impede your opportunities.

Now, if your career plans include a desire to become a doctor, lawyer, or forensic anthropologist, you will certainly need to go back to school for a degree. But so many of the activities adults crave to learn about aren't offered in traditional accredited schools, anyway: knitting, feng shui, decoupage, orienteering, furniture building, painting, gymnastic tumbling, pinhole photography, professional organizing—the list goes on and on. So what are your choices if you want to pursue one of these areas? You either learn from someone else, enroll in informal classes, or engage in self-study. Indeed, the best education is an organic process that takes place between two individuals. Autodidacts see the world, ideally, as one large, free public library. We're all teachers; we're all learners.

My conclusion persists: we each must structure our own adult self-study program, customized to our tastes, needs, and crazy proclivities. I'm certainly pro-education, but ultimately, I advocate for autodidacticism. You end up self-taught anyway, because no matter what you study, you leave behind all kinds of tantalizing subjects on the buffet table. Most people who have been to college harbor a little regret that so many seductive courses in the catalog were off-limits to them, because they had to stay between the rails of the courses required for their major.

In any case, feel free to model the spirit of the following dandy programs for aspiring brain trainers:

- The University of Chicago offers a continuing education program called the Graham School of General Studies. Their master of liberal arts degree is a part-time master's degree program that offers courses in the humanities, social sciences, and natural sciences. Students hail from diverse career fields in business, industry, law, medicine, journalism, or the arts. But they all share a respect for liberal education.

- The Eugene Lang College at the New School for Liberal Arts in New York City is for "students who know that good writing, the natural sciences, new technologies, and civic life do not belong in separate boxes," according to the school's brochures. "The Lang curriculum is a coherent, collaborative, and innovative set of twelve broad areas of study ranging from writing and performing arts to environmental studies, urban studies, public history, and psychology."

- St. John's College, with campuses in Santa Fe, New Mexico, and Annapolis, Maryland, is a coeducational, four-year liberal arts college known for its distinctive "Great Books" curriculum. Students study the classics of literature, philosophy, theology, psychology, political science, economics, history, mathematics, laboratory sciences, and music. I occasionally get inspired to see if I can attract students to a continuing ed class centered on the Great Books; so far, no takers.

The Life of the Mind

Thomas Friedman, syndicated editorial writer for the *New York Times*, has said, "The more I cover foreign affairs, the more I wish I had studied education in college, because the more I travel, the more I find that the most heated debates in many countries are around education." He goes on to say, "Innovation is often a synthesis of art and science, and the best innovators often combine the two." Apple cofounder Steve Jobs, in his compelling Stanford commencement address, recalled how he dropped out of college but stuck around campus and took a calligraphy course, where he learned about the artistry of great typography. "None of this had even a hope of any practical application in my life," Jobs recalled. "But ten years later, when we were designing the first Macintosh computer, it all came back to me. It was the first computer with beautiful typography."

Cultural anthropologist, writer, and "lifehack" Dustin Wax says that most of the skills he's used to make a living are those he's acquired on his own: Web design, desktop publishing, marketing, personal productivity, even teaching. "And most of what I know about science, politics, computers, art, guitar playing, world history, writing, and a dozen other topics I've picked up outside of any formal education." He's not tooting his own horn, though, reminding us that "much of what [everybody] knows how to do they've picked up on their own."

Wax says that being curious (as we saw in Chapter 4) means being troubled by gaps in your understanding of the world. Not indifferent, but troubled. People who lack curiosity see learning new things as a chore rather than an adventure. Wax counsels patience in the same way I counsel kaizen: "There's no field of knowledge that someone in the world hasn't managed to learn, starting from exactly where you are now." On his lifehack.org website, he likewise encourages us to develop an affinity for connectedness (as we'll see Chapter 12). "A new body of knowledge is always easiest to learn if you can figure out the way it connects to what you already know. The more you look for and pay attention to the connections between different fields, the more readily your mind will be able to latch onto new concepts."

Another self-taught man, award-winning drummer and lyricist Neil Peart of the rock band Rush, was a high school dropout. Peart is noted for his complex and sophisticated song content, largely acquired through self-study and travel. He is also a prolific writer, with several published travelogues to his name. Over the years, he has become known for a unique writing style and a propensity for addressing diverse subject matter, including science fiction, fantasy, philosophy, humanitarianism, and libertarianism, including a predilection for the beliefs of objectivist philosopher Ayn Rand. However, "the extent of my influence by the writings of Ayn Rand should not be overstated," he said. "I am no one's disciple."

Musician Frank Zappa is noted for his exhortation, "Drop out of school before your mind rots from exposure to our mediocre educational system," he wrote on the liner notes of his 1965 album *Freak Out*. "Forget about the Senior Prom and go to the library and educate yourself if you've got any guts." Zappa may not have embodied the expected image of an autodidact, but he was clearly a vociferous critic of mainstream education. He is said to have pulled his four children out of school when they were fifteen and refused to pay for college educations for them.

Be Incessantly Insatiable

As the preceding role models would undoubtedly counsel, burrowing your way into a new topic is a matter of research, practice, networking, and scheduling.

Research. Is this too obvious? The most important step in learning something new is actually finding out about it. There are three phases of research. First, build a foundation of the basics. Surfing the Web with the aid of Google or checking out Wikipedia will net you a wealth of information on any topic in seconds. If you want, you can kick it up a notch and browse the work of experts, including researchers' blogs, dedicated websites and forums, magazines, and more.

Your next step is to hit the library. Find books that were referenced online, then scan nearby shelves for related titles that may interest you. Don't forget to consider children's books. I once needed a speedy overview of mythology, without viscous analysis or purple prose, and I found the children's section to be ideal.

Finally, consider building your own small-scale library of reference books. I cherish my reference books as friends, and I return to them again and again. While I'm reading library books, I assess the ones that might merit a permanent place on my bookshelf. Check online booksellers as well the brick-and-mortar variety, but don't overlook thrift stores, used bookstores, library book sales, and garage sales.

Practice. Don't lock your learning up in your head. If you don't share what you've learned with the world, nobody will ever appreciate how much you know about something—and *you* will never realize how much you still don't know.

Network. Social networks can include websites, listservs, e-mail lists—and of course actual human contact with colleagues and friends. These networks can deepen your knowledge in the area you've been learning about, as well as broaden your knowledge into areas where you never imagined you'd go. Networking also allows you to test your newly acquired knowledge against other people's understandings.

"The Wachowski brothers [filmmakers] are unique. Larry and Andy are probably two of the smartest people I know. Larry reads everything. One thing I learned through Larry, through Andy also, is that life is about research. Larry, he's constantly researching. And he's constantly reading. Life is about research."

—Jada Pinkett Smith, actress

Schedule. Can you say "kaizen"? Triumph in Twenty is the way, the truth, and the light. For anything more complex than a simple overview, you'll need to schedule time to commit to learning. Having the books on the shelf, the best websites bookmarked as "favorites," and a shoebox full of contact information does no good if you don't give yourself time to focus on reading, digesting, and implementing.

Smorgasbord Your Brain

It's a sad observation that most of us go through our lives having only the slightest acquaintance with our full range of capabilities. We allow itches to go unscratched. Why do some people make the choice to become autodidacts and others not? We may never know the answer. However, I can affirm this: don't leave it to chance. Take a systematic approach to self-learning, garnished with serendipitous asides. Perpetual learning is the optimal way to extract the best kind of satisfaction this world has to offer. Here are some ideas to get you started and keep you going.

Piggyback your media. Switch from books to movies and vice versa, or from television to the Internet and the reverse. You'll gain a deeper level of understanding of your topic when you explore it in each medium, and you'll gain a deeper understanding of each medium as well.

Start with a history of your topic. If you're not sure where to start in your quest to become an autodidact, begin by learning about the history of your topic. If you start with the history of nutrition, for instance, you'll pick up a sense of the many threads that make up the entire weave, and some will speak to you with a compelling voice. You'll learn about John Harvey Kellogg and his cereal sanitariums, and Horace Fletcher, known as "the Great Masticator," who advocated chewing each mouthful of food one hundred times . . . and on and on.

Always carry reading material. That way you're prepared to be productive when you're stuck in a long line or you have ten minutes between appointments. Use "page pointers" or sticky notes as markers to signify points in the text you want to refer to later—words to look up, references to other books to read, quotes you want to copy and keep.

Keep a "to-learn" list. As mentioned in Chapter 5, each year, create a list of topics you wish to explore that year. Maybe it's a new language; maybe it's an author whose books you intend to read; maybe it's a physical fitness program. If it motivates you, write it down. There is magic in writing things down. There's even more magic in taking action on those things, granted, but kaizen teaches us that we must start with the first small step and move forward from there.

Keep a "books I've read" list. This is your own personal bibliography. It's satisfying to look back and scan what you've read over the last few years. Practically speaking, it also helps to retrieve a book when you're trying to recall a memorable passage.

Find like-minded buddies. If you're taking up ice skating, judo, or portrait painting, cultivate friendships with people who also enjoy those activities. Their habits will rub off on you as you rub elbows with them.

Play against type. Read up on topics you're certain are not your cup of tea, or read the opposition's position on topics that are your cup of tea. We don't learn much from people we agree with.

Argue with authors. Albert Einstein once said, "Any man who reads too much and uses his own brain too little falls into lazy habits of thinking." Flip ideas on their head and examine their undersides. There's almost always merit in the converse.

Hire yourself as your own "lifelong learning manager." Maintain the same expectations of your performance at this "job" as you would if you were paying someone else to do it. Is this "employee" on the job regularly? Is he or she bearing down with stamina and creativity? Does he or she plan well? Execute well? Network with others? Does he or she meet deadlines?

Read—but don't *just* read. If you're interested in horticulture, read up on it, of course. But no one ever legitimately called themselves a horticulturist by just reading about it. Get your hands dirty. Buy some struggling plants at your local plant store and try nursing them back to health.

Teach. As we've seen, the best way to learn is to teach. Plus, you'll meet fellow wood-carvers, Thai cooks, and home remodelers that way.

———

"The man who doesn't read good books has no advantage over the man who can't."

—Mark Twain (1835–1910)

———

Recommit to kaizen. As an autodidact, never lose sight of the power of kaizen. You can get all the way to where you need to go by taking one step at a time. Small increments of consistent action will win the day. Whether you're learning how to cut hair, sing four-part harmony, or become a travel agent, tackling each endeavor bit by bit will end-run overwhelm and harness the forward force of momentum.

Call upon multiple mentors. Instead of choosing a single mentor to guide you in your cross-training efforts, derive the benefit of multiple mentors by conducting a Delphi survey. This is a survey method that uses structured group interaction, unfolding in "rounds" of questionnaires and feedback. After each round, a facilitator provides a summary of the participants' replies. You're next asked to reply to those replies, and possibly revise your earlier answers in light of others' answers. The replies tend to converge toward a synthesis.

Commit to being an autodidact. No one ever became an accomplished cross-trainer without having some intestinal fortitude. There may be few people in your life supporting your endeavor. But once you decide you want it, make it a priority.

EXERCISES

Set against the backdrop of a conscious choice, becoming an autodidact becomes doable for most people. Next, I want to help you implement that autodidactic intention, which is what we'll do in the next chapter with a look at systems thinking. But before we move on, let's gain a little hands-on mastery of self-study tactics with that favorite tool of everyone everywhere: lists.

1. Don't Be Listless

Magazines and websites occasionally publish lists of "Fifty Things Every Person Should Know" (or do, or be), and bestselling books such as *1,000 Places to See Before You Die* tickle our zealous natures. We immediately engage with the material—agreeing, disagreeing, crying out in indignant disbelief. Regardless, many of these admittedly arbitrary lists can be good thought starters for autodidacts. A. S. Byatt wrote on the *New York Times* website that she loves lists. She was defending the Modern Library's lists of the top one hundred books of the century (to which she had contributed), arguing that the public outcry over the partiality of the lists was, in fact, a squeal of pleasure. "All list makers enjoy the misery of indignation about the omitted essentials," she wrote. Lists, in her view, couldn't go wrong. Near the top of a list of things that she believed would define the third millennium, she put lists themselves. The following fanciful lists are irresistibly fun to laugh at and argue with—and just maybe you'll be motivated to scrap them and create your own.

The Vigorous Mind "Essential List"

A whimsical checklist of faux-essential things every vigorously minded cross-trainer needs to do before they pack it in. This list consists of specific cultural-based activities.

- ❑ Read *Goodnight Moon* to a child
- ❑ Read music and understand what an obbligato is
- ❑ Play the cello

- ❏ Dance without resorting to the white-boy shuffle
- ❏ Jump-start a car
- ❏ Read beyond the bestseller list
- ❏ Understand Southern Gothic
- ❏ Finish a half-marathon
- ❏ Know a useful smattering of French, Spanish, Italian, German, and Latin
- ❏ Know how to parallel park
- ❏ Think kaizen is underrated
- ❏ Have informed preferences about fast-food hamburgers; revere slow food
- ❏ Solve quadratic equations and polynomials
- ❏ Know how to spell "miniature" and "occasionally"
- ❏ Make Thai soup
- ❏ Call a plumber when necessary
- ❏ Have a vegetable garden *and* a flower garden
- ❏ Build a cabin in the woods
- ❏ Eschew wine
- ❏ Iron a dress shirt
- ❏ Drive a big rig
- ❏ Hold the attention of a classroom full of twenty-somethings
- ❏ Hold the attention of a classroom full of over-twenty-plus-somethings
- ❏ Write serious haiku
- ❏ Have good sales resistance
- ❏ Play the banjo
- ❏ Make guacamole so good you faint
- ❏ Hang a set of pictures on the wall with mathematical precision (and without losing temper)
- ❏ Drive a stick shift
- ❏ Watch TV
- ❏ Like orienteering
- ❏ Know what *post hoc ergo propter hoc* means
- ❏ Know how to back up a trailer
- ❏ Understand how a circuit breaker works

❑ Make room in your quiver for the subjunctive tense
❑ Abstain from taking photos on vacation just for the sake of taking photos
❑ Know what a subordinate clause is
❑ Respect pumpernickel bread
❑ Feel nostalgic for the debate team
❑ Fearlessly eat dairy products
❑ Own a farm table
❑ Own stationery and use it
❑ Know who Harold McGee is and why he matters
❑ Know the value of shoulder pads
❑ Change a tire
❑ Become unhinged by heartbreak
❑ Build a campfire

2. Back to the Past

Select three items from the following list, which represents the things that every proper Renaissance man should be able to do, circa 1400. Pursue them until the point you're thoroughly grateful you don't live in the year 1400.

The Vigorous Mind "Renaissance Man Essentials" List, Circa 1400

Every "Renaissance" Renaissance man should be able to:

❑ Defend himself with a variety of weapons, especially the sword
❑ Play several musical instruments
❑ Paint and create other works of art
❑ Maintain interest in advancing knowledge and science
❑ Engage in debates regarding issues such as philosophy and ethics
❑ Present himself as a skilled author and poet

3. Back to the Future

Moving back into our present century, the following list is provided for you in case you're not already thoroughly swamped with areas of interest around which to build your vigorous mind cross-training program. Choose at least ten items that immediately appeal to you. Write in your own entries as well, since no list of this kind could ever be comprehensive. Think of this as a loose compendium of a continuing education catalog the way it would appear in an autodidact's mind.

The Vigorous Mind "Contemporary List"

- ❏ Candle making
- ❏ Playing bongos
- ❏ Learning Portuguese
- ❏ Studying hieroglyphics
- ❏ Flying an airplane
- ❏ Theater set-building
- ❏ Reading mythology
- ❏ Studying South Pacific sea turtles
- ❏ Journaling
- ❏ Reupholstering furniture
- ❏ Growing orchids
- ❏ Weaving baskets
- ❏ Making Thai cuisine
- ❏ Dancing the tango
- ❏ Studying ballet
- ❏ Volunteering in a hospice
- ❏ Entering the Pillsbury bake-off
- ❏ Traveling to Turkey
- ❏ Writing a novel
- ❏ Creating a blog
- ❏ Attending tennis camp
- ❏ Practicing tai chi
- ❏ Appreciating classical music
- ❏ Exploring astronomy
- ❏ Studying philosophy
- ❏ Learning about ecology
- ❏ Studying economics
- ❏ Exploring religion or spirituality
- ❏ Fishing
- ❏ Practicing outdoor survival skills
- ❏ Hiking
- ❏ Race car driving
- ❏ Dog grooming
- ❏ Jewelry making
- ❏ Day trading
- ❏ Trading in real estate
- ❏ Mountain climbing
- ❏ Scrapbooking
- ❏ Learning puppetry
- ❏ Boating
- ❏ Restoring antique cars
- ❏ Learning origami
- ❏ Waterskiing
- ❏ Practicing Reiki
- ❏ Palm reading
- ❏ Flamenco dancing
- ❏ Snow skiing
- ❏ Sandcastle building
- ❏ Plumbing
- ❏ Learning Pig Latin
- ❏ Studying ichthyology (fish)

❏ Belly dancing
❏ Repairing cars
❏ Learning sign language
❏ Playing blackjack
❏ Playing the harmonica
❏ Square dancing
❏ Rock climbing
❏ Fur-skin sewing
❏ Lathing
❏ Stone carving
❏ Gift wrapping
❏ Singing the blues
❏ Fundraising
❏ Boat building
❏ Cake decorating
❏ Playing the banjo
❏ Practicing espionage
❏ Learning self-hypnosis
❏ Fly fishing
❏ Gardening
❏ Stamp collecting
❏ Glassblowing
❏ Beekeeping
❏ Animal tracking
❏ Orienteering
❏ Exploring aromatherapy
❏ Bread making
❏ Clogging
❏ Mushroom hunting

❏ Doing massage
❏ Quilting
❏ Learning archery
❏ Kayaking
❏ Scuba diving
❏ Skeet shooting
❏ Playing billiards
❏ Juggling
❏ Golfing
❏ Yodeling
❏ Studying ethics
❏ Making sushi
❏ Joining a wildlife rescue group
❏ Making custom lampshades
❏ Vocabulary building
❏ Learning about the Civil War
❏ Knitting
❏ Tap dancing
❏ Swizzle stick collecting
❏ Taking singing lessons
❏ Flower arranging
❏ Salsa dancing
❏ Trapeze swinging
❏ Taking French lessons
❏ Learning photography
❏ Running
❏ Joining Habitat for Humanity
❏ Studying Latin

Again, use these lists as grist for both fun and further thought. Remember, my take on cross-training contains no designated curriculum per se. You choose its specific content in terms of what pursuits speak most strongly to you.

12

SYSTEMS THINKING: THRIVING AS A GENERALIST IN THE WORKPLACE

In too many corporate contexts, managers and
executives operate with what can be called an utterly
inappropriate "need-to-know" principle, sharing with employees
only what they are convinced those people absolutely
must know to be able to do their jobs. In truth,
the more knowledge we have, the better.

—*Tom Morris, author, from* If Aristotle Ran General Motors

Maybe you're wondering about the practical value of a being a generalist in today's specialist world. How does all this play out where the rubber meets the road—the job market? How best can you capitalize economically on this extraordinary state of affairs—being a generalist? What kinds of vocational choices present themselves?

A Bigger Lens

Entelechy is a Greek word referring to the dynamic purpose that drives us toward realizing our essential self—that "certain something" that reveals to us our higher destiny and directs us toward self-fulfillment. It is the condition of a thing whose essence is fully realized. It is the entelechy of an acorn to be an oak tree, just as it is the entelechy of some human beings to be well-rounded generalists, strivers, reachers, and graspers. With entelechy's lessons in mind, I believe that the most fundamental vocational question is not "What job should I apply for?" but rather the more elemental and difficult "Who am I? What is my nature?" This cuts right to the chase of the question of whether you are a generalist or a specialist by nature. Regardless, our deepest calling is to grow into our own authentic selfhood. Theologian Frederick Buechner says vocation is the place where your deep gladness meets the world's deep need. If your deep gladness is born in undying curiosity, find a way to make a living that honors that life-giving impulse.

Renaissance people are not experts, granted, but in their most evolved incarnation they are "systems thinkers"—big-picture visionary types who work with a wide-angle lens. Systems thinkers have the ability to identify and integrate vitally important interconnections between topics. Systems thinking, also referred to as "holism," has historically been the primary way of viewing the world; today, the pendulum has swung so far in the direction of specialization that we are, I believe, at the vanguard of a corrective trend back toward holism. Surely you've heard of holistic medicine, which refers to the notion that our bodies are made up of interconnected systems; thus, what affects one part of the body also affects all the others. Holistic medicine advances a systems model, where multiple biological, psychological, and social factors are seen as interlinked. This is similar to Ayurvedic medicine, the ancient Indian healing system. Ayurvedic medicine takes into account the connections among body, mind, and soul, with the goal of physical, mental, social, and spiritual harmony.

Systems theory was founded on principles swiped from physics, engineering, and biology. In terms of human evolution, I like to speculate that genetic mutations and the subsequent survival of the fittest is what led to some people to be born generalists and others specialists. Margaret Mead was an influential figure in systems theory—rather ironically, since she is known as a specialist in anthropology. It might be said that she's an example of some-one who specialized in the generalist side of things.

Perhaps a kindred spirit of Mead's is Orit Gadiesh, whom we met in Chapter 2. In Frans Johansson's book *The Medici Effect*, Gadiesh has this to say about systems thinking: "You have to be willing to 'waste time' on things that are not directly relevant to your work because you are curious. But then you are able to, sometimes unconsciously, integrate them back into your work." That is precisely what we have seen demonstrated by the neuro-chemistry of the human brain—how it conspires in just that integration, to remarkable effect. As the world splinters off into ever more spindly special-ties, the people who will thrive in the future will be the ones who can per-ceive the interconnections between all those blinkered, skinny little slices of life.

Systemically Vigorous

Systems thinkers are always keenly attuned to interconnections, tangents, spin-offs, trade-offs, consequences. Cross-trainers are natural systems thinkers—that's our personal passion, as well as our most salient practical value to the grinding engine of the world's commerce. Again, I feel com-pelled to reiterate that the world needs macro-view thinkers as much as it needs micro-view thinkers. The trick is for everybody to identify their own way of being, and then make their particular contribution with gusto, verve, and tenacity. It's practically a sure bet that you make your living as some type of specialist—though if you're lucky enough to have a position that requires you to be a generalist or systems thinker, more power to you. However, I strongly believe specialists should consciously make a point of incorporating tenets of systems thinking into their professional (and personal) lives. That's what this chapter is about.

Aristotle proclaimed, "The whole is more than the sum of its parts." It might be said that specialists are reductionists, and generalists are holists. Ide-ally, you can wear both hats. Think of a Venn diagram, with generalism and specialism represented by two overlapping circles. The area of overlap is the fertile, desirable turf of peak-performing contemporary Renaissance people; it stands for the integration of the best of the specialist world with the best of the generalist world. Another visual representation might be the yin/yang symbol in which the two ways of being are almost intertwined, each curling a tentacle into the other's turf. Holism and reductionism are completely complementary, as are generalists and specialists. This book recognizes that while our modern economy compels most of us to be reductionists, a career-long diet of reductionism can result in mental starvation. That's why engaging in some holistic activities will surely make you a more adept reductionist, as well as a better big-picture thinker and a more well-rounded person.

Voltaire Voltage

Remember Grace Duffy, our motorcycle enthusiast from Chapter 3? Duffy is a sui generis vigorous thinker, a Renaissance woman, and a business consultant cut from a cloth of her own weave. In particular, she's dedicated to quality and process improvement and, as such, she's earned a Six Sigma master black belt. Six Sigma is an industrial methodology that seeks to improve business and manufacturing processes by eliminating defects. And by now it should come as no surprise that one strategy of Six Sigma is kaizen, that stalwart handmaiden of human potential.

Duffy and I sat down over coffee to talk about the fine art of becoming a desultory dilettante. She's a diversely accomplished woman, but rather than calling herself a Renaissance woman, she prefers "Voltaire," in homage to one of the early scientists who was said to know everything. "Machiavelli, too," she says, referring to the Florentine statesman and political philosopher now most famous for his book *The Prince*. In addition to his political theories, by the way, Machiavelli was also a poet, musician, and playwright. The term *Machiavellian* is these days generally considered pejorative, but the judgment against him ignores much of his legacy.)

Duffy grew up in Princeton, New Jersey, as one of six siblings. "My friends were children of university professors," she says. "Instead of playing softball at recess, we'd memorize George Bernard Shaw or talk about Latin Club. I grew up in an intellectual environment." She went on to earn degrees in anthropology and business. A former executive with IBM, Duffy is also a lifelong member of Mensa, the oldest and most famous high-IQ society in the world. We spoke at length about how Renaissance people chart their own course through life, spinning their voracious interests into a highly satisfying web. Here's how she does it:

> *"Be steady and well ordered in your life so that you can be fierce and original in your work."*
>
> —Gustave Flaubert
> (1821–1880), author

I love to read. I subscribe to newsletters on business, human relations, education, training, economics, logistics, management, and quality. Often the subjects in these mailings overlap, which is fascinating. I stay active in three professional societies because, again, there's an incredible overlap in their disciplines. I keep in touch with archaeology and anthropology to understand beginnings, cultural influences, and behavioral patterns. I keep in touch with several theological approaches because they have strong impacts on social relationships.

I agree with your concept of a self-customized, personal Ph.D. This "graduate study" truly takes hold, though, only when the individual has enough self-confidence to accept that we can control our journey. Until we know we can chart our own path, we don't really learn, retain, or use our experiences effectively. Mentors are useful there, to help develop our self-confidence from the inside out.

I am not a specialist. I like the big picture. Given new information, I may find that something I've stuck in one category in my brain needs to be moved around. I move things around all the time. I look at situations and behaviors and look for new patterns. That's what analysis is.

When I was young I was very good in school. I could parrot back all kinds of details. It was only as I got older and more experienced that I was able to combine disparate bits of detail into threads that eventually became systems. All is connected in some way. What I learn in business I should be able to apply in my social relationships. What I learned as an anthropologist strongly supports my efforts in organizational change. Transfer of training is a critical skill. What works in one situation should be modifiable into other situations. The trick is to assess the current situation accurately enough to see a parallel from previous experience. Other terms for that trick are wisdom and experience.

The Vocational Landscape of Your Brain

"Make your work to be in keeping with your purpose."

—Leonardo da Vinci (1452–1519)

The choice of a vocation is often particularly fraught for those of the generalist persuasion. There is so much commotion and anxiety around vocational choice—as well there should be—that I thought I might ventilate the topic a bit by presenting it against a scrim of systems thinking. The choice of a life's work is arguably more agonizing for those of us who go broad and not deep. So many choices, so little time. Quite possibly the most dominant expression of your entire self, I believe, is the immensely ramifying choice of vocation. How you spend the majority of your work time is how you spend the majority of your life, and what could have more repercussions than that? Your vocational footprint will likely accrue as a significant facet of your legacy.

"Far and away the best prize that life offers is the chance to work hard at work worth doing."

—Theodore Roosevelt (1858–1919)

Thoreau cautioned to beware of any enterprise that requires new clothes—or new degrees, I might add. The average person changes careers five to ten times in a lifetime, but that doesn't necessarily require five or ten different degrees. Listen to your inner voice and take what Francis Crick, the codiscoverer of DNA, called the gossip test: What you are really interested in is what you gossip about. Can you make that into a profession?

I work with many clients who feel a disconnect between who they really are and what they're doing to earn a living. They hope to alter their professional lives to be more in accord with the increasingly satisfying and well-rounded personal lives they're fashioning. Frequently, they tell me they want their work to consist of helping others along their paths, and that they want to spend their time dealing with life's more exalted concerns. And of course, at the same time, they feel restless and anxious because there's so much in this throbbing world they haven't had the opportunity to explore. This often leads into a protracted discussion about the realities of forsaking a career as a specialist and somehow forging meaningful work as a cobbled-together generalist. Pursuing a career as a specialist means choosing that specialty very, very carefully—not just falling into it accidentally, as so many people do. The trick is to find your true path, your North Star. It's so very easy to become someone you don't intend to be, just by passively letting life sweep you along.

"Most people go to their grave with their music still in them."

—Benjamin Disraeli (1804–1881), British prime minister and author

"Your work is to discover your work and then with all your heart to give yourself to it."

—Buddha

Are you promoting yourself with sufficient panache? You may wonder what self-promotion has to do with upping your cross-training ante: fair question. I maintain that it's incumbent on us jack-of-all-traders to have our finger on capitalism's marketing pulse to a greater extent than our brethren in the specialist camp, because we already start with one strike against us. The world defaults to preferring specialists—quite often with good reason. Still, it puts us behind the eight ball. We need to convincingly communicate the sometimes difficult-to-grasp value we bring to any professional endeavor, the unique point of view we provide. We need to get articulate and passionate about who we are, rather than *apologizing* for who we are. We possess advantages that our cousins in the next cube would love to have, yet often we ourselves haven't even embraced them. We need to introduce ourselves and promote our wide-ranging skills to people who are in a position to help and appreciate us. In short, we need to "sell" the advantages of being big-picture thinkers. Otherwise, the world will continue to pigeonhole "professional amateurs" as scattered, flakey, spread too thin, and not knowledgeable enough about any slice of the business to be trusted with managing it. Sure, as devilishly interesting people, we'll be invited to parties where the order of business is sparkling conversation, current events, witty bon mots, and Trivial Pursuit board games. But unless we ramp up our efforts to promote ourselves, we run the risk of being admired rather than hired.

"Work is more fun than fun."

—Nöel Coward (1899–1973),
actor and playwright

Do the Right Thing

Business consultant Tom Pearson was "allowed" to be a math and physics major in college, even though he played on the football team—a radical combination in an era when football players were expected to be physical education majors. Pearson's college experiences on the football field worked to his advantage when he was up against engineering specialists in his first job as a government scientist—he'd learned about competition, being a team player, and the importance of a broad, systems-oriented perspective. For instance, Pearson tells me that a great deal of modern cancer or AIDS research is not so much about inventing new formulations as it is about "discovering unusual new substances on the underside of a leaf in the rain forest and investigating their properties." He continues, "[The generalist] scans it all, recognizes the threats and opportunities, and delegates it to a specialist. Left to their own devices, specialists are so focused on their specialty that they never see that seemingly unrelated phenomena may contain the critical clues."

Someone once said this about the difference between a generalist and a specialist: When a specialist finds himself off-point, he immediately drops it. The generalist, when finding himself off-point, says, "Wow, this is interesting." and looks for bridges back to his topic. Pearson has another take on the distinction. "Specialists are critical to 'doing it right,' while generalists ensure that we 'do the right things.'"

Stir the Pot

At some ad agencies, architectural firms, and design houses, management underwrites the expense for creative staffers to attend plays and movies, and even to travel. Other perks might include subscriptions to magazines that, on the surface, have nothing whatsoever to do with advertising, architecture, or design. Creativity is the coin of the realm in these businesses, so they need to keep their employees continually stimulated with fresh ideas; to stir the pot in which inchoate thoughts simmer and stew; to restock their mental pond with imaginative fodder, so they don't fish that pond dry. It's likely that some idea adapted from the world of architecture could result in a new clothing design; that an inspiration borne from reading *National Geographic* ultimately results in a successful advertising campaign; that some weighty tidbit gleaned from the play *Spamalot*, unlikely as it seems, makes its way to the business world. These surprising connections are more apt to occur to a systems thinker who's made the choice to consider input from a multitude of diverse, and especially nonintuitive, sources.

For instance, someone's job in the cosmetics industry is to conjure up the often bizarrely creative names of nail polishes and lip colors. A few to consider: Hot for Chocolate, Fuchsia Fever, Craving Coral, Gold Get Me. According to Revlon president Rory Gevis, "The most creative names are when you are having a cup of coffee, when you leave the everyday environment and go and do something. That's where the inspiration comes from."

Inventors are typically highly inspirational systems thinkers, since they generally possess an ability to take innovations that already exist and combine them in new and revolutionary ways. They see connections where others do not or cannot, building upon component parts that are already available to create something wholly original. A perfect example is the acknowledged inventor of television, Philo Farnsworth, who combined existing technologies to create the first television set. (Later, there were others who challenged Farnsworth's claim as television's inventor.) Only an individual with a systems-thinking perspective could have envisioned the interconnections that ultimately made TV a reality.

It's the unique ability to make these types of connections that is so relevant to generalists in the workplace. Cartoonist Gary Larson borrowed from the Bible when he drew a comic strip of Moses as a kid, dramatically parting the milk in his glass. Velcro was the product of analogical thinking when its inventor went out hiking and came back with burs stuck to his pants. What we now know as the printing press had its humble beginnings as a hybrid of a wine press and a coin-stamping machine. The inventor of Pringles potato chips drew his inspiration from the way wet leaves stacked tightly together. And one final example: the Xerox machine was invented when a fellow named Chester Carlson realized that if the image of an original photograph or document were projected onto a photoconductive surface, current would flow only in the areas upon which that light hit. Carlson, being a physicist, had that flash of inspiration that all inventors covet. That's the peak experience of systems thinking—insight strikes, and two distinct ideas metamorphose into one brilliant new one. Of course, as all inventors know, inspiration doesn't make for an invention. It takes one blinding moment of inspiration to conceive of the solution, but a lifetime to make it work and then get it to market. Still, we can all appreciate the fact that none of these technologies would have been possible without the benefit of systems thinking—that voodoo that cross-trainers do so well.

NEURO NUGGET

What's happening in the brain at that moment when two ideas fuse together to become a new idea? Scientists are unsure—this is new turf. Yet Stanford University's Robert Sapolsky, Ph.D. was willing to speculate. "On a wildly simplistic level, each idea maps, in some way, on a circuit of neurons that are interconnected (in both the sense of synapses and their strength, and in a statistical sense of activating as a unit). The two networks overlap to some degree (i.e., make use of some of the same neurons), and the fusing is when some sort of plasticity/facilitation occurs that strengthens that intersection enough so that activating one of the networks gets you the other as well." Sapolsky is the author of *Why Zebras Don't Get Ulcers*, and any simplistic speculation from his impressive brain is well worth considering.

Playground of the Mind

New Yorker editor David Remnick compares America, memorably, to a big syringe of heroin—the everythingness of American life, he called it. If you're audacious enough to defy modern economic dictates and be a generalist in your professional life—embracing as much of that fertile "everythingness" as you possibly can—my half dozen career suggestions follow. All these occupations are great for calling upon all your brain's capabilities, sometimes called your *wetware*. Not that other jobs don't, or couldn't, but these are my personal Top Jobs for Generalists, Polymaths, Versatilists, Desultorians, and Dilettantes:

Architect: I have a theory that a high preponderance of architects are well-rounded *Uomos Universales*. Architecture is unusual in how distinctly it calls upon both right and left brains: the rational and the poetic. Architecture produces art that functions; in fact, architecture has been called "frozen music." Once you've drawn a solid blueprint, then built a secure foundation that will support the weight of the building, then erected beams and joists and sub-floors, you can move on to flourishes and frills such as moldings, wall coverings, and mosaics. Form and function, soldered together. Architecture has an undeniable romance to it, and is my Path Not Taken.

Writer/Editor: Working as a general-assignment reporter, journalist, writer, or editor is an ideal occupation for a generalist since you're required to delve, short-term, into virtually any topic that presents itself. Spit-spot, then on to the next. For a few days or weeks you're immersed in crime, or fashion, or politics. Writing, essentially the art of thinking, blends especially well with science, which makes science writing the whole enchilada. That combination allows the writer to pull from both major spheres of knowledge. Take, for example, science writer Natalie Angier. She's working her whole brain while writing: the artistic side (the act of writing itself) and the science side (the content of her writing). Actually, though, the niftiest analogy for the way I understand writing is architecture. Both involve the creation of an underlying structure and organization. Once that's honored, you're free to move on to beauty and style if you like. Vocational tests have consistently indicated that I should've been an architect. As a writer, I feel like I am.

Also, writing supports a do-it-all worldview because the old silos separating fiction and nonfiction have broken down almost completely. Writers aren't necessarily the specialists they may once have been, back when they were more or less pigeonholed as either novelists or nonfiction writers. Regardless, working as a writer allows for a wondrous alchemy, since writing, on good days anyway, permits you to transform the dross of your life into gold. And the vigorous-minded generate lots of life experiences to mine.

Musician: I think of music and architecture as practically equivalent, since both involve science-based rationalism (consider the mathematical precision of rhythm) and then emotionalism/beauty/soul/the ineffable layered on top of that math. We saw in Chapter 4 that scientists often spend time musically.

Chef: A career as a chef is also situated at that delicious crossroads of art and science. If you can cook, you are poised between aesthetics and nutrition; hospitality and commerce. If you want your life to be one giant tasting menu, and who wouldn't, cooking is the bomb.

Librarian: In our content-glutted world, to be trained in how to access information is practically as powerful as already knowing the information. Reference librarians these days serve as skilled information retrievers, staying on top of technology and trends. Librarians are also adept at critical thinking, as they must constantly evaluate information sources for legitimacy.

Teacher: Teaching is an epic way to spend your professional life, especially if you have generalist tendencies. Yes, the academy is organized in silos, but that doesn't mean a teacher can't draw the interconnections that exist between those silos. You may be a teacher of the French language, but the history of France, the sociology of the French citizenry, the psychology of Europeans, and everything else is sitting right there in that classroom with you, begging to be set free.

One teacher praised the classroom for allowing her to express herself. "I find it hard to connect with people in life," she explains. "The structure of teaching provides a safe space for me to feel deeply intimate with others, and for our hearts to touch." Writer and educator Parker Palmer says that, "In fact, I could have done no other [than teach]. Teacher is my native way of being in the world." That makes me think of a finance professor I had in college. He was musing that he could make much more money on Wall Street. But what he said next has stayed with me to this day. "Even if I were on Wall Street, I'd still be professing," he said. "Professing is what I do. I profess. So I might as well teach."

The Whole Toolkit

At some point after a particularly invigorating session of photography, running, or bonsai—whatever—ask yourself what about those pursuits really blows your skirt up. Be specific, not general. And try to include how the activity makes you feel. Identify at least three micro-level characteristics that jazz you up when it comes to hieroglyphics, set-building, or antiquing. Those three things—feelings, actually—need to form the basis of whatever you do for a living. Let's try an example. Amy, who's working as a standardized test-grader until she finds higher ground, happens to love mushroom hunting. It's a passion, and sometimes she loses all track of time while 'shrooming. (That means she's likely in that coveted state of flow. This is a huge sign that the universe is trying to get her attention. Something really instructive and wondrous is happening when flow's happening.) Now, Amy has never given much thought to why she loves hunting for mushrooms. After all, it's not like she could become a full-time professional mushroom hunter as her livelihood. Actually, I would advise her to not be so dismissive of that notion. Someone, somewhere, is doing it. But she doesn't want to go that route. So, the key is to extract from mushroom hunting three feelings it elicits in her. After some thought, she says (1) she loves the thrill of a chase, (2) she's okay with long odds, (3) she likes being self-directed. Next, I ask her to think about what jobs might exist that correlate with that same set of criteria occupations that push those same buttons. She thinks about that for some time, and comes back with firefighter, librarian, and postal carrier. Ultimately, she chooses librarian and is working in a major urban library system as she contemplates returning to school for a library science degree. All the things she loves about her favorite pastime are now part of her professional sphere.

> *"I have been trying to think of the earth as a kind of organism, but it is too big, too complex, with too many working parts lacking visible connections. If not like an organism, what is it most like? Then, it came to me: it is most like a cell."*
>
> —Lewis Thomas, author, from *The Lives of a Cell*

Mind Your Metaphors

Systems thinkers are generally skilled at thinking metaphorically. We've all been soaked in years of formal education where we were rewarded for making rational, linear, and literal connections between things. By contrast, metaphor produces a synthesis—often an unexpected, even radical synthesis. Metaphorical thinking is a substitutional mental process by which disparate ideas or entities are compared. Metaphors connect, analogize, evoke. Metaphors are creativity made manifest. Human beings are metaphor machines; our brains are built to seek out interconnectedness, to sense analogies that are hidden from evident perception—although it helps to be somewhat poetic to really do this well. Examples of some simple but powerful metaphors: A car is a horseless carriage. Coffee is liquid energy. Architecture is frozen music.

Panoramic Perception

The advantage of being multidisciplinary is the ability to eventually become *inter*disciplinary. Here's what I mean: First you undertake a Vigorous Mind regimen to cross-train your brain across multiple realms. That's the multidisciplinary part. Before long, you acquire the perspective of a systems thinker, as you begin to notice the interconnectedness of what you're learning. That's the interdisciplinary part. The knack for perceiving interconnections is characteristic of a fully fit brain. This often manifests itself in the use of metaphors and analogies, which are simply linguistic representations of connections between things. In fact, the brain is a metaphor machine, working as a powerful sorter to compare new info to what it already has stored.

Harvard linguist Steven Pinker calls metaphor a "linguistic superhero." Metaphor is how we transform ways of thinking from the realm of concrete actions—like pouring water or throwing rocks or closing a jammed drawer. "But we can leach the content from them and use them to reason about other domains," he tells *Discover* magazine. "When we put together the power of metaphor with the combinatorial nature of language and thought, we become able to create a virtually infinite number of ideas. I believe metaphor is the mechanism that the mind uses to understand otherwise inaccessible abstract concepts. It may be how the mind evolved the ability to reason about chess or politics, which are not really concrete or physical and have no obvious relevance to reproduction and physical survival." Pinker concludes: "Metaphorical insights, the seeing of resemblances and connections, have given rise to countless innovations in science, the arts, and many other fields of endeavor."

But metaphors can lead to paradoxes. Both devices are false statements in a literal sense, but are nevertheless true on a more abstract level. A paradox can be described as a statement in which opposites do not negate each other. Also referred to as "confusion endurance," a paradox is a willingness to embrace ambiguity and uncertainty; it's considered the most distinctive trait of both highly creative and well-adjusted people. For instance, consider the tension that lies within these pairs: joy/sorrow, intimacy/independence, strength/weakness, good/evil, life/death, generalist/specialist. We must embrace both halves of each pair, using their dynamic tension as fuel for our strength, creativity, and personal growth.

Paradox rouses that acutely uncomfortable state called "cognitive dissonance," in which you're unsure what to think because both sides of an argument are equally valid. You will naturally experience discomfort whenever you're faced with two or more contradictory bits of knowledge about yourself or your environment. The choices people make are inherently dramatic because of the potential for cognitive dissonance—that is, for self-doubt. All of us, and most particularly those of us with vigorous minds, must learn to inhabit this uncomfortable space, to embrace the paradox. F. Scott Fitzgerald wrote in *The Crack-Up*, "The test of a first-rate intelligence is the ability to hold two opposed ideas in the mind at the same time, and still retain the ability to function. One should, for example, be able to see that things are hopeless and yet be determined to make them otherwise."

Anyone who seeks to cut a wide swath through this world is inevitably going to run into discrepancies, ambiguities, and inconsistencies. The benefit of embracing paradox is to foster habits of mind that are fluid, flexible, and rangy as opposed to reductionist, literal, and Manichean. Once you become accustomed to recognizing the discrepancies, tolerating the inconsistencies, and embracing the ambiguities, you're much more likely to relax and stop thundering at the absurdity of the world. You're able to get on with your cross-training rather than railing at the parts that don't fit, don't make sense, don't add up. Paradoxes are a good place to invoke wabi-sabi, respecting imperfection and incompleteness.

> *"There are two kinds of truth:*
> *Small truth and great truth.*
> *You can recognize a small truth*
> *because its opposite is a falsehood.*
> *The opposite of a great truth*
> *is another great truth."*
>
> —Niels Bohr (1885–1962),
> Nobel Prize–winning physicist

The most vigorously minded cross-trainers are able to hold many of these opposing ideas in their minds at the same time and still function at a high level. As if that's not challenge enough, I'd like to see you accomplish another paradox: to be both a generalist/ systems thinker and, at the same time, a specialist in the professional field of your choice. In this complex, demanding era, Renaissance people are in the best position to not just "endure" the tension of opposites, but to thrive in an atmosphere of uncertainty, paradox, and ambiguity.

The Italians call this tolerance of ambiguity *sfumato*, which is a metaphoric term borrowed from the art world. It refers to the blurring or softening of sharp outlines in painting by subtle and gradual blending of one tone into another. The classic example is the smokiness around the eyes of the *Mona Lisa*, rendering her expression maddeningly enigmatic. You can't know what she's thinking behind those inscrutable eyes. Ultimately, you may conclude she's both happy and sad, both scheming and docile, both chaste and world-weary. That's the power of art: to convey the sort of complexity that represents the way people really are, and the way life really is. It's true. If we are to live our lives fully, we must choose to embrace our own personal opposites, to live in the creative tension between our generalist tendencies and our specialist realities.

I have heard it said that heroism can be defined for our age as the ability to tolerate paradox and to embrace seemingly opposing forces without rejecting one or the other just for the sheer relief of it. It's about understanding that life is the game played between two paradoxical goalposts: winning is good, and so is losing; freedom is good, as is authority—and the same goes for having and giving, action and passivity, income and outgo, courage and fear, the wide view and the deep view. One doesn't cancel out the other; both are true. As Gregg Levoy writes in *Callings*, these pairs "may sit on opposite sides of the table, but beneath it their legs are entwined."

NEURO NUGGET

Cognitive scientists say that the brain doesn't process information literally. It scans everything through its existing database—the experiences we've had up until that moment. Visual data is interpreted into images; auditory data into sound, music, and language; and experiences into memory. This process renders an otherwise overwhelming, bewildering flood of daily experiences easier to process and recall.

Oops! The Law of Unintended Consequences

As you embark on your kaizen-inspired journey, I urge you to always keep an eye on the big picture. You don't want to make a dramatic change in one area of your life that's going to adversely affect some other aspect of your life. A narrow, purely specialist mind-set—or a failure of imagination, if you will—may render you unable to envision the potential negative consequences of your good intentions. Here's an example: what if, in your excitement to hone your newly acquired skills on the drums, you fail to grasp that you're irritating your spouse and infuriating your neighbors by drumming at all hours? It's highly unlikely that much good will come of that situation. That's the law of unintended consequences (LUC) in a nutshell. Every action you take has repercussions, planned and unplanned, foreseen and unforeseen, intended and unintended, positive and negative. Everything's connected. That's one of the major themes of this book.

Consider these real-life scenarios, taken right out of history: In the 1920s, Prohibition drove many small-time alcohol suppliers out of business and secured the hold of large-scale organized crime over the illegal alcohol industry. Sixty years later, the "War on Drugs," which originated in order to vanquish the illegal drug trade, drove many small-time drug dealers out of business and consolidated the hold of organized drug cartels over the illegal drug industry. That's LUC in action. Other examples include:

- The introduction of low-fat food led to Americans becoming even more obese (People tend to overeat when a food is labeled low-fat, and the fat is often replaced with refined carbohydrates that are potentially more conducive to weight gain than the fat was. Dang!).

- Bringing rabbits into Australia for the sport of hunting them led to an explosive growth in the rabbit population. Today, rabbits are a major feral pest in that country.

- The attempt to censor or remove a certain piece of information instead causes the information in question to become widely known and distributed in a very short time. The fact that a piece of information is restricted assigns to it a previously nonexistent value in the public eye.

- In an attempt to address the problem of congested roads, a city council recommends building more traffic lanes or a bypass. More often than not, that simply attracts more traffic, resulting in the same gridlock as before.

- The stiffening of penalties for driving while intoxicated in the United States in the 1980s led, at first, to an increase in hit-and-run accidents—most of which were believed to have been drunken drivers trying to escape the law.

- Concerned about the increasing number of head injuries suffered by cyclists, Australia made wearing helmets mandatory. The expected reduction in head injuries occurred, but only because fewer people cycled, since wearing a bicycle helmet was not considered to be fashionable.

- Attempts by governments to reduce rent by introducing rent control has led to unfortunate housing shortages, a reduction in housing quality, and even to the creation of slums.

- It has happened, in microbiology, that the elimination of one pesky, disease-causing microbe spawns the evolution of another, more dangerous, microorganism.

- Digital video recorders were initially marketed as a convenient way for us to time-shift our television viewing. But the unintended consequence (and big attraction) has become the ability to skip over all the advertisements.

Whether you're a specialist by birth or by choice, you will likely discover all manner of unintended consequences resulting from your actions (although probably not quite as dreadful and dramatic as those that grew out of Prohibition or the War on Drugs).

Specialists/reductionists, by definition, don't have a systems view; they don't see the whole as they are busily examining its parts. Albert Einstein was indisputably interested in the narrow-view physics of his laboratory environment; the unintended consequence of that singular focus was, of course, the atomic bomb. As Tom Pearson told me, "When your focus is an inch wide and a mile deep, like Einstein, the winds of war in Europe are not on your radar screen. When your marvelous invention gets turned into a bomb, you're surprised and chagrined. The generalist who has the wide-view model, he's not looking for a *detail* in his system but looks for *changes* in his system. A specialist looks at a baseball game and says, 'This hitter is struggling.' If you look at the big picture, you know that all hitters go through down cycles.

The specialist has a very narrow focus and he doesn't notice significant changes outside his narrow area of focus."

Ironically, it was Einstein who said, "The problems that exist in the world today cannot be solved by the same level of thinking that created them." At some level, Einstein must have understood that the world needs systems thinkers to complement its wealth of specialists. Interestingly, Einstein also acknowledged that "imagination is more important than knowledge." And that takes us right back to our discussion about maintaining that big-picture perspective.

All that being said, it's important to note that no one's immune to the law of unintended consequences—not even systems thinkers/generalists. Says Pearson, "Generalists may be so attuned to the big picture that we may miss opportunities." For example, a physician may be so caught up in the big-picture issue of national healthcare reform that she misses a fundamental, crucial diagnosis of strep throat in a patient—with potentially calamitous results. But, on the plus side of the ledger, generalists are more adaptable, according to Pearson: "We're less prone to obsolescence, because a specialty goes obsolete." If you were an expert in transistor radio technology (or eight-track cassettes, or typewriters, or buggy whips—the list is long), you would have backed yourself into a corner as that technology became obsolete.

Accordingly, Pearson says he sometimes refers to his role as that of a "systematic observer of systems"—essentially, he looks at business systems and observes how they're behaving. He adds, "You have to do that in order to anticipate possible unintended consequences."

"I dwell in possibility."

—Emily Dickinson
(1830–1886), poet

This is not to say that unintended consequences are always negative. Indeed, the entire thesis of this book might be described as how to reap the unexpected benefits of systems thinking. If you take up oil painting in your nonwork hours, that endeavor will actually make you more capable at your day job as a property manager. Strange as it may seem, if you study a little anthropology on the side, you will be better suited to your profession as manager of an art gallery. Clearly, these are positive, secondary benefits of pursuing a chosen course of action. Here are a few other serendipitous instances:

- The medieval custom of setting up large hunting reserves for use by the nobility has preserved green space, often as parks, throughout England and other areas of Europe.

- The wartime practice of sinking ships in shallow waters has created numerous artificial coral reefs. Fish don't seem to mind taking refuge in warships that were disposed of in a not terribly environmentally correct way.

- In medicine, most drugs have unintended consequences associated with their use, which are generally known as side effects. Many are harmful and are more precisely called "adverse effects." However, some are beneficial—for instance, aspirin, a pain reliever, can also thin the blood and help prevent heart attacks. The existence of beneficial side effects leads to off-label use—use of a drug for a nonintended purpose.

All Systems Are Go

Let's give Winston Churchill his due as a systems thinker. His stature as a cross-trainer is certainly secure. At the time of his death, an editorial in the *Halifax Chronicle-Herald* eulogized, "We cannot think of Winston Churchill today just in terms of the soldier, the statesman, the parliamentarian, author, orator, artist, and wit. He was all these, and more. He was a Renaissance man, a Leonardo da Vinci of our times, a man larger than the normal, mortal run." Churchill was an epic personality—not just an epic person—who redefined the breadth of the term *Renaissance man*. He was touchingly human, with emotions and desires and faults, some on an Olympian scale. Speaking on British television, Harold Macmillan, a former prime minister of Great Britain, said of Churchill, "His obstinacy was exhausting." But the flip side of the coin was Churchill's "undefeatable determination." Macmillan touched on another aspect of Sir Winston's character: "his puckish sense of humor, his tremendous sense of fun, his quick alternation between grave and gay." Churchill was self-conscious about the inadequacies of his education, and eager to repair the deficits. He set himself upon a self-study program that included history, literature, science, and politics. And it worked.

Connect the Dots

Perhaps the most valuable characteristic of a generalist is the ceaseless drive to connect the dots in an effort to link disparate subjects together. Such cross-disciplinary and cross-cultural cross-pollination is key to moving from incremental innovation to transcendent ideation. In *The Medici Effect*, author Frans Johansson discusses how ideas mixed, crossed, blended, collided with, or seduced by completely different and seemingly irrelevant inspirations are producing some of our era's best cuisines, timeliest medical discoveries, liveliest cities, and most interesting music. Generalists leverage specialist insight to manufacture creative innovation. This is how you end-run a dead end and blaze new paths of potentiality.

> *"The only factory asset we have is human imagination."*
>
> —Bill Gates

Cross-Training as Social Responsibility

Ecologists tend to be generalists, because ecology is a field built on the premise that events do not occur in isolation. A recent story written by Michael Pollan in the *New York Times Magazine* quotes Kentucky farmer and writer Wendell Berry, who observes that the root of all problems of industrial civilization is specialization, which Berry regards as "the disease of the modern character." Pollan:

Our society assigns us a tiny number of roles: we're producers (of one thing) at work, consumers of a great many other things the rest of the time. Virtually all of our needs and desires we delegate to specialists of one kind or another—our meals to agribusiness, health to the doctor, education to the teacher, entertainment to the media, care for the environment to the environmentalist, political action to the politician. As Adam Smith and many others have pointed out, this division of labor has given us many of the blessings of civilization. Specialization is what allows me to sit at the computer thinking about climate change. Yet this same division of labor obscures the lines of connection—and responsibility—linking our everyday acts to their real-world consequences, making it easy for me to overlook the coal-fired power plant that is lighting my screen, or the mountaintop in Kentucky that had to be destroyed to provide the coal to that plant, or the streams running crimson with heavy metals as a result.

Catalytic Intelligence

As systems thinkers, cross-trainers crave choice, creativity, invention, newly minted metaphors, and even thorny paradoxes, because employing these concepts involves more brainpower than a straightforward description or approach. Vigorously minded individuals are all about creative-thinking techniques, not only because the methodologies are cognitively challenging, but also because they're so appealingly catalytic. And *catalytic intelligence* is what we're after. As natural-born skimmers and scanners, generalists want to understand who Machiavelli was and why he's relevant today. We want to understand the role of vitamin D in human health. We want to understand how screenwriting mirrors human nature. But we're not content to stop at that basic level of understanding. We're determined to take it to the next level—to forge connections

> "The meaning of life is: creative love. Loving creativity. Not love as an inner feeling, as a private sentimental emotion, but love as a dynamic power moving out into the world and doing something original."
>
> —Tom Morris, author and philosopher

between Machiavelli, vitamin D, and screenwriting. Doing so may require metaphor; it may not be self-evident; it may require brainstorming; it may yield bewildering paradoxes. But this level of mental engagement is what enables cross-trainers to really catch the slipstream—where they're able to find hidden interconnections between disparate things. That's originality.

To help you develop a propensity for systems thinking, consider some of these ideas:

Another right answer. When thinking, we tend to seize up cognitively, quashing our inborn creativity. Certain beliefs we hold dear tend to create obstacles to creative thinking, according to Roger von Oech on his website Creative Think. Here are some of these stale beliefs we habitually get hung up on:

There is one right answer.

To err is wrong.

Don't be foolish.

Avoid ambiguity.

That's not my area.

Ask yourself if you're subconsciously subscribing to any of these enemies of systems thinking. Then apply Von Oech's mantra: "Look for the Second Right Answer." By doing this, he says, we open our minds to go beyond what's worked in the past to search out unusual contexts that could result in fresh options for the future.

Brainstorming. Brainstorming is by now such a familiar and ingrained technique, we tend to take it for granted and downplay its astonishing power. Recommit to it with fresh eyes. Whenever you suspect your thinking has become narrow or hackneyed, list (either alone or preferably in a group) whatever unexpected thoughts, crazy inspirations, or outlandish solutions pop into your mind when you need to solve a problem or will a creative outcome. The idea is to be completely uncensored. You'll know you've achieved that when your list contains thoughts that run the gamut from the mundane to the preposterous. No judgment allowed while the list is being compiled; you'll cull it later.

Attribute exam. When you need to catalyze your thinking patterns, try an old screenwriters' trick. Screenwriters understand that if you modify just one variable involved in a situation, it can shake things up enough to create a fresh new scenario. For example, the plot of a TV show is composed of a set of attributes (everyone will define these attributes differently; that's okay). Attributes will likely be characters, settings, conflicts, plot, theme, music, dialogue, resolution, and so on. The idea is to tease apart those attributes in order to perceive their interplay and connection with each other. After you've examined and evaluated each attribute, chose just one of them to modify. That seemingly small change has the capacity to turn the entire show on its ear—a desirable thing when you're needing to produce a fresh new TV show every week. Plots for the *Lone Ranger* radio and TV shows were concocted for two decades by modifying attributes that included characters, goals, obstacles, and outcomes. This same technique can help you perceive your own situation with fresh eyes. Tweak just one attribute in your life and watch how that stirs up new energy.

> "*To know one thing, you must know the opposite.*"
>
> —Henry Moore (1898–1986), sculptor

Question stimulus. Check out the modestly famous "73 Idea-Spurring Questions" composed by writer and creativity pioneer Alex Osborn (1888–1966), founder of a creativity institute (and the originator of brainstorming, by the way). His idea checklist encourages fresh combinations, reuses, and rearrangements of existing material. When considering how to re-create something, think about how it can be repurposed, modified, magnified, minified, rearranged, or combined with other objects or ideas. As one example, consider how you might invigorate your cross-training by applying these sample questions from the list:

- Put to other uses? New ways to use as is? Other uses if modified?

- Modify? New twist? Change meaning, color, motion, sound, form? Other changes?

- Magnify? What to add? Exaggerate? Extra value? Duplicate? Multiply?

- Minify? What to subtract? Condensed? Miniature? Lighter? Split up? Understate?

- Rearrange? Interchange components? Other sequence? Change schedule?

- Combine? How about a blend, an assortment? Combine units? Combine purposes?

One client of mine who underwent this process realized that her cross-training efforts could be adapted for training modules in her work as a curriculum-design specialist. Another decided to conduct his cross-training in silence as a sort of silent meditation. Another repurposed kaizen to devote eight-hour stretches of time to learning to knit intricate sweaters and blankets. By undergoing this thinking process—even if you never implement any of your new ideas—you have expanded your abilities as a systems thinker, simply because you've dredged up creative new connections between existing ideas.

The Value of Impracticality

You may be able to sense how the systems thinker in any organization is subject to derision for being pie-in-the-sky impractical. A dreamer! Head in the clouds! Not able or perhaps not willing to deal with day-to-day problems—which is the domain where most employees spend the bulk of their energies, not to mention their careers. If you're inclined to be a systems thinker and you're part of an organization that doesn't encourage systems thinking, you will likely be facing an uphill battle for acceptance and upward

> *"There is always an enormous*
> *temptation in all of life to diddle*
> *around making itsy-bitsy friends and*
> *meals and journeys for itsy-bitsy*
> *years on end. I won't have it.*
> *The world is wilder than that in all*
> *directions, more dangerous and bitter,*
> *more extravagant and bright.*
> *We are making hay when we should*
> *be making whoopee; we are raising*
> *tomatoes when we should be*
> *raising Cain or Lazarus."*
>
> —Annie Dillard, author, from
> *Pilgrim at Tinker Creek*

mobility. It's important to remember that you are always at choice. Options for you fall into three neat categories: depart and find another employer who values your style of thinking; stay put and apply your systems-thinking approach elsewhere in your life; or stay put and persuade leadership of your worth, perhaps asking for reassignment to a role where your contributions can be capitalized upon. For instance, director of research and development is a coveted position for those who've developed a knack for systems thinking; that's often where you'll find an organization's free-thinkers and thought tinkerers.

So a gestalt is what systems thinking ultimately represents: a unified whole that turns out to be more than a rote sum of its parts. I think this was what the writer and Trappist monk Thomas Merton meant when he titled one of his poems "With the World in my Bloodstream." The great Lewis Carroll had a go at it too, with his memorable verse:

"The time has come," the Walrus said,

"To talk of many things:

Of shoes—and ships—and sealing-wax—

Of cabbages—and kings. . . ."

EXERCISES

Systems thinking is one of the more accessible habits of a healthy mind. You can acquire a feel for it by linking it to kaizen: take ten or twenty minutes two or three times a week to mindfully apply it to your cross-training.

1. Metaphor Machine

Don't be passive and simply wait for metaphors or other kinds of analogous connections to present themselves. To really "vigor it up," this kind of systems thinking can be made conscious by strategically and deliberately querying yourself:

What else is like this?

What have others done?

Where can I find an idea?

What ideas can I modify to fit my problem?

How can I make this product better?

Note that you can ask yourself these questions in just about any context: a problem at work, a personal issue, kaizen, an aspect of your cross-training.

2. Poetic Justice

Write a poem that brings together things, events, histories, or people who ordinarily do not come into contact. Explore these, see where the confrontations are, and look for the connections and agreements. Poetry is one venue where this kind of cross-pollinating synthesis is celebrated and encouraged. This exercise will help you cobble together sometimes-radical juxtapositions that can lead to new ways of seeing interconnections between things that you've never before linked.

3. If a Tree Falls in the Woods . . .

How can you live, happily and productively, with the following paradox: We must bring a part of the future into each day; this is how we achieve our goals. Yet—and this is the paradox—we must also live fully and completely in the present, in the Zen sense of not living our lives regretting the past and fretting over the future. Are you able to reconcile the paradox? Is it meaningful to even try? If not, why not? In your own professional and personal life, how are you currently negotiating the tension between living in the present, learning from the past, and planning for the future? If you modified one variable in that mix, how would it restructure the whole?

4. No Good Deed Goes Unpunished

Cogitate on the most recent time you encountered the law of unintended consequences. Was the unintended consequence beneficial? Or did it turn out to be unfortunate? Or might the result have been the opposite of what you hoped would happen? Could more sophisticated systems thinking have helped you avoid the negative results or achieve more useful positive results?

13

THE OMNIBUS OMNIVORE

Develop an interest in life as you see it;
in people, things, literature, music—the world is so rich,
simply throbbing with rich treasures, beautiful souls
and interesting people. Forget yourself.

—*Henry Miller (1891–1980), author*

This book has been a valentine to the liberal arts and a love song to the power of kaizen. Consonant with each of those ideas are the continual choices we all make, choices that often involve our leisure time and that are selected (if even subconsciously) to inspire happiness.

The premise of *The Vigorous Mind* is the call to cultivate the diverse abilities and intelligences you already have; to capitalize on your capable, capacious brain; to improve your fulfillment quotient by stoking that brain with a global range of intellectual possibilities; to create cognitive crescendo; and to bestow upon yourself a perfectly fictitious master's degree in liberal arts. But why stop there? Grant yourself a soi-disant Ph.D. in multidisciplinary studies. For years I've called this quest "The Fine Art of Becoming a Renaissance Person." And it requires choices.

This fine art requires choosing many of the same strategies that the fine art of aging calls into play. The trick to healthy aging is to choose more, not less—cognitively and physically. You can't cultivate a fully vigorous mind in a fully unvigorous body. Physical activity is vitally important to the life of the mind. Apart from improving overall health, exercise promotes neurogenesis—quite literally, remaking the brain. More than even mental gymnastics (for instance, doing crossword puzzles), physical exercise confers protective effects—especially the kind of physical exertion that involves a mental challenge, which is the surest way to coax the brain into releasing a combination of dopamine (which stimulates the pleasure center in the brain) and cortisol (which offsets stress). And although the exact mechanism of these effects is unknown, the implication is clear: exercise protects the brain from stress. Feeling depressed? Exercise. Feeling stressed? Exercise. Feeling great? Exercise. Feeling nothing? Exercise.

Be Experientially Promiscuous

Those who study happiness often describe it as a choice. Happiness is generally a byproduct of discovering what you're meant to do in life and doing it. Since happiness acts more like a verb than a noun, it involves making the choice to engage with the world in a deliberate way. I'm interpreting it like this: I believe people are suffering from mental malnutrition, due largely to a non–intellectually stimulating job and the quotidian grind of adult life. We're *slouching toward entropy*. My recommendation is a return to the quaint notion of the well-rounded person who engages in autotelic self-development.

Aristotle concluded that, more than anything else, men and women seek happiness—more than health, beauty, money, power, romance, or jeans that fit. Those things are valued only because we expect they'll make us happy. What would really satisfy us, though, is not getting slim or rich, but simply feeling better about our lives. But we don't understand happiness and, regrettably, have made no progress in attaining it. Many people feel that their lives

have been wasted, that instead of being
filled with happiness, their years have
been spent in anxiety and boredom.

    Happiness is not something that hap-
pens. It is not the result of good fortune
or random chance. It does not depend
on outside events, but rather on how we
choose to interpret events. Happiness is a
condition that must be prepared for, cul-

> *"With all its sham, drudgery and broken dreams, it is still a beautiful world. Be cheerful. Strive to be happy."*
>
> —Max Ehrmann (1872–1945), lawyer, manufacturer of overalls, and author, from his famous poem "Desiderata"

tivated, and defended privately by each person. People who learn to control
inner experience will be able to determine the quality of their lives, which is
as close as any of us can come to being happy. It is by being fully involved
with every detail of our lives, good and bad, that we encounter happiness, not
by trying to look for it directly. Happiness cannot be pursued, said Viktor
Frankl, the Austrian psychologist who wrote *Man's Search for Meaning*. It is
the unintended side effect of one's personal dedication to a course greater
than oneself. We attain this wonderful side effect by achieving control over
the contents of our consciousness.

    The Declaration of Independence contains the ringing phrase "pursuit of
happiness." Most of us assume we understand what that means, but I believe
our founding fathers did not refer to happiness in the same way we regard it
today. They weren't referring to freedom from struggle or the right to non-
stop bliss. What they meant was freedom to pursue the life of the mind, not
so much the "life of the weekend."

    Someone once said that creating an adult life is a continuous act of will.
Quite unlike some other human emotions (think rage, or joy), satisfaction
doesn't just fall in your lap. You have to manufacture it for yourself, and
doing so requires a certain audacity. In truth, you have to risk fear in order
to gain satisfaction. Until recently, most researchers assumed that some
variation of the pleasure principle governed human motivation. It was Sig-
mund Freud (no, not Janet Jackson) who made popular the phrase "pleasure
principle," but the idea that life consists of the pursuit of pleasure and the

avoidance of pain goes back at least two thousand years. It is a seductive theory, to be sure: we do what brings us joy; we avoid what brings us pain. But the theory is incomplete and overly simplistic. Clearly it's true that human beings avoid certain types of pain (for most of us, physical and psychic) and are drawn to certain types of pleasure. But we're also willing to endure certain types of pain (the discomfort of childbirth, the agony of physical training) and can resist certain types of pleasure (dessert, sometimes) in the name of future reward (winning the Tour de France). The difference is our will, our motivation—our choice.

Higher-Quality Happiness

It is a strange, perplexing irony that the more leisure time you have, the less you do with it. It's a sad thing to realize at the end of another weekend that you really didn't "do" anything, despite being "so very busy." Such is a conundrum of modern life.

As we've seen, people are happiest when they are in flow—that state of utmost concentration or absorption in the activity at hand. You might think this happens all the time, but it doesn't. Usually, our concentration is fractionated by clock-watching; physical discomfort, such as hunger; or the day's temporal worries. However, nearly everyone has experienced flow at some point—a feeling of freedom, deep enjoyment, fulfillment, and mastery. Here's the telltale sign that you've experienced a state of flow: did your usual distractions (time of day, what's for lunch, negative self-talk, what did Fred in Accounting mean by that look he gave me, and so forth) seem to drop away? To forget yourself for a while is a blessing, a burdensome load lifted. Most of us walk around in a state of full-time, mildly agonizing self-absorption. Here's the good news: as a versatilist, you have made a choice to maximize the number of opportunities to experience the much-desired state of flow. If you have no other motivation, the pursuit of flow is enough to justify embarking on a quest to cross-train your brain.

Optimal experiences don't typically occur during occasions when you're passive, receptive, or relaxed. That's not to say that those times can't be enjoyable. But the high points of our lives often occur when we've chosen to undertake a struggle. Optimal experience is thus something we *make* happen. It's a choice. This is as close to happiness as anything we can fathom. And doesn't it sound like what we're up to in this book? A few classic examples of flow-inducing activities: making music, participating in sports, dancing, playing chess, reading, writing, art. Mihaly Csikszentmihalyi, the psychology professor best known as the architect of flow, said the secret to a happy life is to learn to generate flow from as many things as possible—again, in complete accord with the life-structure of a well-rounded person.

As you select a palette of pursuits to embark upon, keep the notion of optimal frustration in mind. To achieve flow, a balance must be struck between the challenge of the task and your level of skill. If the task is too easy, we become bored. If it's too difficult, we become anxious. But if it's just right, flow will sneak in through that window. The small incremental steps involved in kaizen dovetail well with the precepts of flow. You can sidle into a state of flow step by step; it's seldom a full plunge. "The very best moments in people's lives usually occur when a person's body or mind is stretched to its limits in a voluntary effort to accomplish something difficult and worthwhile," Csikszentmihalyi writes in his book *Flow*. What's fascinating is that such experiences are *not necessarily pleasant at the time they occur*. "The swimmer's muscles might have ached during his most memorable race, his lungs might have felt like exploding, and he might have been dizzy with fatigue—yet these could have been the best moments of his life."

_____

"You will never be the person you can be if pressure, tension, and discipline are taken out of your life."

—James G. Bilkey,
motivational quote-meister

_____

NEURO NUGGET

Flow builds brainpower. Scientists have found that pleasure is a key ingredient in building smarts. We learn far more from mental exercises when we enjoy them. Likewise, Csikszentmihalyi found that our minds grow in complexity—literally create new neural circuits—the longer we remain in flow. People in flow experience a profound state of absorption in which time freezes, anxieties fall away, and nothing seems to exist except the task at hand. Humans are able to mentally process 126 bits of information per second, and flow is able to harness and engage all of those precious little bits of conscious attention. No room is left over for negative or distracting thoughts to creep in. At such times, thought becomes focused and orderly, like a laser beam. The mind gains extraordinary power when it acquires order and focus. People in flow work with a degree of speed, talent, and endurance that, at times, can seem almost superhuman.

In a presumptive state of flow, Mozart dashed off entire musical masterpieces in a single night; Babe Ruth hit his sixtieth home run of the 1927 baseball season; rock climbers in Yosemite scale El Capitan; and surgeons perform marathon multi-organ transplant operations. I hesitate to assign to flow every extraordinary achievement that's ever occurred, but I definitely believe flow's had a hand. Additionally, we should note that flow's effects aren't always as dramatic as world records, eternal masterpieces, or life-saving heroics. More often, we move in and out of flow without even realizing it. It can happen when you fall into a rhythm while practicing your tennis strokes against a wall, or when you walk down the street and find yourself so absorbed by the crisp sunlight on the buildings that you forget all your troubles. Virtually any stimulating activity—whether it's African basket weaving or visiting Russian teahouses or bookbinding—if it completely fills your 126 bits per second of conscious attention, it can put you in flow.

The Squandering of Our Leisure

In their leisure time, most people seek to use their minds as little as possible. Lots of TV watching, right? But we need to be careful, because the information we allow into our consciousness is extremely important; it's what determines the content and the quality of our life. Csikszentmihalyi points out that, perhaps surprisingly, more people experience flow at work than in their leisure hours. In this book, we've attempted to create more opportunities for flow in our leisure hours by setting up the conditions (the seven imperatives) that are conducive to it. I've stated else-

> *"All intellectual improvement arises from leisure."*
>
> —Samuel Johnson (1709–1784), lexicographer and author

where that challenge is pleasure; that's flow in a nutshell. Counter to prevailing assumptions, work is a terrific thing for our mental health because it provides opportunities for challenge, even if our work isn't fully engrossing every single second of the day. Nevertheless, many people persist in believing that their coveted leisure hours should be devoted to full relaxation: brain idling, unplugged, unengaged. That's a tragic strategic error in life management. Our leisure hours should instead be spent filling the gaps in our mental circuitry, gaps that our jobs aren't supplying.

We think about Friday all week so we can tumble into free-time mode—but, once there, we often have no good idea what to do with ourselves. Ironically, jobs are actually easier to enjoy than free time, because like flow activities, jobs have built-in goals, feedback, rules, and challenges, all of which encourage us to get deeply involved, to concentrate, and to lose ourselves. Free time, on the other hand, is unstructured, and requires much greater effort to be shaped into something that can be truly enjoyed. It requires conscious choices, in other words, and people often shy from that notion. Understand that this book is not a renunciation of leisure; it is a renunciation of *worthless* leisure. Pursuits that demand skill and discipline make leisure what it is supposed to be—a chance for re-creation as well as for recreation. But on the whole, people miss the opportunity to enjoy leisure. In the name of having fun, we too often get overinvolved in activities that are vicarious: watching others play sports or perform music or cook on TV, for instance. This will mask, at least temporarily, the underlying emptiness of wasted time.

> *"The future will belong not only to the educated man, but to the man who is educated to use his leisure wisely."*
>
> —C. K. Brightbill, leisure theorist

But secondhand observation is a pale substitute for firsthand immersion in real challenges such as participating in sports yourself, playing music yourself, or cooking yourself. The great American sociologist Robert Park memorably declared, "It is the improvident use of our leisure that is the greatest waste of American life."

Operation Saturation

Due to his breadth of interests, ranging from schizophrenia to music, Oliver Sacks, the neurologist and writer, was appointed by Columbia University as its first Columbia artist. The new appointment will allow Sacks, the author of ten books, to range freely across Columbia's departments. "I very much look forward to doing classes that could be about almost anything, from music to psychiatry to whatever." Sacks's appointment exemplifies the university's effort to bridge the gap between the study of neuroscience and other disciplines in which scholars work to understand human behavior, including economics, law, and art history. The appointment aims to incorporate an interdisciplinary approach to the arts into the undergraduate experience at Columbia. Sacks is an exemplar of the "Hey, kids, you can do more than one thing at a time" message.

Carson Cunningham is a history buff, chess player, gardener, pianist, former college basketball player at Purdue University, and independent film producer. Now teaching history at DePaul University, he told me, "I'm a New Age type of nerd. Being well-rounded helps you deal with a lot in life." Cunningham has taken plenty of ribbing from sports-obsessed coaches and buddies over the years who haven't understood his Renaissance worldview. However, even as a very young man, he steadfastly remained committed to his path in the face of the kind of peer pressure that would have caused lesser spirits to capitulate. I think it's hard for most of us to fathom the secure sense of self it would require to buck the macho mind-set of the typical college athlete. Cunningham did that and to this day remains loyal to his preferred way of operating in the world: hitting on all cylinders. He is a wonderful model of a vigorous-minded generalist who supplements his cross-trained mind with a cross-trained body.

"The secret to happiness is this: let your interests be as wide as possible."

—Bertrand Russell (1872–1970), mathematician and philosopher

Irrigate Your Brain

Remember Diogenes, who set out with his lantern twenty-three centuries ago to find one honest man? As tough as that assignment was then, he'd have an even harder time finding one happily well-rounded man today. The roots of our discontent are internal, and each person must untangle them personally. The psychologists call it dysthymia or ontological anxiety or nihilism or existential dread. Basically, it's fear—a fear of living, a fear that there is no meaning to life, or a feeling of having been led on or cheated. Many of us have unconsciously bought into the Cinderella myth that a benign fate would somehow provide for us (women, we hate to admit this). But as well we know, money, power, status, and possessions do not, by themselves, necessarily add one iota to the quality of life.

It *is* hard to live well today. So many choices. And don't you feel like there are so many dams about to burst and so few fingers to stick into them? Following Voltaire's advice, some people throw up their hands in resignation and say, "I'm giving up on the world and will just cultivate my little garden." Aristotle envisioned that garden as a macro-space. His ideal of the good life was known as *eudaimonia*, the word we encountered back in Chapter 9: a life in which the person flourishes, or fulfills his or her true potential.

You stand now at the threshold of becoming an entrepreneur of your own potential. Remember, you don't need endless time and perfect conditions to get your mind vigor'd up with cross-training. And if you're an *opsimath* (one who learns late in life), all the better. Estelle Reiner (mother of actor-director Rob Reiner and wife of actor-director Carl Reiner), who died at ninety-four, was sixty-five when she kicked off a career as a jazz singer. She went on to record seven albums, performing in clubs throughout New York and Los Angeles. Pioneering publisher Max Schuster advised youngsters, "Begin at once to choose some subject, some concept, some great name or idea or event in history on which you can eventually make yourself the world's supreme expert." Good advice—if you're inclined to be a specialist. I'd supplement Schuster's advice by recommending that, no matter what your age, you supplement your specialist status with dabblings in lots of other enriching areas that have no apparent connection to your specialty.

Now is the time to vigor up your mind, whatever time it is. Use the 92nd Street YMHA in New York City as a model for the choices available to a diligent desultorian. I want to become the human incarnation of that place: a bastion of physical, cognitive, and spiritual fitness. As if that weren't enough, it's known for attracting a continuous roster of wide-ranging and top-level speakers. Recent lecturers have included Martha Graham, Yo-Yo Ma, I. M. Pei, Bill Gates, Mikhail Gorbachev, Gloria Steinem, Jimmy Carter, Kofi Annan, Thomas Keller, Mario Cuomo, Geraldine Ferraro, Robert Krulwich, Joyce Carol Oates, Alan Dershowitz, and many others. This renowned facility is all about intellectual, emotional, psychological, physical, spiritual, and cultural health. It offers a wealth of stimulating opportunities for the curious: lectures and public conversations on politics and current events, culture and ideas, business and finance, arts and entertainment, science and discovery, parenting, music, poetry, dance, health, fitness,

"Go confidently in the direction of your dreams. It is time to start living the life you've always imagined."

—Henry David Thoreau (1817–1862)

humanities, languages, music, writing, storytelling, drawing, painting, ceramics, sculpture, cartooning, career, finance, food, wine, and travel. If any organization ever tried to do everything and be everything to virtually everybody, and do it successfully—it's this one. The mission of the 92nd Street Y puts new facets on the word multifaceted.

Develop a Ravenous Intelligence

John Leo, the celebrated columnist for *U.S. News & World Report*, leads the scholarship on the practice of using code words and euphemisms in journalism. For example: *frisky* means slut; a politician who's *constantly growing* is a moron; someone who is *most effective in front of small groups* is incapable of giving a decent speech; a person described as being *experienced* is over the hill; *perky* is shorthand for hyperactive; *soft-spoken* means mousy; *militant* is a nice way of saying fanatic; and *steadfast* is polite language to describe someone who's pigheaded. Leo's list of euphemisms tickled me—until it hit close to home, at which time it became even funnier: *multitalented* means untalented.

It's an interesting paradox: even as the world "silos" and ramifies itself into deeper layers of specialization, it's flattening out in another sense. Membranes are being dissolved between nations; geographic barriers are more porous than ever before; we eat each other's food, wear each other's clothes, speak each other's languages, appreciate each other's art, play each other's music. The tossed salad that was once only New York City is increasingly representative of all cities, with burgeoning ethnic populations and their cacophony of cultural artifacts. Talk about harmonic convergence.

There's so much eclectic thunder to steal from others. Specialism and generalism are irreconcilable only if you choose to frame them as such. In fact, the ultimate goal—the endgame—is to integrate generalist/systems thinking with specialist/reductionist thinking: that's my personal take on how harmonic convergence should work. The exquisite irony at the heart of this book is that you, while engaged in an omnifaceted self-improvement program, may unearth an endeavor you actually wish to pursue as a specialty—a specialty you might not have discovered had it not been for your unbounded romp all over creation.

Indeed, generalists and specialists should not glare at each other across a barbwire fence as would polarized rivals; they should honor each other's strengths and even integrate those strengths into their own approaches. That's the sort of reconciliation we need, so we don't fabricate an Iron Curtain or Cold War between the two camps. The demands of today's world require a synthesis or symbiosis of big-picture interconnectors and small-picture detail-demons. Not a wishy-washy middle-ground compromise, but a harmonizing blend of the two great ways—a complementarity, in the way of yin/yang. Thus, the best Renaissance people possess the ability to drop down from their thirty-six-thousand-foot view of things to perceive problems at the grass roots. That's the grand prix: to mold a mind that's so adept you can elicit both generalist/systems thinking *and* specialist/reductionist thinking at will, calling upon the appropriate tactic as the situation warrants. In other words, I'd like to see everybody using both a microscope and a macroscope. Earlier in the book

> "*Self-expansion is the purpose of life.*"
> —Theodore Roszak, historian

I called this toggle approach the Vitruvian Capability, in honor of da Vinci's Vitruvian Man. This "third way" provides you with one more valuable arrow in your quiver, and don't we all need all the help we can get?

The Promethean Way

Walt Whitman said, "I am large; I contain multitudes." I interpret that as not being afraid to contradict yourself, to freely dabble in all kinds of things without fear of inconsistency. I recently composed an essay that surprised me as it took shape. It appeared to undercut the theme of this book. However, I came to see that it complements my theme, in the same way that yin and yang complement each other, and generalists and specialists complement each other, and bodily fitness and cognitive fitness comple-

ment each other. Yes, even surface-skimming water bugs need to occasionally drop down deep once in a while, and one of those occasions is when visiting an art museum. But before I go into that, first, a memorable 1984
essay written by the late, much-missed *Washington Post* syndicated columnist Art Buchwald to set the stage:

The Six-Minute Louvre

It is common knowledge that there are only three things worth seeing in the
Louvre. They are the Venus de Milo, the Winged Victory and the Mona Lisa. The
rest of the stuff is all junk. For years tourists went to see those three works and
then rushed out to continue their shopping in Paris.

Before World War II, the record for going through the Louvre was seven minutes and thirty seconds held by a man known as the Swedish Cannonball. After
the war an Englishman, paced by his Welsh wife, did it in seven minutes flat—
and pretty soon everyone started talking about a Six-Minute Louvre.

Thus it was in 1950 that the young Peter Stone went in on a Sunday—a day
when you didn't have to pay—and, while thousands cheered, ran around the Venus
de Milo, up past the Winged Victory, down to the Mona Lisa. You always have to
say something when you look at the Mona Lisa. Peter's famous remark was, "I
know the guy who has the original," and then he drove away in a waiting taxi. Peter
did it in five minutes and fifty-six seconds, a record no tourist has ever been able
to beat, making excellent time under perfect conditions, with a smooth floor, excellent lighting, and no wind. As I stood in the courtyard of the palace looking
around me at the seasoned veterans who had come back, I recalled the '50s and
thought, "When it came to sightseeing, we were the best and the brightest."

And now, my piece about experiencing an art museum as a too-superficial
skimmer/scanner/skitterer:

You Can Run but You Can't Glide

Given my propensity to glide through life, shaving off just the top layer and
sprinting off to the next thing, you might imagine that art museums are aerobic

activities to me. Art Buchwald beat me to the punch on this topic when he referred to racing through the Louvre in a record six minutes. He wrote about zooming from the Mona Lisa to the other famous artworks in the museum, making excellent time "under perfect conditions, with a smooth floor, excellent lighting, and no wind."

I'm a competitive museum attender myself, whizzing through the exhibits, applying my philistine gaze to each piece briefly and quizzically. I might glower at the famous ones fractionally longer, taking a few seconds to be stymied by their celebrated attributes but, by and large, I have always employed the (highly unsatisfactory) shotgun approach.

During a trip to Iowa City recently, I puzzled over a sprawling canvas called *Mural* by the revered painter Jackson Pollock. I thought of curmudgeon Andy Rooney on TV's *60 Minutes*, who did a memorable segment decrying the charade of Pollock-style modern art. Then I thought of the recent movie about Pollock starring Ed Harris. I remember the scenes of Pollock spattering paint on canvas and how he did it with such abandon.

I think of writing—my own art form—and how differently I work. There are no haphazard spatterings by the time my pieces reach print, no arbitrary hit-or-miss choices. Every word, thought, and comma is highly considered—even put on trial. Pollock's work strikes me as the equivalent of an embarrassing first draft that is fit for no one's eyes only.

Meanwhile, a class I was part of required us to devote ten minutes of focused attention to a work of art that made us uncomfortable. Nearly all the paintings in this particular museum left me cold. I settled on one that featured a middle-aged couple, presumably married. The man stood imperially over the woman, arm akimbo, leg akimbo, fingers akimbo, even his eyebrow akimbo. His gaze was critical, derision and contempt exuding from his very pores. His upper lip snarled, more supercilious even than the maître d' at the fanciest restaurant. Perhaps most telling, the artist, James Lechay (American, 1902–2001) had chosen to line the man's ears in strokes of bold red paint.

His wife was a vision of oppositeness. Her ears were not lined in vivid crimson; her eyebrow was not cocked—in fact, nothing was akimbo, not even her aspect or attitude. Whatever may be akimbo about her she's probably keeping to herself, because isn't everybody akimbo in some way?

Maybe the artist is suggesting that we are not as we appear. Maybe the wife's tongue is so sharp that she burned the rim of her husband's ears scarlet with her wrath—despite the fact she looks like placidness personified.

Gradually, the worm began to turn for me. The more time I spent engaging with this work of art, the more keenly I felt it. Not affection, quite, but understanding, or at least the beginnings of some questions, the start of a dialogue with the artist. I began to question my devotion to surface-scratching as my technique to a fulfilled life. Without altogether renouncing my modus operandi, I'm beginning to see that skimming at least occasionally requires its counterpart: dropping down deep.

By now, the worm was spinning pretty good. I am actually craving "my" painting, to visit it again, to reunite with it as with an old friend. Next visit, I want to investigate if there's any suggestion of joy in it, looking harder for any gleam in the eyes of that mysterious couple.

This instructive little experience has shown me the light when it comes to museum-going. I have discovered that taking even ten minutes apiece to bear down on two or three works of art is infinitely more satisfying than skittering through a museum, lightning fast, in my usual superficial way.

Another way to think of it: if you try to eat every single item offered on a smorgasbord, you'll surely feel sick afterward. Plus, you probably won't be able to recall any particular dish. Everything will have muddled together on your plate and in your mind. Better to sample, thoughtfully, a few dishes, and form an informed opinion on them—whether it's pâté or Pollock.

So I turn out to be more like Walt Whitman than I thought: I do contain multitudes. As dedicated a superficialist as I am, I found myself realizing that slicing off only the top surface of things is not necessarily the best technique for every endeavor: museum visiting, in this case. Ask yourself what aspects of your own life are best attacked with a generalist gestalt and which with a specialist gestalt.

Mosaic Imperative

It's beginning to happen: more and more people are choosing to equip their worldview with both a wide-angle lens and a zoom lens. In defiance of the hegemony of the specialist, this trend is reassuring. Increasingly, today's master of the universe is a hyphenate. We see actors who are also writer/directors, singers who are painters, painters who are directors, as well as sports stars who are designers, designers who are talk-show hosts, and athletes who are politicians. That infamous phrase from the '60s, *polymorphous perversity* is, in this era, morphing into *polymorphous diversity*.

"There are far too many smart, educated, talented people operating at quarter speed, unsure of their place in the world, contributing far too little to the productive engine of modern civilization. There are far too many people who look like they have their act together but have yet to make an impact. . . . Like most Phi Beta Slackers, [they] are cursed with tremendous ability and infinite choices."

—Po Bronson, author

I've asked myself what the future holds for someone devoted to a cornucopia of liberal arts consumption. I believe skeptics and naysayers will always abound. At the same time, I believe there will always be overachievers who continually strive for more, because some people's natures will be forever hardwired as generalists, as Leonardo da Vinci's was so long ago. So I'm certain a bright future exists for what I've termed cross-training. After all, with the world becoming ever more complex, life regularly supplies more and more fodder for activities spanning the full 360 degrees of curiosity.

The Age of Enlightenment was the period of history when it was decided that all subjects were worth knowing. Let's declare now a Catalytic Age of Enlightenment, an era where we seek to increase the nutritional value of our lives and stave off any trace of mental malnutrition. I want to pig out on life. I want a big, fat, fit life.

Far-Flung Interests

I'll bet Steve Bing has a handle on just that. Steve Bing is a billionaire heir, real-estate developer, producer/screenwriter, and philanthropist. At the age of eighteen, he inherited an estimated $600 million from his grandfather, Leo S. Bing, who had made his fortune in New York real estate in the 1920s. Steve Bing is said to be urbane, easygoing, and charming, besides being an erudite amateur on a vast range of subjects that include politics, business, and movies. He plays the blues on the piano and is passionate about sports, especially basketball. And he's modest and self-effacing. Bing has had considerable success in filmmaking (*Beowulf, Last Man Standing, The Polar Express*, to name a few). As if that's not enough for a breathtaking Renaissance man, Bing is among the nation's leading donors to environmental causes. Despite his low-key personality, he's thought to wield considerable clout within the Democratic Party hierarchy.

"Nearly every man who develops an idea works it up to the point where it looks impossible, and then he gets discouraged. That's not the place to become discouraged."

—Thomas Edison (1847–1931)

Charles Schumann may be the most famous bartender in Germany, but he looks more like a film star. Wiry and tall with silver hair slicked back and up before curling down and over his collar, Schumann presides with authority over two bohemian and cosmopolitan bars in Munich. And, oh yes, he models. He's worked for both Yamamoto and Comme des Garcons and has been the face of Hugo Boss's luxury menswear line. As an author, he's written a manual of mixology, *American Bar*. His life is an eloquent testament to the spirit of a polymathic generalist—he loves music, speaks four languages, follows sport, and maintains a keen interest in interior design. His taste tends toward the spare, but one of his passions threatens to bury him in clutter: "I have books, books, books," he says. "I'll never be able to read all these books. My second problem is newspapers. I collect them for weeks and weeks, and

I never have time to read them. Saturday is my only night off—I spend it leafing through the papers." When Schumann isn't working (or perusing newspapers), he's swimming, running, playing soccer, or studying the piano: "I play very well, but the teacher is a concert pianist, and she insults me every week because I'm not doing my exercises." He surfs, too, and don't forget boxing. "I'm never going to retire," he says.

Elsewhere, David Gregory is said to be cursed and blessed by the *Uomo Universale*'s need for continual inquiry. He's quite a recognizable academic in Canada—said to have the "longest untrammelled hair" at Athabasca University, and "the most historic jeans." He holds the longest conversations in the halls, and he is the longest walker of anyone at AU, having walked trails from his home to work many times, braving bears and weather. He's also walked the length and breadth of England, steering his family through the fog to a hostel shelter that only he could locate. He is an avid devotee of folk music and an aspiring clarinet and guitar player. For about twenty years Gregory has developed and hosted programs on the history of popular music, including the first series, "Ragtime to Rolling Stones," "Blues to Big Bands," and "From Bop to Rock." Another program, called "Writers and Thinkers," covered a wide range of authors, philosophers, and historically noteworthy types. He has also taught history and drama at Oxford University. He and a buddy "holed up in crummy student digs at Pembroke College and Christ Church, to conduct lively conversations about British history and drama, and toured around the countryside in search of English baroque churches, Roman baths, and modernist portraits of Henry VIII and Maggie Thatcher, reminding ourselves that post-colonials do not steal the silverware."

The Revenge of the Generalist

I've tried not to excoriate specialists. To be sure, we generalists have our drawbacks and pitfalls. When you're a generalist, you're seldom the go-to guy. If you find yourself in the middle of an unusual and acute health crisis, I can guarantee you won't be seeking out a generalist. You want the world's number-one specialist in that rare disease—and you sure hope there is one. So I hope I have not indulged in any unwarranted broadsides on specialists. Still, I maintain that chasing one professional specialty for your entire career simply doesn't provide enough cognitive ammunition for your brain, which leads to brain entropy and a generalized malaise. Yet we so need specialists. The world's depending on them; the world is much, much too complex to negotiate without them. We've long since evolved past the point where generalists could serve every purpose. We respect specialists. We *are* specialists, almost invariably, if not by nature then by vocation. In fact, we need specialists so much, we can't allow to risk them burning out on their specialty. In recognition of their contribution, society's unspoken refrain has become "all glory to the specialist," which would surely bamboozle da Vinci, Jefferson, or even Richard Feynman.

In their drive to attract students, our modern universities have largely forsaken the liberal arts and modeled themselves on the attenuation of specialized vocational schools; of course the universities would claim student demand for liberal arts courses is minimal, so it's the chicken-and-egg syndrome. In any case, at this point, it is considered received wisdom and axiomatic gospel that we all be employed as specialists. "You can't make it as a wandering generality," warns author and motivational speaker Zig Ziglar. "You have to be a meaningful specific." Ziglar is implying that the land of big-picture thinkers is a gulag. Compare his advice to that of management guru Peter Drucker. When asked for one thing that would make a person better in business, Drucker responded, "Learn to play the violin."

We don't need to drink the Kool-Aid of abject specialization unless we choose to. If that's the way your brain is organized, your personality constructed, and your worldview constituted, that's terrific—the world needs you desperately. But, as we've seen, for too long we've been funneling our best and brightest into fields of superspecialization and, predictably, many of them have begun to grow restless and dissatisfied. Oversold on the belief that becoming a specialist is the sure route to the good life, they may not even perceive that their career approach could be the source of what ails them.

The good news is baked right into that problem, though. Every movement spawns its opposite. And I believe our culture is poised at the leading edge of a backlash against the tide of superspecialization and the concomitant role of unquestioned "experts." This trend will make way for inquisitive amateurs, systems-minded generalists, Renaissance people, well-rounded liberal arts mavens, and all manner of cross-trained vigorously minded autodidacts to play a heretofore nonexistent role as adjuncts to our friends the specialists. The appointment of Oliver Sacks at Columbia University is, I hope, an encouraging beginning of a trend to recognize generalists elsewhere in academia, where up until now we've been, by and large, pariahs.

One modern symbol for today's cross-trainers is the iPod. You don't listen to a whole album anymore; you select one song from here, one from there. It may be hip-hop, Bob Marley, and the Beatles, all within the same five-minute experience. Here's another analogy: dim sum, the traditional Chinese cuisine in which small portions of a variety of dumplings and other goodies are served in succession. The well-rounded among us skim and sample and scan and nibble from the entire repertoire. But just because we don't focus on one thing for our entire lives doesn't mean we're unable to focus. Focus is overrated anyway; it can lead to blinkered ruts. I'm all for daydreaming, hyperactivity, and divergent thinking—all salutary functions of lack of focus. It takes a pretty stiff backbone to stand up to those who would accuse us of glancing right past the depth, texture, and complexity of things. The fact is, we're highly attuned to the interconnectedness of things, which supplies plenty of depth, texture, and complexity. We exist as human kaleidoscopes with cross-trained synapses.

Liberal arts mavens will also be derided as engaging in an impractical, aristocratic, and anachronistic pursuit, that being a Renaissance person is a vanity enterprise. As we saw in Chapter 12, our worldview provides loads of practical, real-world value. The other accusation that gets thrown at life-of-the-minders is undue earnestness. Neither camp ought to stake any claim to the moral high ground. Generalists are no more guilty of being overly serious than are specialists. Overseriousness ("I read only the classics. . . .") is one of "The Seven Deadly Virtues," according to Roz Chast, the brilliantly perceptive staff cartoonist for *The New Yorker*. The other deadly virtues, by the way, are morning perkiness, uncalled-for thrift ("Dented cans of peas, only 39 cents!"), total honesty ("In fact, that *does* make you look fat. . . ."), gossip prudery ("If you can't say anything nice, don't say it at all."), guilt-mongering ("How can we go to the carnival if people are starving?"), and fitness obsession ("My resting heart rate is two beats a minute.").

The Fulfillment Drench

So buddy up with a partner, if that's your preference; call that person your "intellectual enabler." Help each other create new contours for your lives. Resist the too-common American syndrome of striving to make your life easy and carefree. Elsewhere in the world—I'm thinking Europe here—they emphasize making their lives rich and complex, which is really a much more evolved idea.

Vigorously minded autodidacts are grazers. Show us a buffet table, and we want to sample everything. Connoisseurs of the full buffet, that's us. Greed is our byword. We're maestros of mashup. Being a Renaissance person is like being a rice paddy: acres wide and ankle deep. Or if you prefer a football analogy, you can go deep or you can go wide, and cross-trainers go wide. We have a restless intelligence. We crave a wide wingspan. And it's all here for the taking. Steep yourself in 360-degree curiosity. And if you'll forgive one more woozy metaphor, build a magisterial life out of the bricks and mortar of this treasure chest of a world. You *can* develop the DNA of a dabbler, by making the choice to hitch your wagon to Triumph in Twenty. Take your time and hurry up (see Chapter 12 if that paradox bugs you). The half-life of a dilettante is the length of his or her whole life.

The Endgame

Here's a Zen riddle for you to ponder: Can being a generalist be considered a specialty? It doesn't have to be good versus evil, us against them, generalists versus specialists. I believe that the individual who can see the big picture

> "The road of excess leads to the palace of wisdom."
>
> —William Blake (1757–1827), artist and poet

(the generalist) is the guy who frames the debate, and who will prevail. So we all need to strive to be specialists who behave like generalists. Einstein said everything should be as simple as possible but no simpler.

We've set out to reify the idea of building a vigorous mind. And as we've seen, the key to effective cross-training is to integrate the life of the mind, the body, and the spirit: that's how you hitch a ride on the omnibus. But I would submit that one more element is desirable to leaven the mixture: an attitude of humor, even joyful defiance. Some people are uncomfortable (or is it suspicious?) because the water bugs seem to be having all the fun. "I've never been convinced there's anything inherently wrong in having fun," said George Plimpton (1927–2003), a guy who wrote the book on having fun as an amateur mucking around with the pros. Virtually all the role models profiled in this book seem to possess and even cultivate a lighthearted outlook on life. They manage the neat trick of taking themselves just seriously enough to do good work. After all, these glorious generalists are recalcitrant enough to have chosen a route through life that's considered by many to be idiosyncratic and impractical, if not impossible. Our critics will charge that we're approaching life as a series of aptitude tests—what the writer David Brooks has lampooned as "the ordeal lifestyle." Yes! They get it! An ordeal lifestyle is a good thing!

> "I wanted to live deep and suck out all the marrow of life."
>
> —Henry David Thoreau (1817–1862)

Remember Peggy Lee and her plaintive cry in the song "Is That All There Is?" I don't think she was looking for an answer, but I have one. The answer is yes, that's all there is, and that's all there needs to be, because it's more than enough. Yet most people don't play a big enough game. Still, in an encouraging sign, Americans seem to be developing a fresh hunger for experience, growth, personal cultivation. Men and women of all ages today feel the urge to seek out more in life—to shape a larger self. A well-rounded life isn't something you achieve; it's something you *breathe*, whether you think of yourself as an amateur, an autodidact, a cross-trainer, a Renaissance person, a dilettante, or an interdisciplinarian. It's a way of being in the world; so unconscious you're hardly even aware of it. So consume a high-"protean" diet; binge on life itself. Be the substrate: make the choice to allow life to act upon you, continually. That's the fulfillment drench.

ACKNOWLEDGMENTS

———

There may be such thing as a well-rounded person, but there's no such thing as a self-made person. I owe big to these people and many other formative ones as well. I've been shaped by individuals I've never even met, especially authors past and present. Building a book is involved work. An inchoate thought stirs, an idea is born, and before you know it, the whole thing becomes choate.

Robert Allen, my agent, has been my steadfast prince and stalwart champion. Kind, patient, and good-natured, he's had my back. I commend Michele Matrisciani, my editor, for her good taste, for being so fiercely committed to the project, and for just plain loving it. Mark Chimsky, book doctor, took my early unstructured thoughts, applied discipline and rigor, and helped me produce a proposal that turned out to be almost too good for its own good.

Other seminal helpmates include Christopher Brooks, reader, my altered ego, muse, a Renaissance Man for his time; Samuel Autman; Grace Duffy; Nancy Parker; Mickey Maurer; Caroline Laudig; Kimberly Conrad; Tom Pearson; David Zivan; Amy Wimmer Schwarb; Alex Kosene; Renee Wilmeth; and Mike Knight.

INDEX